Wanderlust USA

The Great American Hike

gestalten

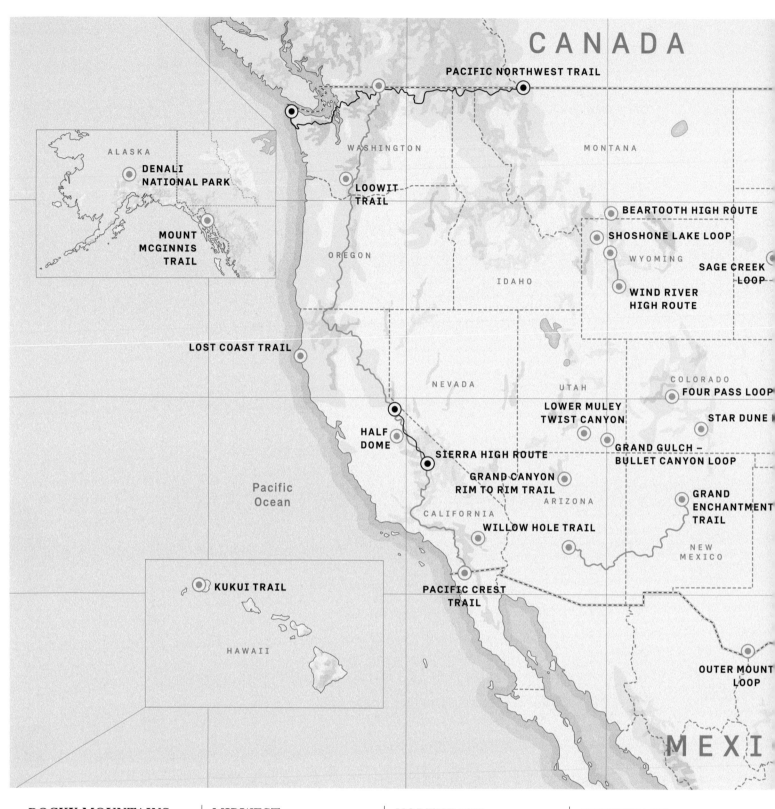

ROCKY MOUNTAINS

MIDWEST

NORTHEAST

SOUTHEAST

SUPERIOR HIKING TRAIL
THE LONG TRAIL
OCEAN PATH
PRESIDENTIAL TRAVERSE
GORGE TRAIL
CEDAR RUN – WHITEOAK CANYON LOOP
BARTRAM TRAIL
OUACHITA TRAIL
DEEP CREEK TRAIL
NORTH DAKOTA
SOUTH DAKOTA
MINNESOTA
WISCONSIN
MICHIGAN
IOWA
NEBRASKA
USA
ILLINOIS
INDIANA
OHIO
PENNSYLVANIA
NEW YORK
MAINE
VT
NH
MA
CT
RI
NJ
MD
DE
WEST VIRGINIA
VIRGINIA
KANSAS
MISSOURI
KENTUCKY
TENNESSEE
NORTH CAROLINA
SOUTH CAROLINA
OKLAHOMA
ARKANSAS
ALABAMA
GEORGIA
MISSISSIPPI
TEXAS
LOUISIANA
FLORIDA
Atlantic Ocean
Gulf of Mexico

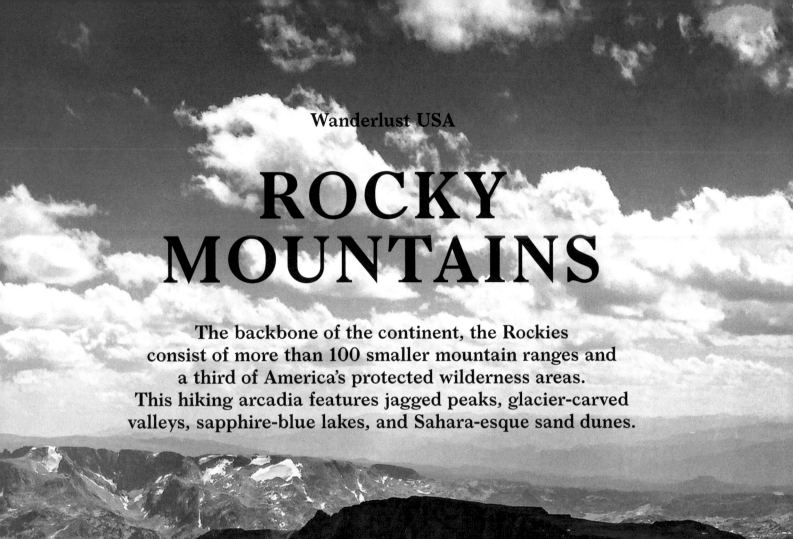

ROCKY MOUNTAINS

The backbone of the continent, the Rockies
consist of more than 100 smaller mountain ranges and
a third of America's protected wilderness areas.
This hiking arcadia features jagged peaks, glacier-carved
valleys, sapphire-blue lakes, and Sahara-esque sand dunes.

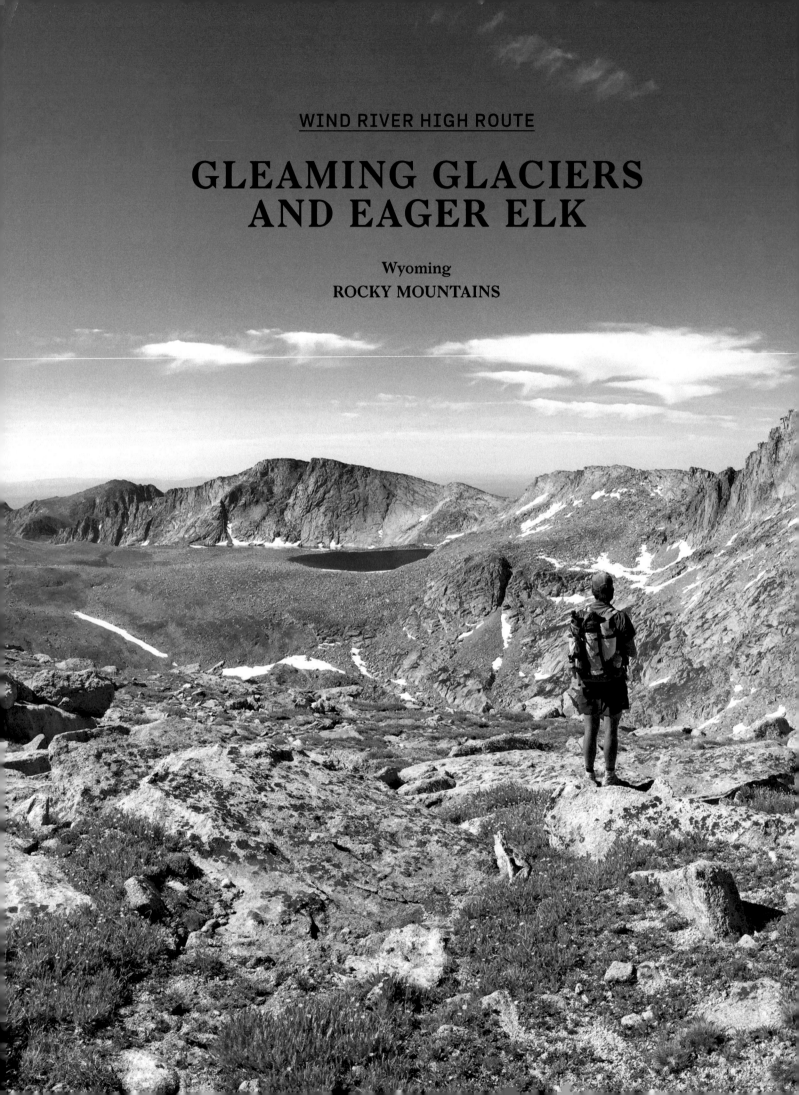

GLEAMING GLACIERS AND EAGER ELK

Wyoming
ROCKY MOUNTAINS

ABOUT THE TRAIL
→ <u>DISTANCE</u> 129 km (80 mi)
→ <u>DURATION</u> 6 to 7 days
→ <u>LEVEL</u> Challenging

The Wind River Range is one of America's best-kept back-packing secrets. In contrast to nearby Yellowstone and Grand Teton National Parks, both of which draw millions of visitors per year, the "Winds" have long flown under the radar of public attention. And therein lies part of their charm. Unlike the range's famous neighbors to the northwest, the Winds do not require you to procure permits, reserve campsites, or book a hotel weeks in advance. All you need is a sense of adventure, a fair amount of backcountry experience, and a healthy set of lungs to deal with the lofty elevations.

Following the crest of the Continental Divide, the Wind River Range is approximately 160 km (100 mi) long and is located in the western part of Wyoming. The highest subrange of the Rocky Mountains outside of Colorado, the Winds boast countless granite peaks, more than 1,500 alpine lakes, and an impressive collection of 63 glaciers—the second-highest number of any range in the contiguous United States after Washington's

Cascade mountains. If you're a seasoned hiker searching for a challenging, off-the-beaten-track adventure in a jaw-droppingly beautiful location, look no further.

Among a multitude of trekking options in the Wind River Range, the Wind River High Route (WRHR), pioneered by Alan Dixon and Don Wilson, is one of the best. Stretching 129 km (80 mi) from Green River Lakes Trailhead in the north to Big Sandy Campground in the south (the direction that it's typically walked), the rollercoaster route goes up and over nine passes between 3,505 m (11,500 ft) and 3,719 m (12,200 ft), with a total elevation gain of more than 6,096 m (20,000 ft). More than half of the WRHR consists of off-trail travel, and during its course, hikers will negotiate talus slopes, glacial ice, granite slabs, and lingering snowfields.

As with any long trek through the Wyoming wilderness, wildlife is a highlight. The Wind River Range is home to brown bears, moose, bighorn sheep, wolverines, marmots, and mountain lions. And if you arrive here in September, you will also witness the rutting (mating) season for elk. During this period, male elk (bulls) do their best to win over their female counterparts (cows) by any and all means necessary. Occasionally this can mean locking antlers with other bulls to establish dominance. But generally, it involves showing off, most notably with a distinctive call referred to as bugling. Oscillating between a high-pitched cry,

"All you need is a sense of adventure, a fair amount of backcountry experience, and a healthy set of lungs to deal with the lofty elevations."

↖ An abundance of clear mountain streams means that great drinking water is rarely hard to find on the WRHR.

↑ Horse packing through the Winds.

← The snowmelt reveals a colorful blanket of wildflowers.

9

a throaty bellow, and a series of low, deep grunts, the sound of an elk bugling is something you are not likely to forget, much like the intimidating roar of a nearby grizzly, the jump-provoking buzzing of a too-close-for-comfort rattlesnake, or even the pecking of an industrious woodpecker.

For those who hike the WRHR earlier in the summer, an equally memorable wildlife experience—though less enjoyably so—awaits in the form of mosquitoes. Thanks to a watery combination of heavy snowmelt, verdant meadows, and a landscape dotted with lakes, July (often stretching deep into August) brings hordes of mosquitoes to the Winds. This can be a maddening experience for wayfarers, especially during morning and evening when the little bloodsuckers are at their most formidable. A head net, mosquito repellent, a long-sleeve shirt, and pants can be sanity savers. A healthy dose of stoicism can also come in handy.

For every talus-scrambling pass or mosquito-swatting evening in the Winds, there is another gorgeous mountaintop vista, wildflower-carpeted alpine meadow, or lake-filled basin in which the blue shimmer of the waters will hold you transfixed. And as for bearing witness to one of nature's most fascinating courting rituals if hitting the trail in September, just be sure to keep your distance. There is no surer way to put a damper on a long-distance trek than by incurring the ire of a pointy-racked, testosterone-filled 300 kg (661 lb) bull elk who is out to find a girlfriend.

↑ Watch your step on glacier crossings!
↓ Alpenglow illuminates the granite peaks.
→ Boulder fields and soaring pinnacles.

GOOD TO KNOW

START / FINISH
Northern Terminus
Green River Lakes Trailhead
Southern Terminus
Big Sandy Campground

TOTAL ELEVATION GAIN
Approximately 6,096 m (20,000 ft)

SEASON
July to mid-September. Late summer is ideal, as the snowfields have melted out and the mosquitos have abated.

ACCOMMODATION
On-Trail
Wild camping is possible throughout the Wind River High Route (WRHR).
Off-Trail
Big Sandy Lodge. Located just a few minutes from the campground of the same name, these beautifully set rustic cabins make for an ideal place for some post-hike rest and recreation.

HIGHLIGHTS
1. Knapsack Col
2. Alpine Lakes Basin
3. Cirque of the Towers
4. Golden Lakes
5. Bugling elk during their rutting season
6. Titcomb Basin
7. Knife Point Glacier
8. Indian Pass
9. Alpenglow illuminating the granite peaks
10. The feeling of relief as you zip your tent up to escape a ravenous horde of mosquitoes

HELPFUL HINTS

NAVIGATIONAL TOOLS
Even if you have a GPS application on your phone, be sure to carry paper maps and a compass on the WRHR (and most importantly, know how to use them). Batteries can die, electronics can fail, signals don't

always come through. GPS has its limitations, and if a worst-case scenario occurs, having a navigational backup can potentially be a lifesaver. This especially holds true in extreme environments above tree line like the Wind River Range, where the margin for error is slimmer, and the possible consequences of getting lost are far greater.

GEAR TIPS
10 items to bring on the WRHR:
1. Head net
2. Microspikes (a lightweight traction device for lingering snowfields and the Knife Point Glacier crossing)

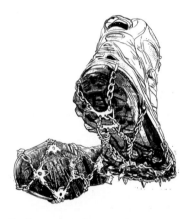

3. Trail running shoes
4. Compass and paper maps
5. Lightweight, light-colored long-sleeve shirt
6. Bug repellent
7. Ursack (bear-proof food storage bag)
8. Sunglasses
9. Sunblock
10. Trekking poles (which help with balance on the glacier crossing and while descending talus slopes)

TRANSPORTATION
The Wind River High Route is bookended by two relatively remote trailheads accessed via dirt roads. From a logistical perspective, the easiest way to reach them is to organize a shuttle with the Great Outdoor Shop, a hiker-friendly store in the town of Pinedale (population: 1,890), located on the western slopes of the Wind River Range.

BONUS TRACK

Near the Wind River Range is a hydrological oddity known as the "Wedding of the Waters." Located 7 km (4.2 mi) south of the town of Thermopolis, it is the point at which the Wind River becomes the Bighorn River—however, what sets this mysterious place apart, is that

the name change doesn't occur at a confluence, as is the case with other watercourses.

The Wedding of the Waters is also known for its inordinate amount of aquatic vegetation, which every winter attracts thousands of waterfowl to the area. Notable among the feeding avifauna are predatory bald eagles, who migrate here during the colder months in search of the river's abundant spawning trout.

The bald eagle (*Haliaeetus leucocephalus*) is the United States' national bird. A part of the sea and fish eagle group, this large raptors is endemic to North America, and typically live close by coastlines, large bodies of water, or rivers with large fish populations. Their nests can be found in tall trees with branches that are strong enough to support their massive bulk—measuring up to 2.5 m (8.2 ft) wide and weighing over 907 kg (one ton), they are the largest nests in the avian kingdom. Bald eagle numbers dwindled in the late twentieth century, but have since made a comeback thanks to widespread conservation efforts. The bird was officially removed from the U.S. government's List of Endangered and Threatened Wildlife in 2007.

Thanks to its status as the national bird, killing a bald eagle is a federal crime—it violates the Bald and Golden Eagle Protection Act. But the birds are facing a new threat in the form of wind farms. Wyoming sits in a wind corridor that makes it an important location for turbine installations, which are capable of generating almost 10 percent of the total energy consumed in the region.

Unfortunately, some bird species such as the bald eagle have trouble spotting these structures and have become victims of the spinning blades. This has become problematic enough that in December 2016, the U.S. Fish and Wildlife Service set a threshold for the total number of bald eagles that can be accidentally killed by the wind industry at 4,200 per year. This law has raised many concerns among animal rights and conservationist groups, who have opposed the measure.

But it's not all bad news. Scientists and engineers are focusing on tackling the problem and have proposed solutions that range from proximity alarms that shut down engines and stop the blades when an animal is too close, all the way to adapting each wind station with sound-emitting boxes that would help divert America's national bird from a direct collision.

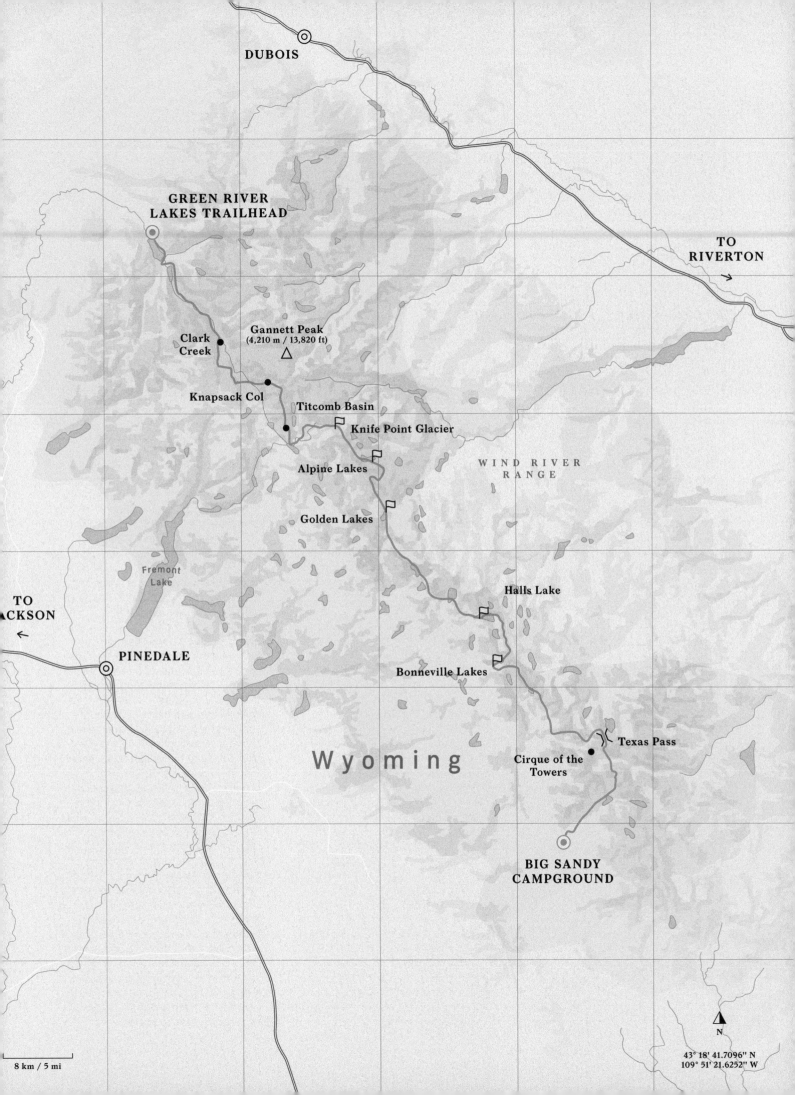

DUBOIS

GREEN RIVER
LAKES TRAILHEAD

TO
RIVERTON

Clark
Creek

Gannett Peak
(4,210 m / 13,820 ft)

Knapsack Col

Titcomb Basin

Knife Point Glacier

Alpine Lakes

WIND RIVER
RANGE

Golden Lakes

Fremont
Lake

Halls Lake

TO
JACKSON

PINEDALE

Bonneville Lakes

Texas Pass

Wyoming

Cirque of the
Towers

BIG SANDY
CAMPGROUND

8 km / 5 mi

N

43° 18' 41.7096" N
109° 51' 21.6252" W

FOUR PASS LOOP

THE MAJESTY OF MAROON BELLS

Colorado
ROCKY MOUNTAINS

ABOUT THE TRAIL
→ <u>DISTANCE</u> 45.1 km (28 mi)
→ <u>DURATION</u> 3 days
→ <u>LEVEL</u> Moderate

Colorado is a mecca for backpackers. Glacier-carved peaks, glistening lakes, and flower-laden alpine meadows abound. With so many hiking options, sometimes the hardest part is deciding where to go. Among myriad excellent choices, the Four Pass Loop stands out as one of the finest. Situated in the Maroon Bells-Snowmass Wilderness, it arguably packs in more jaw-dropping mountain vistas per kilometer than any other trail in the state.

The 45.1 km (28 mi) loop begins and ends at beautiful Maroon Lake. From this vantage point, prepare to be treated to a triple-take view of Colorado's most photographed mountains—the claret-hued twin peaks of Maroon Bells, both measuring in excess of 4,267 m (14,000 ft). The peaks are composed of mudstone, a fine-grained sedimentary rock that distinguishes them from most of Colorado's other prominent mountains, which are made up of granite and limestone. The mudstone gives the Bells their famous reddish color, and its soft, crumbly consistency makes ascending to their summits a dangerous proposition for even the most experienced of climbers.

The Four Pass Loop circumnavigates the Maroon Bells by way of a rollercoaster-like course that traverses a quartet of high mountain passes—all over 3,780 m (12,400 ft). In between, you'll find sweeping valleys boasting verdant forests of aspen, alder, spruce, and willow. This lofty landscape is also sprinkled with meandering streams and inviting meadows that call out to the foot-weary hiker to stay and rest for a while.

It's difficult to imagine a more idyllic alpine environment, but a hike around the Maroon Bells is not without its perils. Principal among these are stormy weather and high altitude. The summer months in Colorado coincide with monsoon season and the likely delivery of rumbling thunderstorms during the early afternoon. At this time of day,

↖ Drinking in the views from a lofty perch.
↑ Vertiginous photo opportunities abound at Maroon Bells.

you should avoid being on top of the passes if storms are fore-casted. As for altitude, it's the number one reason some hikers have difficulty on the Four Pass Loop. The entire trail is situated above 2,920 m (9,580 ft), so it's of paramount importance to be well acclimatized beforehand in order to avoid altitude sickness, also known as Acute Mountain Sickness (AMS).

AMS is the name given to the collection of symptoms that can occur when a person attempts to ascend too quickly at altitudes above 2,500 m (8,202 ft). Fortunately, it's almost entirely preventable by following some basic precautions:

1. If you're coming to Colorado from sea level, plan on spending at least two to three days in Denver (1,600 m [5,249 ft]), the state's capital city and home to its international airport. During that stay, it's important to gradually increase your exercise workload, ideally going for a day hike or two up to approximate elevations of 2,743 m (9,000 ft), before heading back to the Denver area to sleep. This is referred to as "climbing high and sleeping low," and it's a time-tested acclimatization strategy used by mountaineers.

2. Plan on spending the final night before your trek in Aspen, situated at 2,498 m (8,000 ft) and a short drive or shuttle ride away from the trailhead.

3. Drink a lot of water—at least 3 or 4 liters a day—before and during your hike. The air is drier and thinner at high altitude, and due to cooler temperatures, many hikers make the mistake of not drinking enough H_2O.

4. Don't overdo it with the alcohol and coffee, both of which increase the likelihood of dehydration.

5. When you eventually hit the trail, remember to pace yourself. Your body needs time to adapt to its new environment. Think tortoise rather than hare. If you take these precautions, the chances of you completing the Four Pass Loop without any altitude issues increase exponentially.

Colorado is to hikers what New Orleans is to jazz lovers—a mecca steeped in inspiration. And to extend the analogy just a wee bit further, the Maroon Bells is the backpacking equivalent of Miles Davis's "Kind of Blue"—hugely popular, but for very good reason. Quite simply, it's a masterpiece. And like the illustrious trumpeter's signature album, a visit to Maroon Bells moves the spirit in ways which words can never do justice. It has to be experienced to be understood.

"Among myriad excellent choices, the Four Pass Loop stands out as one of the finest. Situated in the Maroon Bells-Snowmass Wilderness, it arguably packs in more jaw-dropping mountain vistas per kilometer than any other trail in the state."

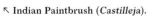 Indian Paintbrush (*Castilleja*).
← Water-loving moose are a familiar sight on the Four Pass Loop.
↑ Mountain goats comb rocky ledges.
→ Carpets of fireweed (*Chamaenerion angustifolium*).

GOOD TO KNOW

START / FINISH
Maroon-Snowmass Trailhead (Maroon Lake)

TOTAL ELEVATION GAIN
2,473 m (8,115 ft)

SEASON
Mid-July to late September

PERMITS
All hikers overnighting in the Maroon-Snowmass Wilderness are required to self-register at the trailhead. The permits are free, there are no quota limits, and you should keep a copy of your registration on you at all times during your trek.

BEAR CANISTER
Due to the prevalence of black bears in the area, backpackers are required to carry either a bear canister or an Ursack (a bear-resistant food sack). If you own neither, it is possible to rent canisters at outdoor stores in nearby Aspen.

HELPFUL HINTS

CAPITOL CREEK CIRCUIT
A lightly trafficked and more challenging alternative to the Four Pass Loop, the Capitol Creek Circuit begins and ends at the Capitol Creek Trailhead near Carbondale or Snowmass Village. The circuit is approximately 64.4 km (40 mi) in length and meanders by four gorgeous alpine lakes. Just like its more trafficked neighbor, it goes up and over four high-altitude passes, all of which exceed 3,048 m (10,000 ft) above sea level.

THE TIMES LESS TRAVELED
The Four Pass Loop is a very popular trail. If you are looking for a little more in the way of solitude, consider the following strategies:

1. Try hiking at dawn and dusk when the trails are virtually empty. Plan to have a long break in the middle of the day when temperatures are at their hottest.
2. Avoid public holidays, weekends, and the peak summer season.
3. Late September is a particularly lovely time of year to hike—cooler weather, fewer people, and the ubiquitous Rocky Mountain aspens turning a vivid shade of gold.

FLORA & FAUNA

Apart from bears, wildlife in the Maroon-Snowmass Wilderness includes elk, mule deer, Canada lynx, mountain goats, and bighorn sheep.

BACKGROUND

RUNNING THE FOUR PASS LOOP
Backpackers aren't the only ones who complete the Four Pass Loop—it's also popular with ultramarathon runners. As of 2019, the record time for completing the full circuit stands at 4 hours and 17 minutes.

JOHN DENVER SANCTUARY
If there is one song synonymous with Colorado's High Country it is John Denver's 1975 classic, "Rocky Mountain High." In nearby Aspen it's possible to visit the John Denver Sanctuary, a picturesque park on the banks of the Roaring Fork, which features the legendary singer's lyrics engraved into giant river boulders.

BONUS TRACK

For those runners that aren't sure about tackling the lofty 3,658 m (12,000 ft) heights of the Four Pass Loop, but nonetheless want to test their mettle in the Rocky Mountains, the Aspen Valley marathon provides a more manageable alternative. Held every July, the scenic route has a maximum altitude of just under 2,438 m (8,000 ft), and the course affords runners spectacular views of Aspen Valley and the Maroon Bells. In addition to the full marathon, the race also has half marathon and 5K events.

ALL PACKED

For centuries, llamas and alpacas have been used in South America to help transport heavy loads in the Andes Mountains; the Incas in Peru revered these animals and considered them an important part of society. These fuzzy and sturdy creatures can carry up to nearly a third of their weight without much hassle and are known to be reliable companions; they were key in transporting rocks and other material used in the building of mountain cities, such as Machu Picchu, during the pre-Columbian era.

Llamas and alpacas have a much shorter history in North America. However, since the 1980's, they have gained increasing popularity as fiber producers, guard animals, pets, and pack animals. Cue Paragon Guides, a travel company that has been operating out of Vail (around two hours away from Aspen) since 1978. Paragon offers several llama-packing itineraries, including a five-day trek that goes all the way to Aspen. Other multi-day options include the Colorado Trail and an ascent of Mount of the Holy Cross. Llama trips are a particularly good option for trekkers who like to bring extra equipment such as a high-end camera gear or telescopes for star-gazing—items that may be too heavy to carry solo for extended periods.

Llamas are part of the Camelidae family, and are perhaps most famous for their propensity to spit when stressed or agitated. Nonetheless, over the decades the Elliot family—the owners of Paragon Guides—haven't received too many complaints about these generally sociable woolly creatures. Indeed, it is said that llamas can spot threats such as bears and wild cats before humans can, and their high-pitched audible alarm can help alert accompanying hikers.

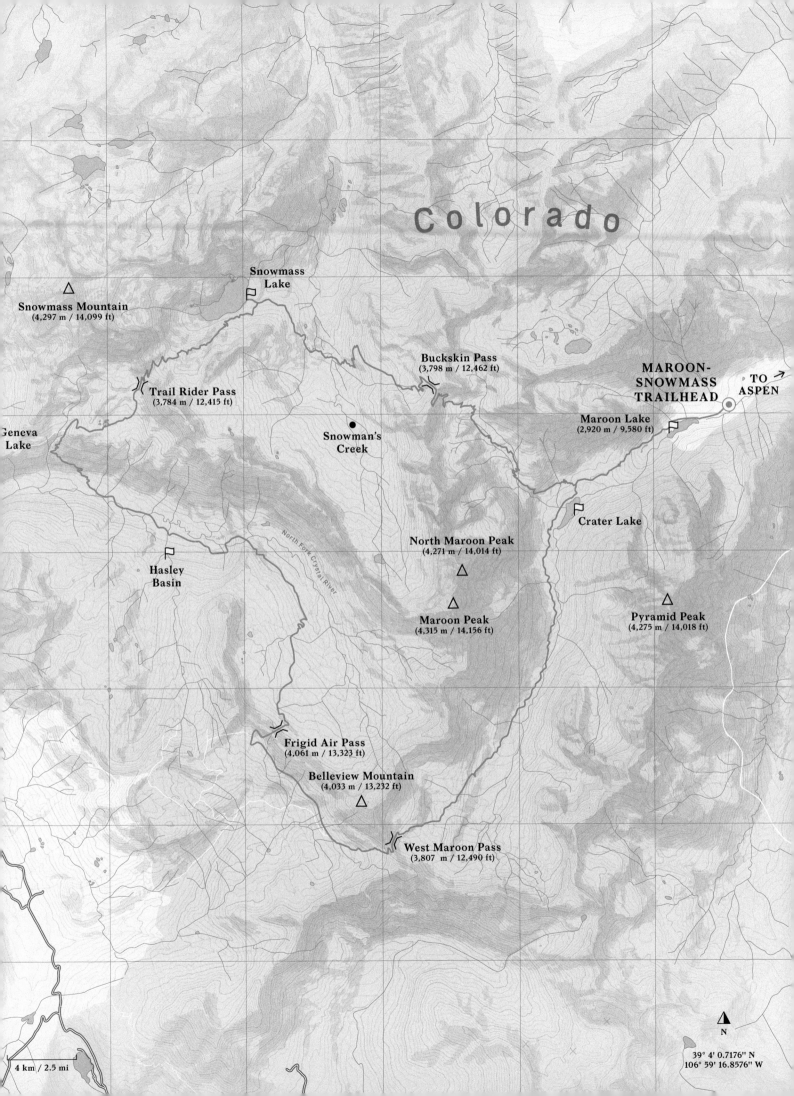

C o l o r a d o

Snowmass Mountain
(4,297 m / 14,099 ft)

Snowmass
Lake

Buckskin Pass
(3,798 m / 12,462 ft)

MAROON-
SNOWMASS
TRAILHEAD

TO
ASPEN

Trail Rider Pass
(3,784 m / 12,415 ft)

Maroon Lake
(2,920 m / 9,580 ft)

Geneva
Lake

Snowman's
Creek

Crater Lake

North Maroon Peak
(4,271 m / 14,014 ft)

North Fork Crystal River

Hasley
Basin

Maroon Peak
(4,315 m / 14,156 ft)

Pyramid Peak
(4,275 m / 14,018 ft)

Frigid Air Pass
(4,061 m / 13,323 ft)

Belleview Mountain
(4,033 m / 13,232 ft)

West Maroon Pass
(3,807 m / 12,490 ft)

N

39° 4' 0.7176" N
106° 59' 16.8576" W

4 km / 2.5 mi

SHOSHONE LAKE LOOP
(YELLOWSTONE NATIONAL PARK)

A GEOTHERMAL WONDERLAND IN THE ROCKY MOUNTAINS

Wyoming
ROCKY MOUNTAINS

ABOUT THE TRAIL
→ <u>DISTANCE</u> 46 km (29 mi)
→ <u>DURATION</u> 2 to 4 days
→ <u>LEVEL</u> Moderate

In 1872, Yellowstone was established as the first national park in North America. Spanning three states and 8,903 sq km (2.2 million acres), it's home to massive lakes, roaring waterfalls, abundant wildlife, and the largest geothermal area on Earth. More than four million people per year come to experience Yellowstone's unparalleled collection of natural wonders, yet less than one percent of these visitors head off the beaten track to go backpacking.

There are more than 1,449 km (900 mi) of hiking trails in Yellowstone National Park. Options range from short board-walked strolls among bubbling mud pots, burping geysers, and snap-happy tourists, to exacting multi-day excursions into the park's backcountry, where you are likely to encounter more bears, bison, and elk than you are fellow hikers. The Shoshone Lake Loop falls somewhere in the middle on the hiking difficulty scale. Measuring 46 km (29 mi) in length, the trail is suitable for intermediate to advanced backpackers, or beginners accompanied by an experienced companion. During its course, the path meanders through peaceful forests, wild-flower-laden meadows, and one section of shoe-sucking swampland. Opportunities for viewing wildlife abound, but the trail's twin highlights are undoubtedly Shoshone Lake and the Shoshone Geyser Basin.

Stretching across more than 32.4 sq km (8,000 acres), Shoshone Lake is the largest body of water in the contiguous United States that doesn't have road access. You'll find nothing but black sand beaches, deep-blue water, sweet-smelling pine forests, and—if you happen to be hiking in June or July—a few billion mosquitos putting out the welcome mat (you knew there had to be a catch). There are plenty of established camping areas (advance reservations are required) around the lake's shoreline, and drinking in the sunrises and sunsets from these scenic sites is one of the highlights of any trip. But the mosquitoes are also at their most ferocious during dawn and dusk, so be sure to bring repellant and appropriate clothing (see info box) to enjoy the sun's hellos and goodbyes without constant swatting and colorful language.

On the lake's western shore lies the impressive Shoshone Geyser Basin, the biggest backcountry geyser area in Yellowstone National Park. Among its hundreds of geothermal features are fumaroles, hot springs, bubbling mud pots, over 80 geysers, and an entrancing collection of multi-hued pools that smell of sulfur. Unlike the popular Upper Geyser Basin to the northwest, which contains the world-famous Old Faithful Geyser (see info box), the Shoshone Geyser Basin has no boardwalks and receives relatively few visitors. And therein lies part of its appeal. Long preserved due to its remote location, it remains in virtually the same pristine

↑ **Gazing northwards towards Shoshone Lake.**
→ **Shoshone Lake.**

condition as when it was first visited by non-natives (fur traders) in the early 1800s.

After soaking in the marvels of this geothermal wonderland, there are two alternative routes by which to finish the hike. You can either complete the circumambulation of Shoshone Lake back to the DeLacy Creek Trailhead, or head north toward Lone Star Geyser and Old Faithful Village. The former option provides more lake views and less in the way of foot traffic, while the latter gives you the chance to witness one of Yellowstone's most impressive and least-visited geysers—Lone Star Geyser. If you have the chance, go with the latter.

Yellowstone is home to more than 4,000 bison, the nation's largest herd on public land.

"More than four million people per year come to experience Yellowstone's unparalleled collection of natural wonders, yet less than one percent of these visitors head off the beaten track to go backpacking."

← Lone Star Geyser.
↓ The gem-like pools of Biscuit Basin—a short walk north from Old Faithful Geyser.
→ Lower Falls in the Grand Canyon of the Yellowstone.

Lone Star Geyser is located a 4.8 km (3 mi) walk from Old Faithful Village. It erupts approximately every three hours for about 30 minutes at a time, shooting water 13–17 m (40–50 ft) into the air. Its secluded forest setting beside the Firehole River is quite lovely—no roads, no lodges, no elbowing tourists looking for the perfect camera angle. It's an incredible sight to behold, and if you time your visit for dawn or dusk, you might even enjoy a private viewing. (Tip: Camp close by at either the OA1 or OA2 campsites.)

Lone Star Geyser and the entire Shoshone Lake Loop showcase many of the natural wonders for which Yellowstone is world-renowned. Although far from under the radar, it's an accessible trail that is well within the capabilities of most hikers. While walking along the serene forest pathways and gazing in awe at the mystical geysers, you will receive confirmation of something that holds true in most of the popular national parks around the United States: if you want to escape the crowds and experience natural places in relative solitude, nothing rivals hiking, backpacking, and giving yourself over to Mother Nature's schedule.

Mammoth Hot Springs Terraces.

GOOD TO KNOW

START / FINISH
DeLacy Creek Trailhead (alternate finish point: Old Faithful Village)

SEASON
May to September. It's worth noting that Yellowstone National Park is situated on a high plateau (also named Yellowstone) and has an average elevation of 2,400 m (8,000 ft). Even during the summer months, nighttime temperatures can hover near freezing or below.

PERMITS
All backcountry camping in Yellowstone requires a permit/reservation. Due to the popularity of some of the campsites around Shoshone Lake (especially during July and August), reservations should be made well in advance.

HELPFUL HINTS

BEAR SPRAY & BEAR POLES
Yellowstone is home to a large population of bears—both grizzly and black. Although not obligatory, park rangers recommend that backpackers carry a can of bear spray when hiking. Also, food storage poles can be found at all campsites along the Shoshone Lake Loop. At the end of each day, hikers hang their food from these poles in order to protect it from bears and other critters.

GEAR RECOMMENDATIONS
Bear spray; bug repellant; trail running shoes; rain jacket; warm insulation layer; beanie; double-wall tent; head net; small multi-tool; broad-brimmed

hat; lightweight binoculars; 11–15 m (36–49 ft) of rope for food hangs; quick-drying shorts that perform double duty for both hiking and taking a swim in Shoshone Lake.

FIVE (OTHER) RECOMMENDED OVERNIGHT HIKES IN YELLOWSTONE
1. Lamar River Trail (53 km [32.9 mi])
2. Sky Rim Loop (32.2 km [20 mi])
3. Black Canyon of the Yellowstone (30.6 km [19 mi])
4. Specimen Ridge Trail (27.5 km [17.1 mi])
5. Bechler River Trail (45 km [28 mi])

FIVE RECOMMENDED DAY HIKES IN YELLOWSTONE
1. Mount Washburn (10 km [6.2 mi])
2. North Rim Trail (Grand Canyon of Yellowstone) (10.9 km [6.8 mi])
3. Observation Point Trail (1.8 km [1.1 mi])
4. Artist Point – Point Sublime Trail (4.8 km [3 mi])
5. Bunsen Peak (7.1 km [4.4 mi])

FLORA & FAUNA

MAMMALS IN YELLOWSTONE
With 67 different species, Yellowstone National Park is home to the highest concentration of mammals in the United States. Among its most notable are grizzly bears, black bears, bison, moose, otters, wolves, elk, mule deer, wolverines, and bighorn sheep.

THE RETURN OF THE WOLF
Gray wolves are native to the Yellowstone area but were hunted to extinction by 1926. After an absence of almost seven decades, they were reintroduced into the park in 1995, and there are now 13 packs and more than 370 wolves in total living in the Greater Yellowstone Ecosystem.

WHERE THE BISON ROAM
Yellowstone is the only place in the United States where free-ranging bison have lived continuously since prehistoric times. The national park's

herd of over 4,000 is the largest herd in the country on public land, and according to the National Park Service, they are "among the few bison herds that have not been hybridized through interbreeding with cattle."
Fun fact: Bison are the leading cause of traffic jams on the park's roads during the summer.

BACKGROUND

OLD FAITHFUL GEYSER
The world's most famous geyser is situated only a few miles from the DeLacy Creek Trailhead. Named in 1870 by members of the Washburn Expedition who were amazed at the regularity of its eruptions, Old Faithful goes off every 60 to 90 minutes—on average 17 times a day—and shoots water 32–56 m (106–185 ft) into the air.

THE GRANDDADDY OF GEYSERS
The word "geyser" derives from the Icelandic term *geysir* (to gush). The original geyser, sometimes known as the Great Geysir, is located in the Haukadalur Valley in southwestern Iceland. It spurts water up to 70 m (230 ft) in the air, and the oldest account of its activity dates back to 1294. These days the Great Geysir is mostly dormant, but its far more active and almost as famous neighbor, Strokkur, goes off every few minutes and shoots water up to 30 m (98 ft) high.

FIVE FACTS ABOUT YELLOWSTONE NATIONAL PARK
1. Yellowstone has been inhabited for more than 11,000 years. The most well-known of the Native Americans to live either full-time or seasonally in the region were the Tukudika tribe.
2. Yellowstone National Park was established on March 1, 1872, making it North America's first designated national park (see next page).
3. It is home to more than 500 geysers, more than half of the total geysers on the planet.
4. The park is located on top of an active supervolcano and

experiences between 1,000 and 3,000 earthquakes per year. The last time the Yellowstone Caldera erupted was approximately 640,000 years ago, with the explosion estimated to be about 2,500 times larger than that of Mount St. Helens's devastating event of May 18, 1980.

5. At 8,900 sq km (2.2 million acres), Yellowstone is bigger than Delaware and Rhode Island combined. Of its total area, 96 percent is located in Wyoming, 3 percent in Montana, and 1 percent in Idaho.

Is Yellowstone the World's Oldest National Park?

Although technically speaking Yellowstone National Park was the first of its kind in the world, it was not the first government-protected natural area. That honor goes to Bogd Khan, one of the holiest mountains in Mongolia. Since as early as the thirteenth century, Bogd Khan has been considered sacred by Mongolians. In 1783, the mountain and its immediate surroundings were declared a protected site by the Qing dynasty government. To this day, Buddhists continue to make the pilgrimage to Bogd Khan, which is situated about one hour's drive southeast from the capital of Ulaanbaatar.

BASE CAMP TALES

Throughout Yellowstone National Park there are more than 10,000 hydrothermal features—by far the largest such collection on the planet. These can be divided into five separate categories: hot springs, geysers, mudpots, travertine terraces, and fumaroles:

Hot Springs
- Also known as thermal springs, hot springs are naturally occurring pools of water that are hotter than 36.7°C (98°F). They most commonly form when rainwater or groundwater is heated by molten rock below the earth's surface. A buildup of pressure then forces the heated water back up to the earth's surface via the same cracks and faults by which it was absorbed. Some of Yellowstone's thermal springs contain water that is suitable for bathing, however, most are far too hot for soaking. Two places that are ideal for visitors to enjoy a relaxing dip are the popular Boiling River located in the Mammoth area, and the not-so-easily accessible Mr. Bubbles Hot Springs. The latter is reached via the scenic Belcher River Trail, a 51 km (32 mi) out-and-back hike from Old Faithful.

Geysers
- Geysers are essentially blocked hot springs that periodically erupt in order to release the buildup of pressure. Apart from Old Faithful and Lone Star, other notable geysers in Yellowstone include Echinus, Castle, Grand, Riverside, and Steamboat— currently the world's tallest active geyser, capable of shooting water more than 91 m (300 ft) into the air.

Fumaroles
- Fumaroles are openings in the earth's surface that emit steam and volcanic gases, often with a distinct hissing or whistling sound. The most common hydrothermal feature in Yellowstone, fumaroles (also known as steam vents) are dry geysers that have so little water in their system that the H_2O boils away before it reaches the earth's surface.

Travertine Terraces
- According to the National Park Service, travertine terraces are "hot springs that rise up through limestone, dissolve the calcium carbonate, and deposit the calcite that makes the travertine terraces." These dazzling snow-white cliffs with shimmering tiered pools rank among the most singular and bizarre geological features on the planet, and one of the foremost examples is Yellowstone's Mammoth Hot Springs Terraces.

Mudpots
- A mudpot is a bubbling, burping, acidic hot spring, with very little water. The acidic content in mudpots is such that it dissolves the surrounding rock into mud and clay. The most well-known mudpots in Yellowstone are the Artist Paint Pots located 4.8 km (3 mi) south of Norris Geyser, and the Fountain Paint Pots which can be found in the Lower Geyser Basin just north of Old Faithful.

POINT OF VIEW

Measuring approximately 90 m (295 ft) wide and with a depth of 50 m (160 ft), the rainbow-colored Grand Prismatic Spring is the largest hot spring in North America and the third largest in the world. Its vivid multi-hued waters are due to heat-loving thermophilic bacteria, and even among Yellowstone's unparalleled collection of natural wonders, Grand Prismatic rates as something truly extraordinary. For views of this marvel of the Midway Geyser Basin, take the 1.9 km (1.2 mi) out-and-back Grand Prismatic Overlook Trail starting at the Fairy Falls Trailhead.

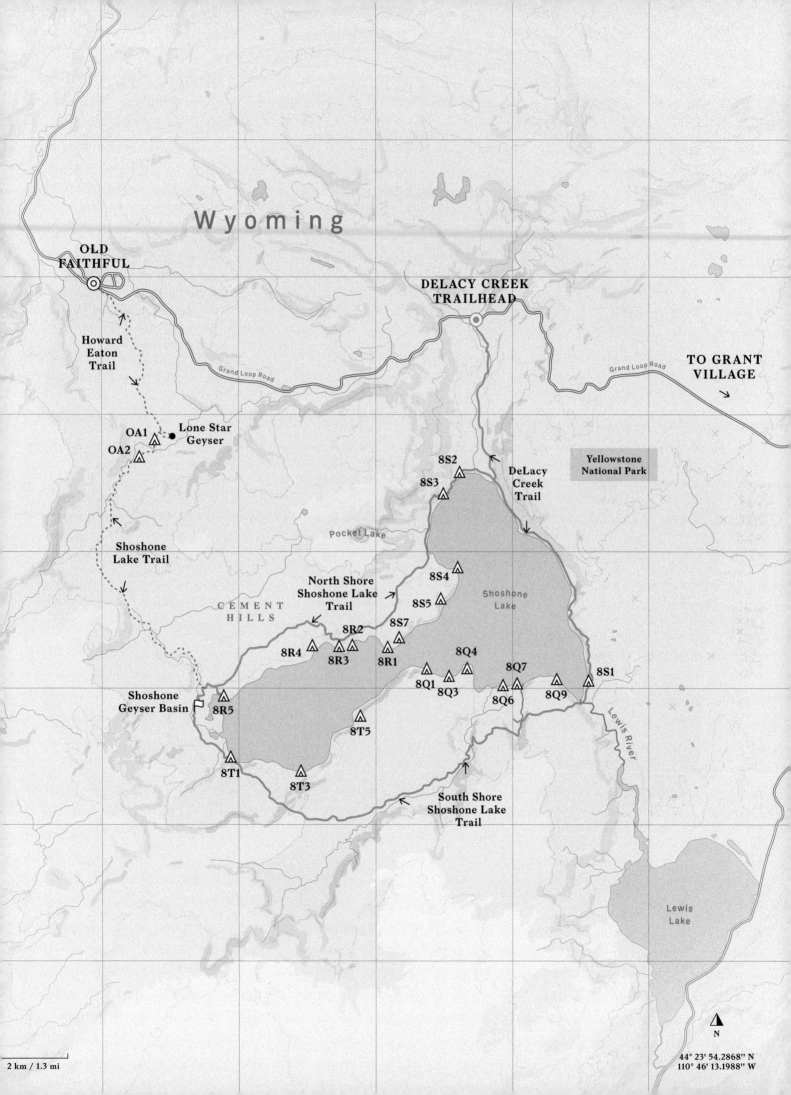

Wyoming

OLD FAITHFUL

Howard Eaton Trail

Grand Loop Road

DELACY CREEK TRAILHEAD

Grand Loop Road

TO GRANT VILLAGE

OA1

• Lone Star Geyser

OA2

Shoshone Lake Trail

Pocket Lake

8S2

8S3

DeLacy Creek Trail

Yellowstone National Park

North Shore Shoshone Lake Trail

8S4

8S5

Shoshone Lake

CEMENT HILLS

8R2

8S7

8R4

8R3

8R1

8Q4

8Q7

8S1

Shoshone Geyser Basin

8R5

8Q1

8Q3

8Q6

8Q9

Lewis River

8T5

8T1

8T3

South Shore Shoshone Lake Trail

Lewis Lake

2 km / 1.3 mi

N

44° 23' 54.2868" N
110° 46' 13.1988" W

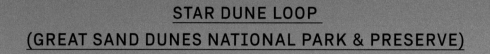

SANDY LEAPS AND SOARING PEAKS

Colorado
ROCKY MOUNTAINS

↑ Ridge-walking in the dunes.
→ Heading above tree line in the Sangre de Cristo Mountains.

ABOUT THE TRAIL
→ <u>DISTANCE</u> 10 km (6.2 mi) approx.
→ <u>DURATION</u> 5 hours
→ <u>LEVEL</u> Moderate

The Colorado Rockies are renowned for their lofty summits, shimmering lakes, and sweeping valleys. Yet nestled among these storied, arcadian mountains is an outlier tract of wilderness like no other in the United States. A four-hour drive south from Denver, Great Sand Dunes National Park & Preserve (GSDNP) is home to the tallest and most dramatic sand dunes in North America. Set at the foot of the Sangre de Cristo Mountains (a subrange of the Rockies), these Sahara-esque dunes combine with snow-capped peaks to make the most striking juxtaposition between desert and alpine scenery anywhere on the planet.

The dunes sit at an altitude between 2,439 and 2,743 m ([8,000 and 9,000 ft]) in the San Luis Valley, and cover 78 sq km (30 sq mi) within the boundaries of GSDNP. Dating back 500,000 years, they were formed when the sediment left behind by receding lakes was funneled by the predominantly southwest winds toward a low curve in the surrounding Sangre de Cristo Mountains, eventually forming the massive sea of sand that exists today.

The Star Dune Loop measures approximately 10 km (6.2 mi) in length and rates as one of the most exotic and downright fun treks in the United States. Over the course of five hours, you'll be channeling your inner Lawrence of Arabia as you traverse the highest dunes on the continent, while catching periodic glimpses of the towering white-topped mountains to the east. The route begins at the Great Sand Dunes parking area, and soon crosses Medano Creek (see info box), a snow-fed watercourse that runs along the side of the dune field. During years of above-average snowpack in the Sangres, keep an eye out for "surge flow," a naturally occurring hydrological phenomenon where water flows in waves across underwater sand ridges. During the warmer months, you often spot children—or those who are young at heart—riding the surges on inflatable tubes. (Tip: Bring one along to enjoy a post-hike rapids ride!)

Once Medano Creek has been forded, you will zigzag northwest along well-trodden ridges to the top of High Dune (198 m [699 ft] from base to top), the tallest dune visible from the parking lot. This is the most popular hiking destination in the park, and for those looking for something shorter and less demanding, an out-and-back trip takes about two hours. From the apex, the featured hike continues west across the loose and undulating terrain toward the pyramid-shaped Star Dune; at 230 m (755 ft), it's the highest dune in North America. The 360-degree panorama from the summit is breathtaking, in no small part due to the mountain of soft sand you will have just finished climbing.

Crossing Medano Creek.

↑ A sea of rippling sand.
↓ The wooded lower valleys of the Sangres.

There are a handful of noteworthy tips to keep in mind when hiking in GSDNP: 1. Bring sunglasses, a sun hat, and perhaps even a bandana to protect your face from the sand in case of strong winds; 2. Wear lightweight, breathable running shoes that are easy to slip on and off when they fill with sand; 3. The first section from Medano Creek to High Dune can be crowded after 9:00 a.m. Make a dawn start to increase the chances of having this incredible wonder almost all to yourself; 4. There is no trail as such in the dunes. While ascending, be sure to walk along the ridgelines and use other people's footprints where possible to make the going easier; 5. Focus on taking shorter steps and breathing steadily while climbing; 6. When descending from the high points, do so in leaps and bounds accompanied by lots of hooting and hollering. There's an incredible sense of freedom inherent to letting it all hang out when dropping down the face of a steep sand dune—it brings out the little kid in even the most seasoned of ramblers!

The Star Dune Loop is usually done as a day hike. But if you would like to make your time in the dunes even more extraordinary, consider stretching the trek out over two days and overnighting in America's premier sea of sand. Do so by starting out in the late afternoon in order to catch the sunset from High Dune. As the light fades, head west toward Star Dune until you find a solitary valley to make camp. Or even better—sleep under the night sky if rain isn't on the cards. Once you've set up, go for a wander in any direction that strikes your fancy. Gaze up at the star-filled heavens or look east toward the shadowy pinnacles of the Sangre de Cristo Mountains. It's enlivening to have places such as Great Sand Dunes all to yourself, and soon the throbbing and gleaming to which Saint-Exupéry so eloquently alludes will become acutely apparent. It's the heartbeat of Mother Earth, and only you can hear it pulsing.

"I have always loved the desert. One sits down on a desert sand dune, sees nothing, hears nothing. Yet through the silence something throbs, and gleams."

—

ANTOINE DE SAINT-EXUPÉRY,
THE LITTLE PRINCE

↑ Gazing north from the summit of Blanca Peak
(4,372 m [14,351 ft]).
← Prairie sunflowers (*Helianthus petiolaris*).

GOOD TO KNOW

START/FINISH
Great Sand Dunes parking area

SEASON
Year round. During the winter months, temperatures can drop below freezing and snow is a possibility. Summer brings with it the potential for electrical storms and high winds.

PERMITS
All visitors to Great Sand Dunes National Park & Preserve (GSDNP) will need to pay an entrance fee. If you're interested in doing an overnight backpacking trip in the dunes or other parts of the park, free backcountry permits are available only in person at the visitor center.

HELPFUL HINTS

WATER
Once you cross Medano Creek, there are no water sources in the dunes. Plan on taking at least two to three liters for the Star Dune Loop; more if you intend to stay overnight.

CAMPING
Camping in the sand dunes is an ethereal experience. Due to the park's isolated location, the night skies can be incredible. When it comes to pitching your shelter, note that snow/sand tent pegs with a broad profile provide more holding power in the soft terrain. If the forecast is for clear weather, consider sleeping under the stars sans tent.

FLORA & FAUNA

PRAIRIE SUNFLOWERS
In wet summers, the grasslands surrounding Great Sand Dunes come alive with a blanket of prairie sunflowers (*Helianthus petiolaris*). Pockets of these gorgeous blooming plants can also be seen in the dunes during this time, creating a striking contrast with the otherwise barren terrain.

KANGAROO RAT
Within the national park's alpine and grassland areas, it's possible to spot bighorn sheep, black bears, mule deer, pikas, and marmots. If you're very fortunate—or unfortunate, depending on the proximity—you might also see a mountain lion. However, the only mammal capable of living its entire life in the dune field is the Ord's kangaroo rat. According to the National Park Service, these nocturnal creatures "collect seeds from various grasses and sunflowers, and hide them in moist sand below the surface. After a couple of days collecting moisture, the seeds now provide a little water to these rodents that can live their entire lives without drinking." *Fun fact: Ord's kangaroo rats are so named because of their uncommon jumping ability. In order to avoid predators, they are able to leap up to 1.5 m (5 ft) in the air. When jumping doesn't work, they commonly kick sand in their would-be attacker's face.*

BACKGROUND

SACRED BLANCA PEAK
The towering Sangre de Cristo Range forms the most dramatic of backdrops for Great Sand Dunes National Park & Preserve. Of the many prominent mountains in the chain, the highest, as well as one of the most scenic and accessible, is Blanca Peak (4,372 m [14,345 ft]). Located at the southern end of Colorado's Sangres, Blanca Peak is one of the Navajo people's four sacred mountains. They call it *Sisnaajiní* (or *Tsisnaasjini'*), which means the Dawn or White Shell Mountain. Fit and acclimatized hikers can make the ascent to the summit via a 35 km (22 mi) out-and-back trek from Lake Como Trailhead, located just off SH-150, a 30-minute drive south of the GSDNP Visitor Center.

AUTHOR'S ANECDOTE

SANGRE DE CRISTO TRAVERSE
In September 2016, I hiked the length of Great Sand Dunes National Park & Preserve as part of an eight-day traverse of Colorado's Sangre de Cristo (Blood of Christ) mountains. My route began at the town of Salida in the north, and finished on the summit of Blanca Peak (4,372 m [14,351 ft]) in the south. The trek was largely an off-trail affair, measuring approximately 180 km (112 mi) in length, with a cumulative elevation gain of more than 12,192 m (40,000 ft). The rugged terrain encountered during my journey was mostly above tree line, and the knife-edged profile of the Sangre crest meant that when thunderstorms rolled through, bailing off the ridge was by no means an easy proposition. That said, when you're hiking at around 4,000 m (13,123 ft) on treeless mountaintops and lightning is striking all around you, seeking lower ground is the only safe option available. *Note: Lightning generally zaps the tallest object or point in the vicinity.* When not shrouded in a blanket of thick storm clouds, the alpine scenery in the Sangres was sublime. There were jagged peaks, crystalline lakes, and dramatic glacier-carved valleys on both sides of the crest. Equally spectacular was the relatively short section through Great Sand Dunes. Measuring around 17 km (10 mi) in total, I loved every undulating yard, especially the galloping descents of the steeper dunes!

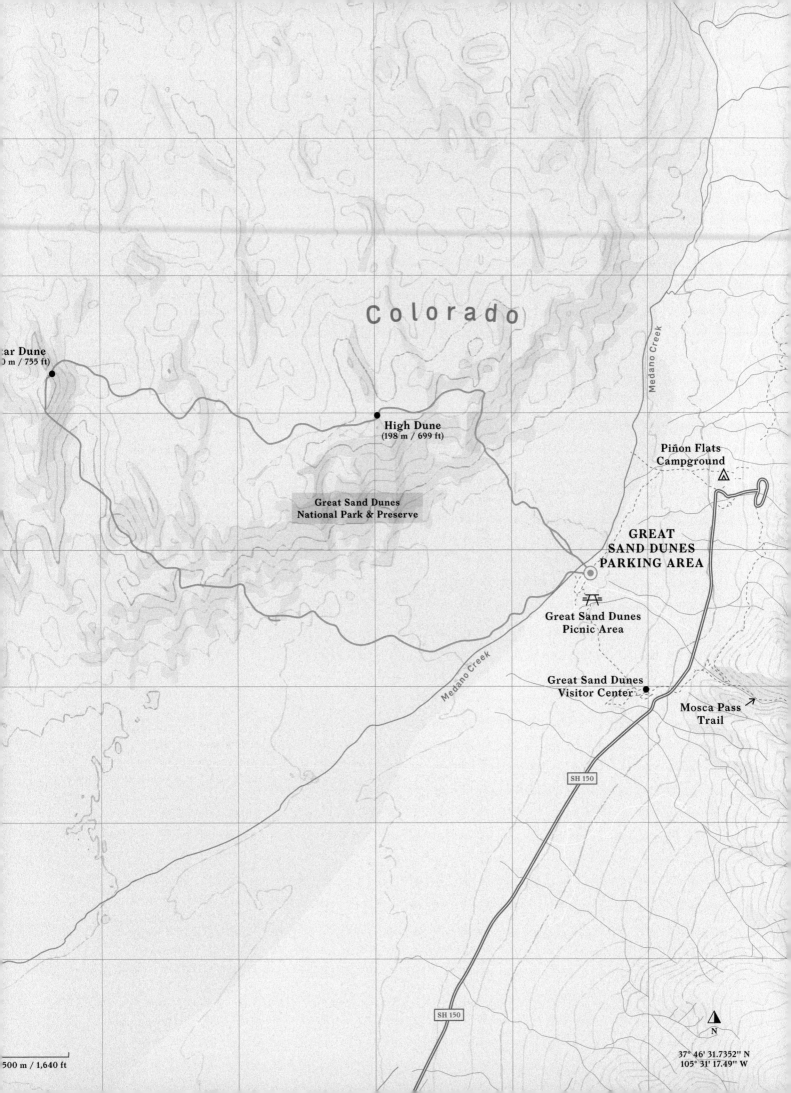

Colorado

ar Dune
0 m / 755 ft)

High Dune
(198 m / 699 ft)

Great Sand Dunes
National Park & Preserve

Medano Creek

Piñon Flats
Campground

GREAT
SAND DUNES
PARKING AREA

Great Sand Dunes
Picnic Area

Medano Creek

Great Sand Dunes
Visitor Center

Mosca Pass
Trail

SH 150

SH 150

N

37° 46' 31.7352" N
105° 31' 17.49" W

500 m / 1,640 ft

PEAKS, PLATEAUS, AND ALPINE BAPTISMS

Montana
ROCKY MOUNTAINS

ABOUT THE TRAIL
→ <u>DISTANCE</u> 106 km (66 mi) approx.
→ <u>DURATION</u> 5 to 7 days
→ <u>LEVEL</u> Challenging

Montana's Beartooth Range is one of the most dramatic, challenging, and solitary places to hike in the contiguous United States. Located just over 100 km (62 mi) northeast of Yellowstone National Park, the mountains resemble a fusion between the Swiss Alps and the Tibetan Plateau. As with the Alps, they contain towering granite peaks, glacier-sculpted valleys, and serene alpine lakes (not much in the way of chocolate, unfortunately). And just as with Tibet's "Rooftop of the World," the Beartooth Mountains are also known for their treeless, windswept, and bone-chillingly cold plateau landscape.

The Beartooth Mountains are one of two distinct ranges that form the Absaroka-Beartooth Wilderness (3,820 sq km [944,00 acres]) of Montana and Wyoming. The Absaroka Range is lower in elevation, more forested, and—unlike the granite-laden Beartooths—it consists primarily of volcanic and metamorphic rocks. Together, they constitute one of the most pristine and unheralded regions of America's West. However, if you had to choose just one of the two areas in which to spend a hiking holiday, it's hard to go past the higher and more spectacular Beartooths.

The trekking possibilities here are practically limitless. For newbies and intermediate ramblers, the best choice is the appropriately named Beaten Path. Measuring 42 km (26 mi) in length, it runs in a southwesterly direction across the range from East Rosebud Trailhead to just outside of Cooke City (population: 140). As you might expect, the Beaten Path is a well-maintained and easy-to-follow trail that sees a relatively high amount of foot traffic. Most importantly, it includes oodles of beautiful mountain scenery, and though it may not be as difficult as other hiking options in the Beartooths, it's by no means a poor man's option.

For those who aspire to go beyond the Beaten Path—both literally and metaphorically—an excellent choice is the Beartooth High Route (BHR). The BHR is a mostly off-trail 106 km (66 mi) loop hike pioneered by American long-distance hikers Steven Shattuck and Andrew Bentz in 2016. From a logistical standpoint, it has the advantage of starting and finishing at the same place, meaning that you don't have to worry about long shuttles or unpredictable hitchhikes back to your vehicle. (Note: There are no public transport options for the Beartooth Range.)

"Be sure to go for at least
one swim during your time
in the Beartooth Range.
There are very few things in life
as invigorating as taking
a dip in a remote mountain lake
surrounded by nothing
but peaks and blues skies."

← Striding out on the Beartooth High Route.
↑ The view from Granite Peak (3,904 m [12,087 ft]),
  looking south towards Sky Top Lakes.
← Crystal-clear lakes and soaring peaks.

Bears Tooth—the distinctive granite spire which gives the mountain range its name.

↑ The Beartooth Highway between Red Lodge and Yellowstone National Park is one of America's most scenic drives.
↓ The Beartooth Mountains are home to more than a 1,000 alpine lakes.

From an aesthetic perspective, the BHR encompasses an amazing cross section of the range's geographical features, including 8 named peaks, 33 named lakes, and above-tree-line plateaus. One of the other advantages of this particular route is that it can easily be cut short if the weather takes a turn for the worse by linking up with the Beaten Path (see overview map). Having a Plan B (and even a Plan C) is no small matter in a region renowned for its extreme meteorological conditions.

The BHR is one of the most demanding treks covered within these pages. However, if you're fit and experienced, your senses will reap what your legs and lungs have sowed—the scenery is dizzyingly beautiful throughout its course! One of the standout features of the trek comes in the form of a challenging 2.4 km (1.5 mi) out-and-back side trip to the summit of Granite Peak. The highest mountain in Montana, its ascent involves a Class 3 scramble up steep and loose talus. The reward is a 360-degree quadruple-take (one for every 90 degrees) panorama encompassing glaciers, tooth-like spires, lonely valleys, unforgiving plateaus, and a remarkable collection of lakes that come in every shade of blue imaginable.

Speaking of lakes, be sure to go for at least one swim during your time in the Beartooth Range. There are very few things in life as invigorating as taking a dip in a remote mountain lake surrounded by nothing but peaks and blues skies. You will emerge spiritually recharged and physically reborn after the bracing plunge—an alpine baptism courtesy of Mother Nature herself!

↑ Lakeside camping.

GOOD TO KNOW

START/FINISH
East Rosebud Trailhead

There are three other alternative start/finish points for the Beartooth High Route, but the only other option that doesn't include a lengthy approach hike is the Camp Senia Trailhead, located near Silver Run Plateau.

HIGHEST / LOWEST POINT
Granite Peak
(3,904 m [12,808 ft])
East Rosebud Trailhead
(1,914 m [6,230 ft])

SEASON
Mid-July to mid-September

PERMITS
You do not need a permit to hike in the Beartooth Mountains.

HELPFUL HINTS

FISHING FOR DINNER
If you've ever thought about bringing a lightweight, collapsible fishing rod on a hike, the Beartooth High Route is the hike for you. The crystal-clear lakes of the Absaroka-Beartooth Wilderness are renowned for having some of the finest trout fishing in the Rockies; varieties of trout include rainbow, brook, cutthroat, and golden. You can pick up a fishing license in either Red Lodge or Cooke City before your hike.

POST-HIKE FEAST
The nearest town to the East Rosebud Trailhead is Red Lodge, Montana. After finishing your trek, a great place to enjoy a well-priced celebratory meal is Red Lodge Pizza. The extensive menu offers organic burgers, an excellent salad bar, and—you guessed it—tasty pizzas. There is also beer on tap and wine by the glass.

FLORA & FAUNA

In the forested valleys of the Beartooth Range, moose, mule deer, elk, and grizzly bears can be spotted. Higher up on the ridges and plateaus, keep an eye out for pikas. And if you're lucky, you may spot a bighorn sheep or a mountain goat.

BACKGROUND

HOW THE BEARTOOTH MOUNTAINS GOT THEIR NAME
The mountains are named after a spire on the east ridge of Beartooth Mountain (3,766 m [12,356 ft]), one of the most prominent peaks in the range. The area's original inhabitants, the Crow Tribe, called it *Na Pet Say*— the Bear's Tooth.

BEARTOOTH HIGHWAY, AN ALL-AMERICAN ROAD
Since its opening in 1937, the Beartooth Highway has been recognized as one of the most scenic drives in the United States. Stretching 109 km (68 mi) from Red Lodge, Montana, to the northeast entrance of Yellowstone National Park in Wyoming, it affords visitors breathtaking views of the Absaroka and Beartooth Mountains. It also takes drivers over the highest-elevation highway in the Northern Rockies, with high points of 3,155 m (10,350 ft) in Montana and 3,337 m (10,947 ft) in Wyoming. Due to heavy snow conditions at these lofty elevations, the road is usually only passable between mid-May and mid-October, weather permitting. *Tip: For a spectacular panorama and a small but fascinating museum, don't miss the short side trip off the Beartooth Highway to Clay Butte Lookout Tower, a refurbished fire tower with an observation deck.*

AUTHOR'S ANECDOTE

RIDING OUT THE STORM
I ended day four of my 2016 trek in the Beartooth Mountains camped a few hundred meters northeast of Aero Lakes. The elevation was a little over 3,100 m (10,171 ft), and the last hour of hiking had been done in a light and steady drizzle. It turned out this was just a meteorological teaser for what was to come. Literally moments after I'd finished pitching my tarp, the wind picked up and the heavens opened. Over the next couple of hours the elements raged all around me (thunder, lightning, driving winds, and heavy precipitation), but warm and dry in my sleeping bag, I was at peace. After eating a spartan dinner of cold dehydrated beans and corn chips, I fell into a deep sleep, listening to the rapid-fire pitter-patter of rain on my low and taut Cuben Fiber rooftop.

The following day I awoke to clear skies and a gentle breeze. Even after all these years of hiking, I still get a kick out of opening my eyes the morning after a huge storm to find that all my gear is dry, my shelter held up well, and, most importantly, I'm safe and sound—small, but meaningful confirmations that I've been diligent and taken nothing for granted.

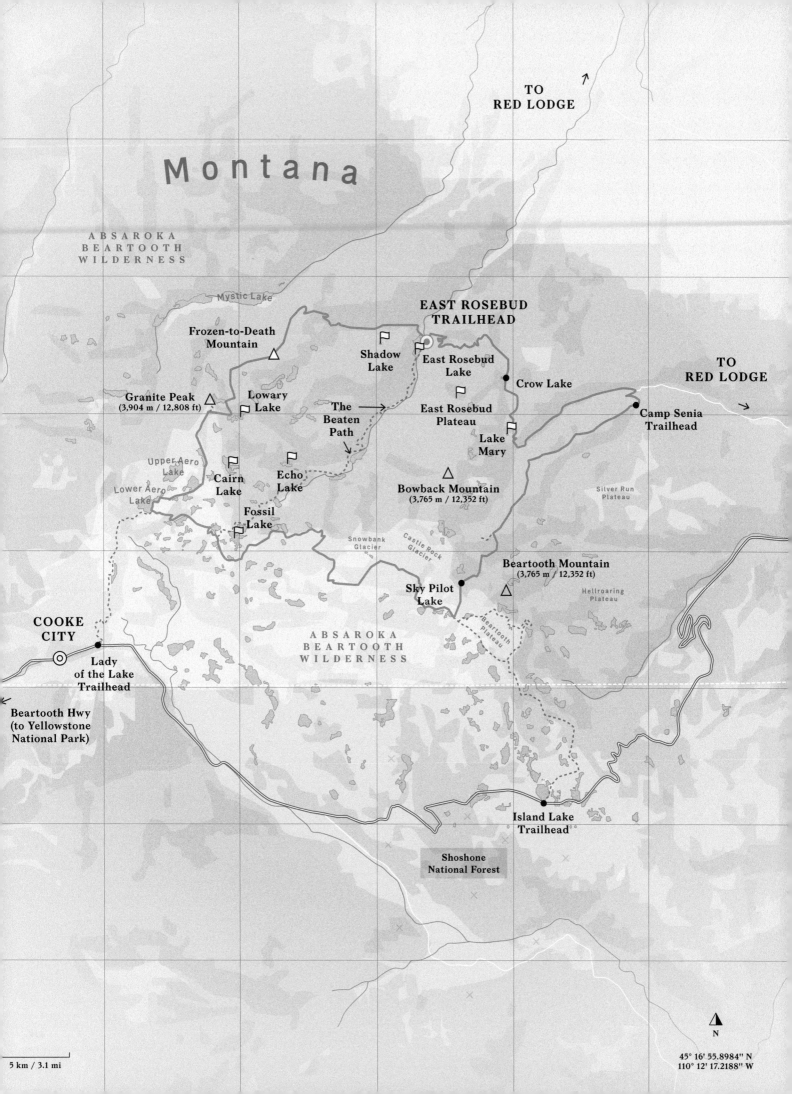

Montana

TO
RED LODGE

ABSAROKA
BEARTOOTH
WILDERNESS

Mystic Lake

Frozen-to-Death
Mountain

EAST ROSEBUD
TRAILHEAD

Shadow
Lake

East Rosebud
Lake

Crow Lake

TO
RED LODGE

Granite Peak
(3,904 m / 12,808 ft)

Lowary
Lake

The
Beaten
Path

East Rosebud
Plateau

Camp Senia
Trailhead

Lake
Mary

*Upper Aero
Lake*

Cairn
Lake

Echo
Lake

*Silver Run
Plateau*

*Lower Aero
Lake*

Bowback Mountain
(3,765 m / 12,352 ft)

Fossil
Lake

*Snowbank
Glacier*

*Castle Rock
Glacier*

Beartooth Mountain
(3,765 m / 12,352 ft)

*Hellroaring
Plateau*

Sky Pilot
Lake

*Beartooth
Plateau*

COOKE
CITY

ABSAROKA
BEARTOOTH
WILDERNESS

Lady
of the Lake
Trailhead

Beartooth Hwy
(to Yellowstone
National Park)

Island Lake
Trailhead

Shoshone
National Forest

N

5 km / 3.1 mi

45° 16' 55.8984" N
110° 12' 17.2188" W

MIDWEST

Often overlooked in favor of the iconic ranges to the east and
west, America's heartland contains a diverse array of hiking
options, including the fantastical Badlands, the shores of
mighty Lake Superior, and one of the country's best-kept
backpacking secrets—the Interior Highlands.

SUPERIOR HIKING TRAIL

BETWEEN
THE CELESTIAL
AND THE AQUATIC

Minnesota
MIDWEST

"Try to time your hike so as to reach these high points at sunrise or sunset, when the shine of the rising or setting sun blends seamlessly with Superior's famously clear waters, creating a sublime union of the celestial and the aquatic."

↑ Waves pound Lake Superior's wooded shoreline during a heavy storm.
→ Surveying the route ahead.
↗ A bridge over rapid waters.

ABOUT THE TRAIL

→ <u>DISTANCE</u> 499 km (310 mi)

→ <u>DURATION</u> 17 to 20 days

→ <u>LEVEL</u> Moderate

Minnesota's Superior Hiking Trail is fittingly named for its location, purpose, and quality. Tracing the ridgeline above Lake Superior's northern shore, this pedestrian-only footpath showcases a remarkable collection of plunging waterfalls, sheer cliffs, tranquil ponds, and roaring rivers. Quite possibly the finest long-distance trail between the Rockies and the Appalachians, it plays peekaboo with its namesake lake for much of its 499 km (310 mi) course, regularly oscillating between deep gorges and scenic high points.

Accessibility is one of the attributes that sets the Superior Hiking Trail apart from many other long-distance pathways in the United States. It is very much a "trail of the people," one that is open to hikers of all ages and levels of fitness and experience. It is well marked with blue blazes, has plenty of campsite options (93 in total), and thanks to its myriad trailheads, can be enjoyed equally by day hikers, long weekenders, or thru-hikers out for multiple weeks at a time.

The Superior Hiking Trail stretches between Jay Cooke State Park in the south and the 270 Degree Overlook on the Canadian border in the north. The trail can be hiked in either direction, and generally takes between two and three weeks to complete in its entirety. Between mid-September and late October, the skies above the north shore of Lake Superior play host to thousands of eagles, hawks, ospreys, falcons, and kestrels all heading south from their summer breeding grounds near the Arctic Circle to their warmer winter homes in South America.

During the annual exodus, many raptors are drawn to the ridgeline along Superior's northern shore, where they receive a volitant assist from upward-moving thermal drafts; in other words, more gliding and less flapping. This is no small thing on a multi-thousand-kilometer journey—saving as much energy as possible is paramount (not dissimilar to long-distance hiking!).

The ridgeline above Superior's northern shore is not only ideal for taking in the birdlife, but it also presents periodic lookout points to soak up the vast and timeless beauty of Lake

Overlooking Bear Lake, with Bean Lake in the distance.

↑ A boardwalk crossing at Sawmill Creek.
← The trail often undulates between high
   scenic lookouts and dramatic river valleys.

Superior. The largest freshwater lake in the world by surface area (82,100 sq km [31,700 sq mi]), Superior is bigger than the Czech Republic, and almost the same size as the state of South Carolina. If at all possible, try to time your hike so as to reach these high points at sunrise or sunset, when the shine of the rising or setting sun blends seamlessly with Superior's famously clear waters, creating a sublime union of the celestial and the aquatic.

In between these scenic lookouts, the landscape regularly drops into picturesque river and creek valleys that feature ample opportunities for spotting a variety of wildlife (see info box). Although there is more than 11,278 m (37,000 ft) of total elevation gain and loss, the pathway does not have long ascents or descents, instead boasting a multitude of short, sharp climbs and dips. And despite its name, the Superior Hiking Trail actually spends very little time routed along the lake itself. Because much of the northern shore is privately owned, there is only one short stretch north of Grand Marais, Minnesota, where the trail and the lakeshore are contiguous.

The Superior Hiking Trail is the crown jewel of long-distance pathways in America's Midwest—a 499-km-long (310-mi-long) invitation from Mother Nature to immerse yourself in the Minnesotan wilderness and its wonders. Thanks to the trail's singularly accessible, well-maintained character, your footfall will always be welcomed, regardless of how much fitness, experience, or time you have at your disposal.

↑ Singing in the rain.
↓ Gazing eastward towards Lake Superior, the largest freshwater lake in the world by surface area (82,100 sq km [31,700 sq mi]).

GOOD TO KNOW

START / FINISH
Southern Trailhead
Jay Cooke State Park
Northern Trailhead
270 Degree Overlook (1.9 km [1.2 mi]
north of the Otter Lake Road Trailhead)

HIGHEST / LOWEST POINT
Rosebush Ridge (557 m [1,827 ft])
Lake Superior (183 m [602 ft])

SEASON
May to October

ACCOMMODATION
On-Trail
As of 2019, there are 93 campsites
located along the trail. Stealth or
wild camping is not permitted on
the Superior Hiking Trail.
In-Town
If you are looking for a hot shower
and a comfortable bed, the best
accommodation options are available
in the towns of Finland and Grand
Marais (Minnesota).

HELPFUL HINTS

LAKESHORE TRAIL
For hikers looking for a shorter
alternative, consider the 68 km (42 mi)
Lakeshore Trail. Situated on Lake
Superior's southern shore in the state
of Michigan, the Lakeshore Trail is
a gorgeous trek between Munising
and Grand Marais (Michigan), which
encompasses lighthouses, sand dunes,
shipwrecks, beaches, and, of course,
magnificent views of Lake Superior.

FLORA & FAUNA

In regard to wildlife on the Superior
Hiking Trail, there are moose, eagles,
black bears, grouse, deer, and, if you're
lucky—or unlucky depending on the
proximity—wolves. The prevalence of
beaver dams throughout much of the
hike means that water along the SHT
should be treated.

BACKGROUND

THE BIRTHPLACE OF BOB DYLAN
The southern terminus of the trail is
a few miles south of the Minnesota
city of Duluth. With a population of just
under 90,000, Duluth is the fourth-
largest city in the state, and alongside
its interstate neighbor, Superior,
Michigan, it represents the largest port
on Lake Superior. For many die-hard
music fans, Duluth's claim to fame
is that it's the birthplace of Robert
Zimmerman (aka Bob Dylan), the
legendary folk singer and Nobel Prize
winner for literature. During your hike,
it's possible to visit Dylan's birthplace
on North Third Avenue, a nondescript
duplex house with no blazing signs to
show you that you've found the right
place. There is simply a small plaque
embedded in the sidewalk out front
that reads, "In Bob We Trust."

BONUS TRACK

OLD LOG THEATER
If you're flying into or out of Minnesota,
chances are you'll be doing so from
Minneapolis, part of the famous "Twin
Cities," a moniker shared with the
state capital of St. Paul. If you have
the time, try to catch a show at the Old
Log Theater, the oldest continuously
operating professional playhouse in
the country. Opened in 1940, the theater
was revamped in 1965 by architect
Herb Bloomberg. Inspired by the barn
design emblematic of the Midwest,
Bloomberg expanded the building to
fit 655 people. 48 years later, Greg and
Marissa Frankenfield—theater fanatics
and owners of a major Minnesota IT
firm—acquired the venerable landmark.
Estimates suggest the Old Log Theater
has welcomed over six million people
since it opened its doors almost eight
decades ago.

TRANS SUPERIOR YACHT RACE
In August of every odd year since 1969,
Lake Superior has been the site of the
Trans Superior International Yacht
Race. The competition started off as a
challenge between two longtime friends,
John Pierpoint and Jack Soetebier, both
of whom hail from White Pine, Michigan.

The course is 326 nautical miles
(the equivalent of 603 km [375 mi]) in
length, and it extends between Gros Cap
Light near Sault Ste. Marie, Michigan,
and the Duluth Ship Canal in Minnesota.
The world's longest known freshwater
sailboat race, competitors often have to
deal with exacting conditions, with high
winds and waves up to 3 m (10 ft) high
being commonplace.

CANADA

270 DEGREE
OVERLOOK

Rosebush Ridge
(557 m / 1,827 ft)

Pincushion
Mountain

Judge C.R. Magney
State Park

Cascade River
State Park

Oberg
Mountain

Grand
Marais

Lake Superior

Finland

Crosby Manitou
State Park

Silver Bay

Minnesota

Gooseberry Falls
State Park

Split Rock
Lighthouse
State Park

Two Harbors

U.S. Hwy 53

DULUTH

JAY COOKE
STATE PARK

Wisconsin

I-35

TO
INNEAPOLIS

U.S. Hwy 53

TO
EAU CLAIRE

N

40 km / 25 mi

46° 38' 29.5836" N
92° 20' 50.1432" W

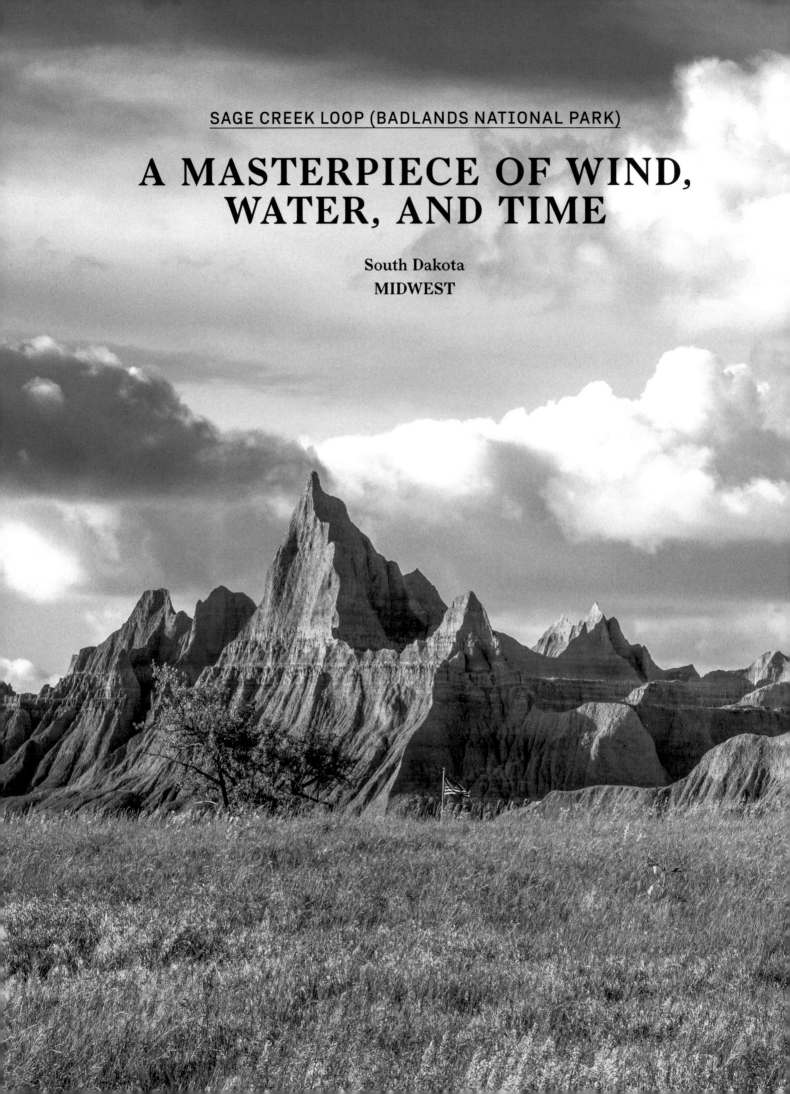

SAGE CREEK LOOP (BADLANDS NATIONAL PARK)

A MASTERPIECE OF WIND, WATER, AND TIME

South Dakota
MIDWEST

ABOUT THE TRAIL

→ <u>DISTANCE</u> 36 km (22.4 mi)

→ <u>DURATION</u> 2 to 3 days

→ <u>LEVEL</u> Moderate

Badlands National Park encompasses one of the most surreal and unique landscapes in North America. Situated among the prairies of southwestern South Dakota, its defining feature and raison d'être is the Wall, a sprawling escarpment of sheer cliffs, labyrinthine ravines, and fantastical rock formations that stretches for approximately 100 km (62 mi) from east to west. It is a place that has long inspired both awe, as well as trepidation, in those who have gazed upon it. The area's original

inhabitants, the Oglala Lakota, called the harsh landscape *mako sica*, which translates to "land bad"; and when French-Canadian fur trappers arrived centuries later, they similarly dubbed it *les mauvaises terres à traverser* (bad lands to travel through).

Considering its foreboding moniker, it's no surprise that the Badlands is not exactly a backpacking mecca. It isn't easy to get to, and there's a dearth of potable water and trail infrastructure. Throw in an almost complete lack of shade and summer temperatures that regularly top 40°C (104°F), and you'll begin to understand why most people who tour the area do so from the comfort of their air-conditioned vehicles. Indeed, visits to the Badlands generally consist of taking a few snapshots from the lookouts along the park's scenic loop road, followed by a 30-minute to 1-hour stroll along one of the short, manicured pathways close to the visitor center.

"Situated among the prairies of southwestern South Dakota, its defining feature and raison d'être is the Wall, a sprawling escarpment of sheer cliffs, labyrinthine ravines, and fantastical rock formations."

← Upon first seeing the Badlands, French-Canadian fur trappers dubbed it *les mauvaises terres à traverser* (bad lands to travel through).
↓ Ladder climbing on the Notch Trail, one of Badlands National Park's most popular day hikes.

However (and you knew there was going to be a "however"), for experienced hikers looking for an off-the-beaten track adventure, the Badlands offers an atypical combination of geology, flora, fauna, and solitude. Exploring its backcountry requires no special permits or reservations; however, given its lack of trails, those considering a multi-day trip in the Badlands should be comfortable navigating with a map and compass and/or GPS. Among a multitude of rambling possibilities, an excellent option that covers all the renowned elements in the park is the Sage Creek Loop (SCL).

Starting and finishing at the Conata Picnic Area, the SCL measures 36 km (22.4 mi) in length and can be completed in two or three days. When planning your trip, perhaps the most important consideration is water. In short, you'll have to carry a lot of it—at least four liters per day—as there are no potable sources to be found along the route (see info box). During its

The colors of the Badlands geological layers tell the story of 75 million years of Earth's history.

↑ Roaming bison in the Sage Creek Wilderness Area.

course, the loop traverses wide-open grasslands and serpentine washes while meandering its way through the Badlands' singular collection of spires, buttes, cliffs, jagged ridges, and pinnacles. Among the highlights of the SLC, two of its most memorable sections are Deer Haven and the Sage Creek Basin.

Hiking in a counter-clockwise direction, Deer Haven is located less than two hours of easy walking from the trailhead. An elevated oasis of junipers surrounded by implausible rock formations, it appears as an island of verdant green set among a sea of desert hues. Its cool confines act not only as a magnet for the park's wildlife (it is one of Badlands' few forested areas), but also represent a great campsite option for those who make a late start to the trek. With the Wall as your backdrop and the sweeping prairies in the foreground, the sunsets from Deer Haven are magnificent.

Leaving the shady trees behind, climb steeply to the highest point of the route—a scenic narrow ridge at 884 m (2,900 ft)—before descending into a maze-like wash that eventually leads to Sage Creek Basin. It's during this section that you'll likely encounter North America's largest land animal, the bison.

A small herd of 50 were reintroduced into Badlands National Park in 1963, and as of 2019 their numbers have swelled to more than 1,200—one of the largest federal bison herds in the country. Observing them as they roam the open prairies is a wondrous experience; however, it's worth remembering that they are wild animals, and despite their massive bulk—mature males can weigh up to 900 kg (1,984 lb)—they are capable of moving at speeds of up to 65 km/h (40 mph). Keep a distance of at least 100 yards (90 m) at all times, and be careful not to camp on or near the bison trails that crisscross much of the Badlands. There's no surer way to put a damper on your hiking trip than by having your tent, with you in it, trampled by a bison.

Despite its name, the Badlands is a place that's more inviting than foreboding for those who come prepared for its exacting conditions. While the alien-like landscape may not seem of this planet, in reality the colors of its geological layers tell the story of 75 million years of Earth's history. And while walking among its collection of rock treasures, it's difficult not to be awestruck at what the erosive forces of wind and water can carve out if given enough time.

GOOD TO KNOW

START / FINISH
Conata Picnic Area Trailhead

HIGHEST / LOWEST POINT
Ridge above Deer Haven
(884 m [2,900 ft])
Conata Picnic Area Trailhead
(791 m [2,595 ft])

SEASON
April to June and mid-September to November. With temperatures often exceeding 40°C (105°F), backpacking during the height of summer is not recommended.

PERMITS
All visitors to Badlands National Park are required to pay a park entrance fee, but permits are not required for camping/backpacking in the Badlands backcountry. Note that there is a backcountry register at the Conata Picnic Area Trailhead, where you can leave the details of your trip itinerary.

HELPFUL HINTS

BADLANDS HYDRATION STRATEGIES
There are no reliable potable water sources on the Sage Creek Loop. Therefore, you will need to haul all H_2O from the beginning of your trek. It's recommended to carry at least four liters per day, drink small amounts at regular intervals, and, if possible, try to find a shady spot where you can rest during the middle of the day. Other hydration tips include:

1. Try to do as much hiking as possible during the early morning and late afternoon.
2. Consider eating cold food for the duration of your trip, as this means you won't have to lug extra water for cooking.
3. Plan to complete the hike in two days, rather than the often recommended three days. This will also mean you don't have to carry as much water. The distances

are not that great for experienced backpackers, so as long as you wake up early and take advantage of the cooler temperatures, the shorter timeframe should be well within your capabilities.

FLORA & FAUNA

THE RETURN OF BIGHORN SHEEP
Bighorn Sheep are one of the Badlands' most iconic species. These magnificent creatures are native to the region, but by 1916 they had been exterminated in the Badlands due to overhunting. In 1964, nearly five decades later, the National Park Service reintroduced 22 Rocky Mountain bighorns (*Ovis canadensis*) from Colorado. According to recent estimates, they now number over 100 and are once again thriving in their natural habitat. *Fun fact: The species is named after their unusually large curling horns, which can weigh up to 14 kg (30 lb). The male bighorn sheep are called rams, and the size of their horns are a symbol of their rank in the herd. The females are called ewes, and they have smaller horns that don't exceed half a curl.*

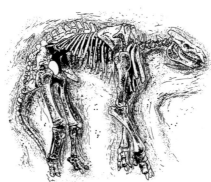

BACKGROUND

FORMER RESIDENTS
Badlands National Park is renowned for preserving one of the world's richest deposits of mammal fossil beds from the Oligocene epoch (33.9–23 million years ago). Over the years, fossil research conducted in the Badlands area has significantly contributed to the science of vertebrate paleontology, and skeletons discovered in the region

include hornless rhinoceros, three-toed horses, saber-toothed cats, small deer-like creatures, and marine reptiles (the Badlands began as a shallow inland sea 75 million years ago). A good way to gain insight into the area's natural history is to take a stroll on the Fossil Exhibit Trail, a short 400 m (1,312 ft) boardwalk near the visitor center, which contains fossil replicas housed in display cases.

AUTHOR'S ANECDOTE

"IT'S THE BADLANDS, BABY"
In September 2016, I pioneered a 145 km (90 mi) full-length traverse of Badlands National Park. The most challenging aspect of the trip was the dearth of potable water along the route. In light of the parched landscape, I began my journey carrying 12 liters of H_2O—enough to get me through to the tiny ghost town of Scenic on the park's western outskirts, where I knew I could fill up for the second and final stage of the trek.

Not more than 25 minutes after setting out from Ben Reifel Visitor Center, I was just about to leave the Badlands Loop Road for the path less traveled, when a yellow and white combi van pulled up beside me. Inside was a bohemian-looking couple who looked to be in their early to mid-sixties.

The lady in the passenger seat asked me if I needed a ride. "No thank you," I replied. She then asked me where I was going, to which I gave her a quick synopsis of my plan to hike from one end of the park to the other. She seemed genuinely concerned for my welfare. After a minute or two of assuring her that I knew what I was doing, her less talkative husband piped up and said in a deadpan voice: "It's the Badlands, baby, it ain't meant to be easy."

All three of us broke out laughing. And with that memorable line, we said our goodbyes, and I continued on my way. Over the next five days I couldn't get those words out of my head. Every time I encountered a difficult situation, I'd repeat, "It's the Badlands, baby…" and start to chuckle. It has been almost three years since completing the route, yet those simple words have continued to be a tough-moments mantra of mine—a surefire way of making me smile and lightening the mood when I'm faced with challenging obstacles.

OFF THE BEATEN PATH

For the astronomically inclined, summer is the optimal time of year for stargazing in the Badlands. Light pollution is minimal, allowing visitors to sift through the sky for planets and constellations. It's estimated that up to 7,500 stars can be spotted in a single night in the Badlands, in and around the thick streak of the Milky Way.

From Memorial Day weekend (celebrated on the last Monday of May) through to Labor Day (the first Monday of September), park rangers organize nightly night-sky viewings at the Cedar Pass Campground Amphitheater, after which visitors are invited to make use of top-notch telescopes. Additionally, every year in early July, the park has partnered with NASA South Dakota Space Grant Consortium to host the Badlands Astronomy Festival. The event brings together space science professionals, educators, amateur astronomers, and regular visitors for a three-day celebration that includes guest presentations, planetarium shows, and equipment demonstrations.

PEAK PERFORMANCE: RECOMMENDED GEAR

Broad-brimmed hat; sunscreen; six to eight liter water-carrying capacity; sunglasses; trail running shoes; light and breathable long-sleeve shirt; hiking pants; a topographic map; compass; gaiters (to keep the sand out of your shoes); and a small pair of binoculars for wildlife viewing.

Another item which you may consider carrying while trekking in the Badlands is a lightweight umbrella. In the long-distance backpacking world, umbrellas have become popular in recent years for the cooling shade they provide while traversing arid regions. Indeed, on the Pacific Crest and Continental Divide Trails, each and every year an increasing number of thru-hikers are using them while negotiating the desert sections of California and New Mexico.

DEEP ROOTED

The Badlands are considered to be sacred by members of the Lakota tribe. The South Unit of the park is home to the Pine Ridge Indian Reservation and managed by the National Park Service. While exploring this infrequently visited area, visitors may come across signs of native worship such as prayer sticks: wood that has been carved and adorned with beads, seeds, feathers, or leather. Some religious objects might appear much simpler: fabric or yarn tied to a bush or bundles fixed to branches. These sacred items should always be respected as such, and should not be meddled with or removed.

Also located in the South Unit is Stronghold Table, which holds a particularly special place in Lakota culture. It is thought that Stronghold Table was the site of the last Ghost Dance of the nineteenth century. This was a revered ceremony that recalled the dead, summoned buffalo herds, and willed great forces of nature to drive the colonists out of Native land. To this day, young men of the Lakota Tribe continue to make pilgrimages to both Stronghold Table, as well as nearby Sheep Mountain Table, in order to fast and pray, in the hope of both connecting to their collective pasts, as well as gaining foresight into their futures.

For those interested in experiencing the South Unit, be sure to stop by the White River Visitor Center before you go. This is done not only to ensure your own safety (there is very little in the way of infrastructure), but also to guarantee you won't be trespassing, as certain sections of this remote region are private property of the Oglala Sioux Tribe (a subtribe of the Lakota people).

IN & OUT

A measure of the Badlands National Park's remote location is that the nearest major airport is Denver, about a six-hour drive away. A smaller, regional airport in Rapid City is located only an hour by car from the Pinnacles Entrance. While more convenient, keep in mind that flight options into Rapid City will be limited, and generally more expensive than their Denver equivalents.

Before or after your trip to the Badlands, be sure to stop at the nearby town of Wall, named for the national park's fantastical escarpment. The town is most famous for the Wall Drug Store, which opened as a small pharmacy in the 1930s. Over the decades it transformed into a Western-themed tourist venue, and with more than two million visitors passing through its swinging doors per year, it now rates as one of America's most popular roadside attractions. *Fun fact: One of the things for which Wall Drug has become known is free ice water. During the hot summer months, up to 20,000 cups of H_2O are given away per day to visiting tourists— no small thing in an area famed for its parched, arid landscapes.*

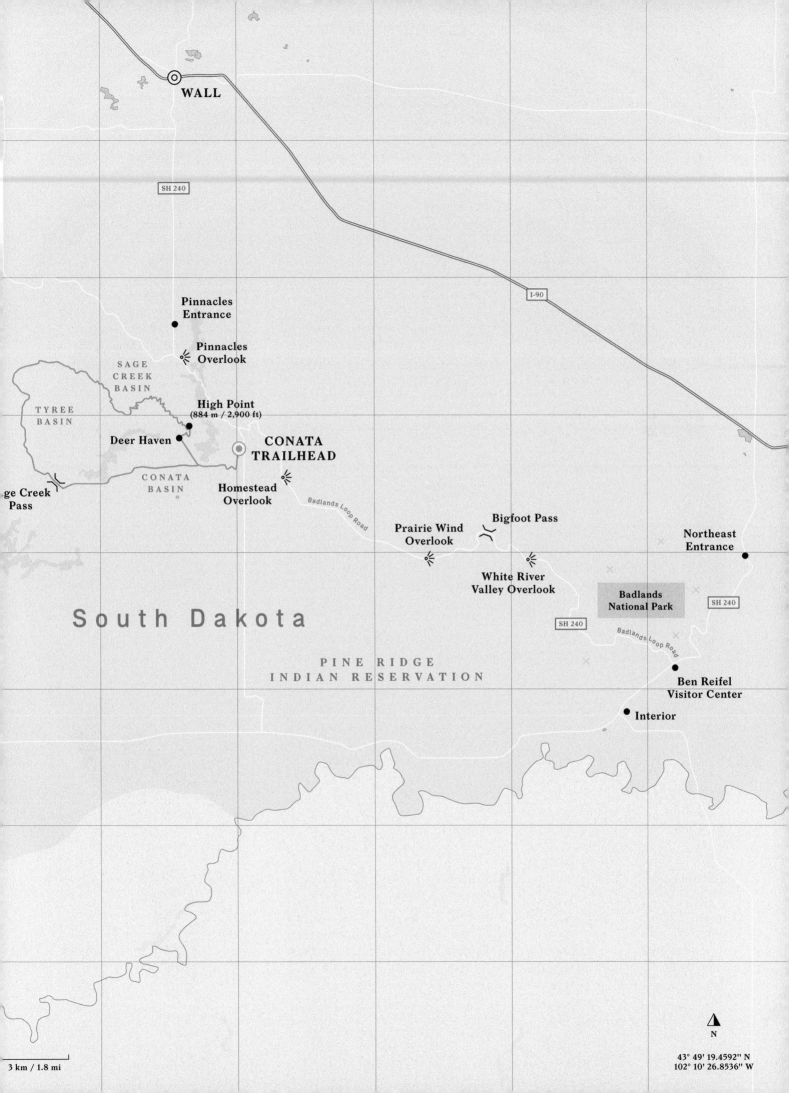

WALL

SH 240

I-90

Pinnacles Entrance

Pinnacles Overlook

SAGE CREEK BASIN

High Point
(884 m / 2,900 ft)

TYREE BASIN

Deer Haven

CONATA TRAILHEAD

ge Creek Pass

CONATA BASIN

Homestead Overlook

Badlands Loop Road

Prairie Wind Overlook

Bigfoot Pass

Northeast Entrance

White River Valley Overlook

Badlands National Park

SH 240

SH 240

Badlands Loop Road

South Dakota

PINE RIDGE INDIAN RESERVATION

Ben Reifel Visitor Center

Interior

3 km / 1.8 mi

N

43° 49' 19.4592" N
102° 10' 26.8536" W

THE SOUNDS OF SILENCE IN AMERICA'S HEARTLAND

Arkansas and Oklahoma
MIDWEST

"The beauty of the Ouachita Trail is rarely found in spectacular vistas, but instead in a subtle combination of solitude, rolling hills, and a diversity of flora and fauna."

↑ Early morning views from the shore of Lake Ouachita.

↗ Looking over Lake Ouachita from the summit of Pinnacle Mountain.

→ Rectangular blue blazes mark the entire length of the 359 km (223 mi) Ouachita Trail.

ABOUT THE TRAIL
→ <u>DISTANCE</u> 359 km (223 mi)
→ <u>DURATION</u> 11 to 14 days
→ <u>LEVEL</u> Moderate

For mountain-loving hikers in America, there isn't much on offer between the Rockies and the Appalachians. The principal exception to this geographic rule comes in the form of the Ouachita (pronounced wa-she-ta) Mountains and Ozark Plateaus, which together make up the Interior Highlands region of the United States. While their alpine siblings to the east and west may dwarf them—the highest point of the Highlands, Mount Magazine, is a mere 839 m (2,753 ft) above sea level—this often overlooked region sports some fantastic backpacking opportunities, not least of which is the Ouachita Trail (OT).

Loping its way for 359 km (223 mi) through the Ouachita Mountains of Arkansas and Oklahoma, the OT has remained off the backpacking world's radar since its completion in 1981. Stretching across one of the only east-to-west ranges in the country, the OT is a non-motorized single-track trail that is well marked and maintained from start to finish, thanks to the tireless efforts of the Friends of the Ouachita Trail volunteer organization (FoOT).

The beauty of the Ouachita Trail is rarely found in spectacular vistas, but instead in a subtle combination of solitude, rolling hills, and a diversity of flora and fauna. The trail also brings with it a colorful history of American outlaws. During the mid to late 1800s, the rugged and wild terrain of the Ouachitas created the perfect refuge for famous bandits such as Jesse James, the Dalton Gang, and Belle Starr. Such was the region's reputation as a haven for the lawless, it served as the setting for the classic Western novel by Charles Portis, *True Grit*. The book was made into two Hollywood feature films, the first starring John Wayne in an Oscar-winning role, and the other, a Coen brothers production featuring Jeff Bridges and Matt Damon.

Though it may have been wild and wooly in centuries past, the Ouachita experience for modern-day wayfarers is a much friendlier affair. This convivial spirit is embodied in the not-to-be-missed town of Story, Arkansas. Situated close to the halfway mark of the Ouachita Trail, Story (population: 197) is the OT's

main resupply point. Any visit to the blink-and-you-miss-it hamlet revolves around the Bluebell Cafe & Country Store—a restaurant, grocery store, gas station, live-music venue, and de facto community center all rolled into one. The cafe's meals are well priced, the servings are large, and if there is any place that encapsulates the South's legendary hospitality along the OT, it is the Bluebell. The staff may even shuttle you back to the trail for a small fee if you ask nicely!

While you are likely to receive a warm welcome when stopping at such places, any long hike through the Ouachita Mountains will be a quiet and solitary experience on the whole. And this is one of the trail's most endearing features. The OT is a pathway that invites a heightened sense of connection with your surroundings. With little in the way of conversational possibilities, Mother Nature's soundtrack will amplify—the songbird's melody at dawn, the meditative bubbling of a meandering stream, or the patter of rain on nylon as you drift off to sleep at day's end. These are the sounds of silence on the Ouachita Trail.

"The trail also brings with it a colorful history of American outlaws. During the mid to late 1800s, the rugged and wild terrain of the Ouachitas created the perfect refuge for famous bandits such as Jesse James, the Dalton Gang, and Belle Starr."

← Freezing rain and foggy ridgetops on the OT during winter.
↙ Welcome to the Ouachita Trail! The beginning point of the OT at Pinnacle Mountain State Park Visitor Center.
↓ The sunrise from Pinnacle Mountain.
→ Paddling on the Little Maumelle River, located just a few kilometers away from the trail's eastern terminus.

GOOD TO KNOW

START / FINISH
Western Terminus
Talimena State Park, Oklahoma
Eastern Terminus
Pinnacle Mountain State Park, Arkansas

HIGHEST / LOWEST POINT
Rich Mountain
(800 m [2,610 ft])
Pinnacle Mountain State Park
(82 m [270 ft])

SEASON
Autumn through spring is ideal. The summer months in the Ouachita Mountains can be very hot and humid, and water sources are less reliable than at other times of the year.

PERMITS
Permits are not required to hike the Ouachita Trail (OT).

ACCOMMODATION
On-Trail
Camping is possible throughout the OT. Additionally, there are lean-tos (three-sided wooden shelters) located every 13 to 16 km (8 to 10 mi) during its course.
Off-Trail
If you're looking for a bit of luxury during your OT hike, consider spending the night at the Queen Wilhelmina Lodge. Located 80 km (50 mi) from the western terminus, the lodge was established in the late 1800s and boasts

40 comfortable rooms, a spectacular mountaintop setting, and a reasonably priced restaurant. *Tip: North-facing rooms offer the best views.*

HELPFUL HINTS

PINNACLE MOUNTAIN SUMMIT
The best views on the Ouachita Trail are not actually on the official OT. They are found via a 3 km (2 mi) return trip to the summit of Pinnacle Mountain, located close to the eastern terminus.

BACKGROUND

THE SPA OF AMERICA
Less than a 30-minute drive south of the Ouachita Trail on Highway 7 is the town and national park of Hot Springs, Arkansas. For centuries its thermal waters, with an average temperature of 62°C (143°F), have been renowned for their restorative qualities. Hot Springs is America's second smallest national park (after Gateway Arch, St. Louis), and due to its designation as a federal reservation in 1832, it also holds the distinction of being the oldest protected area in the national park system, predating Yellowstone National Park by 40 years. The perfect spot for some post thru-hike rest and recreation!

QUARTZ CAPITAL OF THE WORLD
Nestled deep in the Ouachita Mountains is the small town of Mount Ida (population: 1,007), which proclaims itself to be the "Quartz Capital of the World." While this moniker may be a bit

hyperbolic, geologists have found that the finest quartz crystals on Earth do indeed come from Brazil, Madagascar, and the 64-km-wide (40-mi-wide) quartz belt that runs through the heart of Arkansas's Ouachita Mountains.

AUTHOR'S ANECDOTE

FROM THE PENTHOUSE TO THE OUTHOUSE
After enjoying a night of luxury at the Queen Wilhelmina Lodge, I was forced the following evening to take refuge in a restroom at the Winding Stair Campground during the mother of all electrical storms. When the elements are raging, and you're stuck on an exposed mountain ridge, beggars can't be choosers. But all things considered, I was pretty pleased with my find. The bathroom was clean, dry, spacious, and even had one of those little hand sanitizer dispensers in the corner. Most importantly, it was a safe haven from the lightning strikes that had been happening all around me. It was the final night of my 2012 winter thru-hike of the Ouachita Trail, and I slept like a baby.

It wasn't until the following day that I found myself pondering: "I wonder if it's a sign that you've spent too much time in the wilderness when you start thinking about the inside of a toilet like it's the presidential suite at the Hilton?"

BONUS TRACK

The Ouachita Mountains are named after a Native American tribe that resided in northeastern Louisiana. The word itself is the result of the French transliteration (the process of transferring a word from the alphabet of one language to another) of *washita* from the Caddo Nation, a confederation of multiple southeastern indigenous tribes. Its original meaning was "good hunting grounds." A different version of Ouachita's etymology is that it derived from combining the Choctaw words *ouac* and *chito*, which together mean "country of large buffaloes."

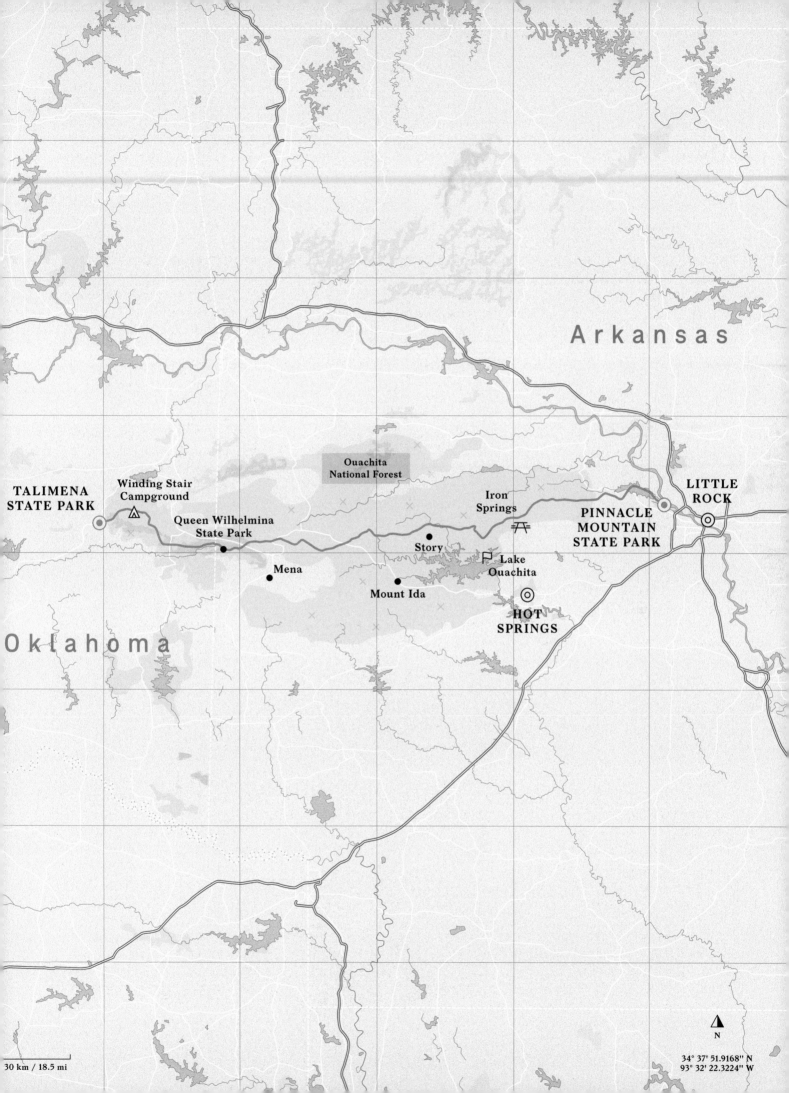

NORTHEAST

Where dense forests meet icy sea and historic towns dot
the bucolic countryside, the Northeast is the cradle of long-
distance hiking in America. It is a place in which heritage and
landscape are intertwined, and every pathway has a tale to tell.

VERMONT'S FOOTPATH
IN THE WILDERNESS

Vermont
NORTHEAST

ABOUT THE TRAIL
→ <u>DISTANCE</u> 439 km (273 mi)
→ <u>DURATION</u> 19 to 22 days
→ <u>LEVEL</u> Challenging

Built between 1910 and 1930, the Long Trail (LT) is the oldest long-distance hiking trail in the United States. Winding its way through the Green Mountains of Vermont, it stretches 439 km (273 mi) from the state line with Massachusetts in the south, to the border with Canada in the north. Passing through the heart of Vermont's wilderness, it goes up and over the summits of 53 named peaks, skirts dozens of lakes and ponds, and negotiates a multitude of rocky ravines, roaring rivers, and shoe-sucking bogs. Serenely beautiful and frequently challenging, if the Long Trail's views don't take your breath away, its legendary treadway—both steep and rugged—most certainly will.

The idea for the trek was conceived by James P. Taylor in 1909, in order to "make the Vermont mountains play a larger part in the life of the people." Over the next two decades, Taylor's dream was realized through the labors of the Green

Mountain Club (GMC), which was formed precisely for this singular purpose. Almost 90 years after its completion, the trail's principal steward remains the GMC, which, as of 2019, boasts more than 10,000 members. So synonymous is the club with the trail that it's actually recognized by the Vermont state legislature as "the founder, sponsor, defender, and protector" of the Long Trail System.

Appropriately for a pathway that is maintained by such a large and diverse group of volunteers, the Long Trail can be enjoyed by hikers of all descriptions. Because it's well marked from beginning to end, and it has an abundance of trailheads and camping options, it's equally accessible to everyone from day hikers to overnighters to those out for multiple weeks at a time. However, take note that very few sections of the trail can be considered "easy," regardless of how short or long you make your trip. The path is invariably rocky, rooty, and muddy—the "big three" of the Long Trail. Though the altitudes reached are not as high as in parts of the western United States, a great deal of ascent and descent is involved nonetheless (38,404 m [126,000 ft] of total elevation gain and loss).

For those who aspire to walk its complete length, the Long Trail offers much more than a backcountry experience. It also provides a window into Vermont's cultural heritage. Hikers

↖ Enjoying a moment of sunshine as the clouds roll in.
↑ The Long Trail is marked from beginning to end with rectangular
 white blazes. Side trails off the main pathway are blazed with blue.
↓ An Eastern Milksnake (*Lampropeltis triangulum*).
↘ Hikers must negotiate multiple ladders during the ascent of Mount
 Mansfield (1,339 m [4,393 ft]), the highest point on the Long Trail.

have the opportunity to visit historic towns and villages along the way such as Manchester, Bennington, and the state capital, Montpelier. In Bennington, you will find an impressive museum that boasts the world's largest collection of Grandma Moses (aka Anna Mary Robertson) paintings. Moses was one of America's most singular and beloved artists of the twentieth century. An unknown farmer's wife who didn't take up painting until her late 70s, her joyful and nostalgic works depicted scenes from rural American life and vividly captured the beauty of the natural world.

Bennington is also the burial place of another American cultural icon, the four-time Pulitzer-Prize-winning poet Robert Frost. For more than four decades, Frost resided in a farmhouse close to the town of Ripton, where he produced many of his finest works, including the poetry collection *A Witness Tree*. A celebrated community member, Frost was named Poet Laureate of Vermont two years before his death in 1963.

You can't talk about the Long Trail without also making mention of the world-famous pathway that it inspired, the Appalachian Trail (AT). Stretching 3,541 km (2,200 mi) between Georgia and Maine, the AT and the southernmost section of the Long Trail run concurrently for 167 km (104 mi). Both marked by iconic white blazes and an extensive shelter system, they are also similar in that they're widely known for the legendary characters who have hiked their entire spans (known as thru-hikers).

Among the most famous of the Long Trail's prolific ramblers were a trio of trailblazing ladies known as the "Three Musketeers." In 1927, Catherine Robbins, Hilda M. Kurth, and Kathleen Norris became the first women to hike it from end to end. At a time when conventional wisdom said it wasn't possible (or proper), these three adventurers endured both the elements and the naysayers to make it all the way from Massachusetts to Canada. In doing so, they inspired generations of other women to follow in their footsteps.

Since its inception in the early 1900s, the Long Trail has affectionately been referred to as "Vermont's footpath in the wilderness." Yet its 439 kilometers (273 mi) represent much more than a hiking trail mirroring the state's renowned natural beauty. From rocky peaks to valley bottoms, the Long Trail showcases the spirit, pride, and hard work of the people who tirelessly maintain this excellent pathway. It's Vermont's gift to America's national trail system, and a testament to the vital relationship between nature and community; the more we engage with and value the land, the more likely we are to work toward preserving it for future generations.

"Since its inception in the early 1900s, the Long Trail has affectionately been referred to as "Vermont's footpath in the wilderness." Yet its 439 kilometers (273 mi) represent much more than a hiking trail mirroring the state's renowned natural beauty."

← Enjoying Vermont's fall colors from a rocky outcrop.
→ Mushrooms and moss.
↓ Corliss Camp. Lean-tos (three-sided shelters) and/or huts are
   situated roughly every 16 km (10 mi) throughout the Long Trail.

GOOD TO KNOW

START/FINISH
Vermont-Massachusetts state line, near Williamstown, Massachusetts
Vermont-Canadian border, near North Troy, Vermont

HIGHEST/LOWEST POINT
Mount Mansfield (1,339 m [4,393 ft])
Jonesville (99 m [326 ft])

SEASON
Mid-June to mid-October. Unless you've got a thing for black flies and knee-high mud (the locals call it "vermud"), you won't want to start the Long Trail before the second week of June. If you can swing it with the dates, it's best to hike between mid-September and early October. By that time the crowds have thinned, there are no bugs, and most importantly, you'll give yourself the opportunity to witness some of the finest fall colors New England has to offer.

ACCOMMODATION
On-Trail
There are some 70 overnight sites along the trail; a combination of lean-tos (three-sided shelters), huts, and tent sites. Shelters are situated roughly 16 km (10 mi) apart. Despite the abundant "indoor" options available, you should definitely bring along your own shelter. This particularly holds true during the summer months, when lean-tos and huts can be crowded.

In-Town
Situated just off trail at the 167.4 km (104 mi) mark on Route 4 is the Inn at Long Trail. This iconic establishment offers comfortable accommodation, meals, and a great Irish pub atmosphere. For Long Trail thru-hikers looking to treat themselves to a bit of indoor luxury (as well as a soothing redwood hot tub), it ranks as a must-stay. *Note: As an added bonus, they will hold hiker resupply packages.*

BACKGROUND

CULINARY PILGRIMAGE
For ice cream devotees of a pilgrimesque bent, it is worth noting that Vermont is home to world-famous Ben & Jerry's. If you would like to pay a visit to their factory, head east to the picturesque town of Waterbury once you reach I-89 (between Camel's Hump and Mount Mansfield).

LONG TRAIL ALE
Another homage comes via their collective taste buds; the state's most popular craft beer for more than two decades has been a full-bodied amber by the name of Long Trail Ale.

BONUS TRACK

In addition to being the home of Ben & Jerry's ice cream, Vermont is also famous for producing some of the world's finest maple syrup. The sweet stuff is made by boiling the sap of the sugar maple tree until most of the water has been evaporated, and the syrup reaches a concentration of 66.9 percent sugar. Approximately 151.4 liters (40 gallons) of sap are required to make 3.8 liters (one gallon) of syrup.

In 2018 alone, Vermont produced more than 7.34 million liters (1.94 million gallons) of maple syrup, accounting for 47 percent of America's total. However, not all maple syrup is created equal. According to the Vermont Maple Sugar Maker's Association (founded in 1893), syrup is separated into four distinct color classes:

1. Golden Color with Delicate Flavor: Delicious on pancakes, waffles, French toast, or combined with yogurt.
2. Amber Color with Rich Flavor: Ideal for all around use. Equally as good with pancakes as it is with salad dressing, cocktails, and sweetened barbecue sauce.
3. Dark Color with Robust Flavor: Also good for all around use. With a heartier taste, it can be used as a glaze for vegetables and meat, combining well with "smoky and spicy flavors like chipotle peppers, sriracha, or bourbon."
4. Very Dark Color with Strong Flavor: Almost the same color as molasses, and typically used for cooking and baking.

So who produces the best maple syrup in Vermont? That's like trying to decide on who makes the best chocolate in Belgium or Switzerland—practically impossible. However, among a plethora of excellent options, some of the most highly regarded brands in the Green Mountain State include Slopeside Syrup, Brown Family Farm, Bragg Farm, Gagne Maple, and Butternut Mountain Farm.

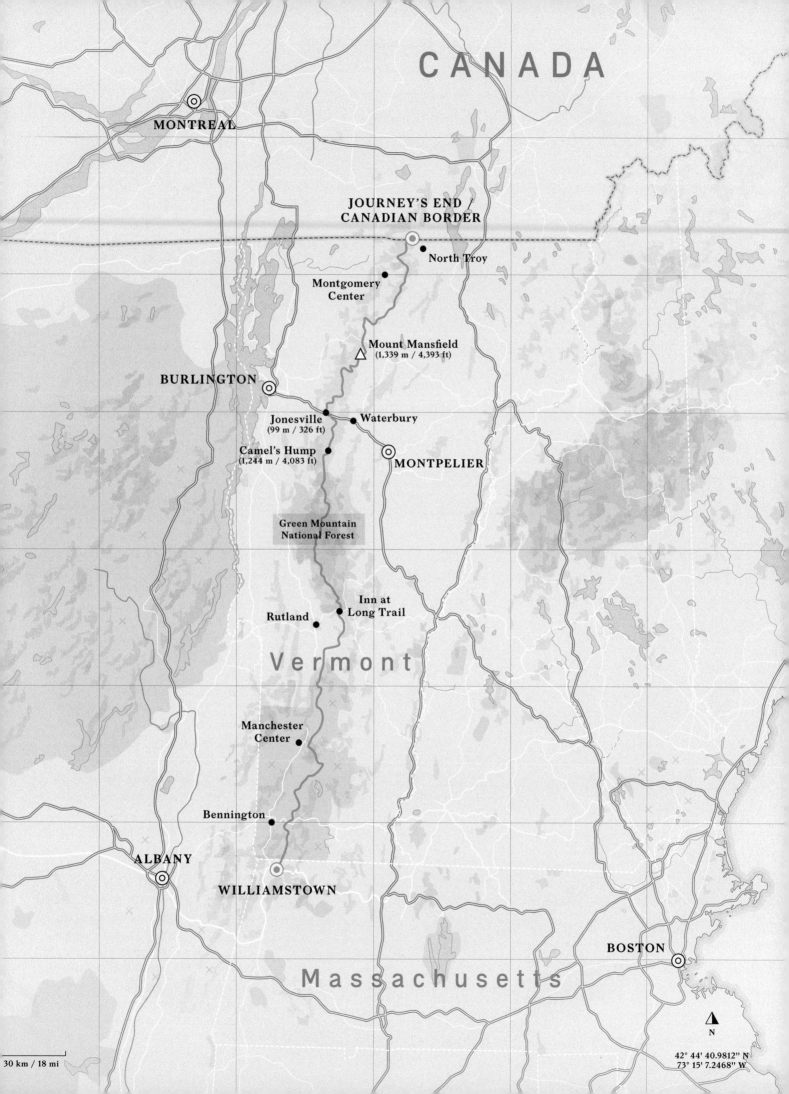

CANADA

JOURNEY'S END /
CANADIAN BORDER

North Troy

Montgomery
Center

Mount Mansfield
(1,339 m / 4,393 ft)

BURLINGTON

Jonesville
(99 m / 326 ft)

Waterbury

Camel's Hump
(1,244 m / 4,083 ft)

MONTPELIER

Green Mountain
National Forest

Inn at
Long Trail

Rutland

Vermont

Manchester
Center

Bennington

ALBANY

WILLIAMSTOWN

MONTREAL

BOSTON

Massachusetts

30 km / 18 mi

N

42° 44' 40.9812" N
73° 15' 7.2468" W

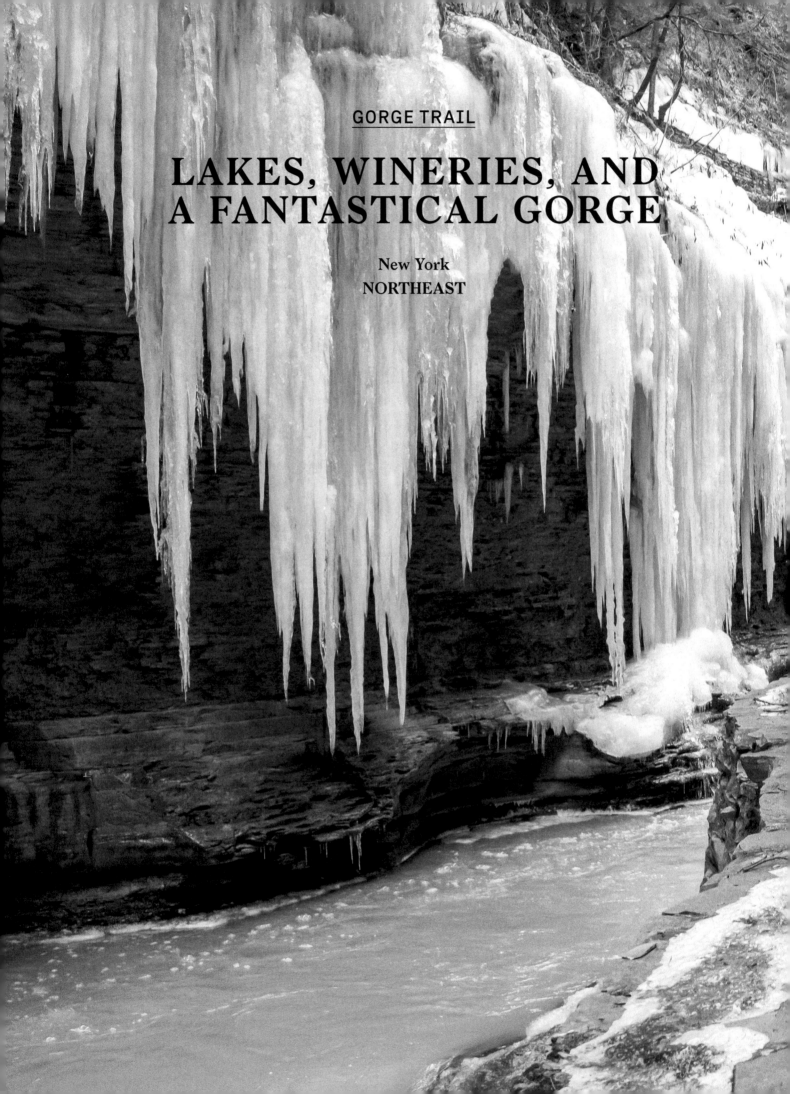

LAKES, WINERIES, AND A FANTASTICAL GORGE

New York
NORTHEAST

← With fall foliage in full swing, October is a great time to hike the Gorge Trail.
↑ The village of Watkins Glen.

ABOUT THE TRAIL

→ <u>DISTANCE</u> 4.8 km (3 mi) (Gorge Trail/Indian Trail Loop)
→ <u>DURATION</u> 2 to 3 hours
→ <u>LEVEL</u> Easy

Watkins Glen State Park is a glacier-carved master-work more than 10,000 years in the making. Situated in New York's picturesque Finger Lake region, its centerpiece is a fantastical 120-m-deep (400-ft-deep) gorge that delights with fairytale stone bridges, atmospheric caverns, emerald pools, and a series of 19 waterfalls. Winding its way through all of these chasmic marvels is a 2.4 km (1.5 mi) pathway known simply as the Gorge Trail.

First opened to the public in 1863 as a privately owned tourist attraction, Watkins Glen was officially designated a state park in 1906. The gorge's original trails were destroyed during massive floods some 24 years later, after which the stone staircases, bridges, and walkways of today were constructed. Hiking season runs from mid-May to late October, and the Gorge Trail is often combined with the Indian Trail, which traverses

the northern rim of the gorge, to form a scenic 4.8 km (3 mi) loop through the heart of the state park.

When planning your Gorge Trail hike, one of the most important considerations is timing. Given its easy accessibility and dramatic beauty, it's understandably a very popular tourist attraction. If you would like to bypass the crowds, it's best to avoid weekends, particularly during the summer months when school is out of session. And if you make the effort to arrive at the park as soon as the gates open in the morning, it will pay off—chances are you'll have one of America's most breathtaking ravines almost all to yourself.

Spring and fall are the best times to hike the Gorge Trail. The temperatures are cooler, and the former sees Glen Creek at peak flow due to the melting of the winter snows. The runoff means that the gorge's collection of cascades will be at their most spectacular. The path runs very close to some of the falls, even passing beneath two of them (Cavern Cascade and Rainbow Falls), which creates a powerful sight, sound, and feeling to behold; the roaring water is almost deafening and the ground literally vibrates beneath you. Autumn is an equally memorable time to hike the Gorge, but for different reasons. Fall foliage is in full swing in Watkins Glen during the month of

The Gorge Trail in winter—frozen waterfalls and Rainbow Bridge.

"Situated in New York's picturesque Finger Lakes region, its centerpiece is a fantastical 120-m-deep (400-ft-deep) gorge that delights with fairytale stone bridges, atmospheric caverns, emerald pools, and a series of 19 waterfalls."

← Rainbow Falls is one of two waterfalls that the Gorge Trail passes under during its course (the other is Cavern Cascade).
↓ The main entrance to Watkins Glen.
→ The Gorge Trail consists of 19 waterfalls and a knee-crunching 832 steps.

October, and the combination of magnificent autumnal hues, moss- and lichen-covered walls, and Rivendell-esque cataracts makes for an enchanting experience. You almost expect to see elves bounding effortlessly along the stony paths and dwarves darting in and out of the gorge's damp and dark caverns.

Watkins Glen State Park is located at the southern end of Seneca Lake, the deepest and largest of New York's 11 Finger Lakes. There are a multitude of vineyards around its sloping shores that are renowned for producing world-class riesling. Once you've finished taking in the wonders of the gorge on foot, celebrate by giving your palate an equally satisfying workout on the Seneca Lake Wine Trail. As New York's largest wine trail, it visits more than 30 local vineyards; in addition to riesling, other varietals on offer include pinot noir, chardonnay, gewürztraminer, and cabernet franc.

The Gorge Trail/Indian Trail is a family-friendly loop, and the shortest hike we cover in this volume of the *Wanderlust* series at only 4.8 km (3 mi). However, like one of Chekhov's short stories or the 100-meter sprint final in the Olympics, it packs a powerful punch into a brief space. And when tripled with beautiful Seneca Lake and myriad excellent wineries, it's no surprise that the Gorge Trail is one of those hikes that people return to time and time again.

GOOD TO KNOW

START/FINISH
A loop hike starting and finishing at the main entrance to Watkins Glen State Park

SEASON
Mid-May to late October

ACCOMMODATION
If you plan on arriving early at the state park in order to avoid the crowds, it is recommended that you stay in nearby Watkins Glen village. Located less than one mile from the main entrance on the southern shore of Seneca Lake, the village has multiple accommodation options; the pick of the bunch is undoubtedly the lakefront Watkins Glen Harbor Hotel.

HELPFUL HINTS

DIRECTION OF CHOICE?
For the best views, start your hike at the bottom of the gorge at the park's main entrance. That way you're facing the cascades during the ascent. Those who choose to take a shuttle around to the upper entrance to avoid climbing the gorge's 800-plus steps will find themselves constantly having to turn around during the descent to see the waterfalls in all their glory.

MOTHER NATURE'S CALL
Before beginning the Gorge Trail/Indian Trail Loop, keep in mind that the park's only bathroom facilities are at the entrances. This is important because for most of the hike you will be accompanied by the sound of running water, especially during peak flow in the spring.

GEAR FOR THE GORGE
The gorge tends to be cool and wet, and the stone path that dissects it is often slippery. In addition to a rain jacket, it is best to have lightweight, quick-drying running shoes with good tread.

BACKGROUND

WINEMAKING AROUND SENECA LAKE
Seneca Lake boasts an ideal microclimate for grape growing, thanks to a combination of deep water (193 m [632 ft] at its deepest) and rolling hillsides around its shore. The origin of viticulture in the region dates back to the mid-1800s; however, the industry was dealt a major blow during the Prohibition era (1920–1933), when only the larger companies survived by making grape juice and sacramental wine. It wasn't until the 1970s that wine-growing around

the lake took off again. And it has continued to go from strength to strength since the founding of the Seneca Lake Wine Trail in 1986, which draws more than half a million visitors annually.

BONUS TRACK

FINGER LAKES
Located in central New York State, the Finger Lakes are a collection of 11 long and skinny lakes that resemble the outstretched fingers of a pair of hands. From east to west they are as follows: Otisco, Skaneateles, Owasco, Cayuga, Seneca, Keuka, Canandaigua, Honeoye, Canadice, Hemlock, and Conesus. The lakes were formed at the end of the last Ice Age, when the glacial retreat left behind not only these elongated shale valleys filled with water, but also other notable geologic features such as the incredible gorge of Watkins Glen.

OTHER HIKES IN THE REGION
Apart from the featured Gorge Trail, there are many other excellent day hiking options in the Finger Lakes area. Four of the best are as follows:

1. **Grimes Glen:** A short 1.6 km (1 mi) out-and-back hike to an 18 m (60 ft) waterfall. There's a wonderful pool at the bottom that's perfect for a cooling swim during the hot summer months.
2. **Conklin Gully 12 Falls Trail:** Located near the town of Naples, this waterfall-laden 5.5 km (3.4 mi) trail is one of the more challenging hikes in the region. An excellent option for experienced ramblers looking for a little more in the way of solitude.
3. **Letchworth State Park:** Known as the "Grand Canyon of the East," Letchworth is arguably the most beautiful of the Finger Lakes' 24 state parks, and contains more than 100 km (62 mi) of hiking trails from which to choose.
4. **Keuka Lake Outlet Trail:** Located in the heart of the Finger Lakes region, this 11.3 km (7 mi) long multi-use trail follows the path of the historic Crooked Lake Canal, which once joined Keuka and Seneca Lakes.

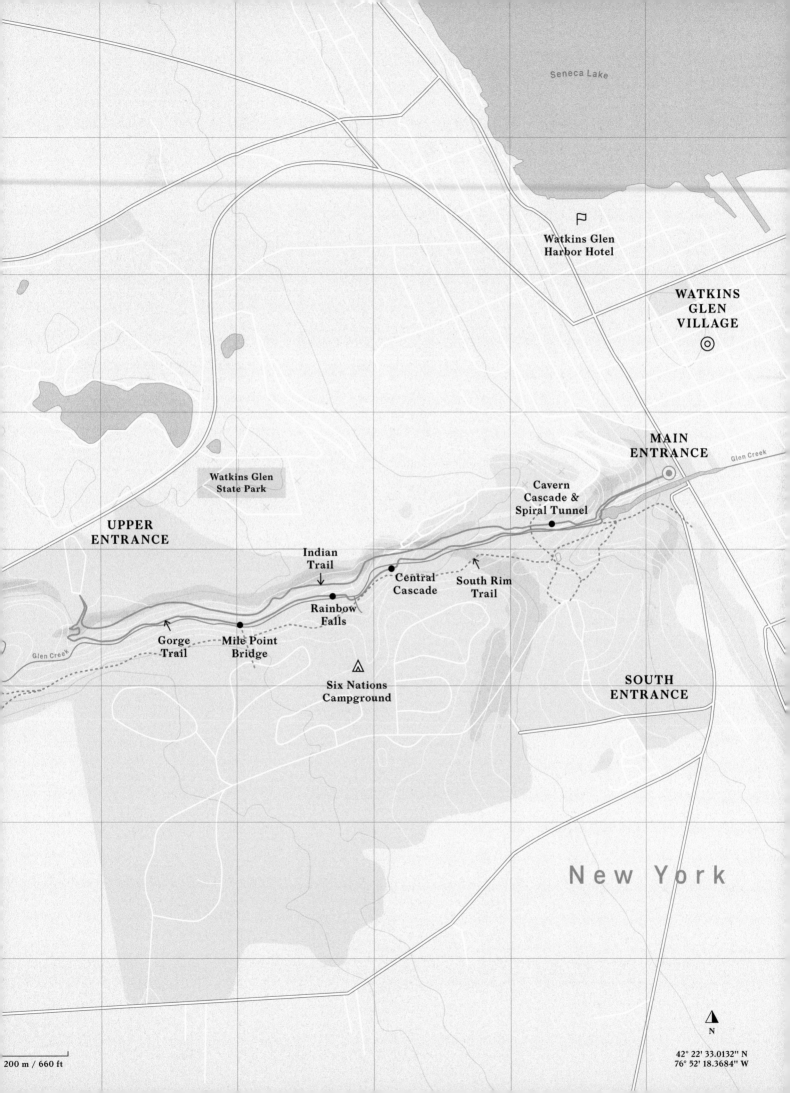

Seneca Lake

⚑
Watkins Glen
Harbor Hotel

WATKINS
GLEN
VILLAGE
◎

MAIN
ENTRANCE
Glen Creek
◉

Cavern
Cascade &
Spiral Tunnel
●

Watkins Glen
State Park

UPPER
ENTRANCE

Indian
Trail
↓

Central
Cascade
●

South Rim
Trail
↑

Rainbow
Falls
●

Gorge
Trail
↗

Mile Point
Bridge
●

SOUTH
ENTRANCE

Glen Creek

⛺
Six Nations
Campground

New York

▲
N

200 m / 660 ft

42° 22' 33.0132" N
76° 52' 18.3684" W

PRESIDENTIAL TRAVERSE

ACROSS THE ROOFTOP
OF NEW ENGLAND

New Hampshire
NORTHEAST

ABOUT THE TRAIL
→ <u>DISTANCE</u> 40.2 km (25 mi)
→ <u>DURATION</u> 2 to 3 days
→ <u>LEVEL</u> Moderate to Challenging

The Presidential Traverse is an arduous trek across the highest and most exposed section of New Hampshire's White Mountains. One of the premier backpacking adventures east of the Continental Divide, this classic 40 km (25 mi) trail has an elevation gain and loss of almost 6,096 m (20,000 ft) and has long been regarded as a rite of passage among New England hikers. The trail's rollercoaster profile is only part of what makes the Presidential Traverse so challenging, with the weather potentially being a far more significant obstacle. With snowstorms, brutal winds, and driving rain constant considerations, the White Mountains are renowned for having the "worst weather in America."

The standard Presidential Traverse begins at the Appalachia Trailhead on U.S. Route 2 and finishes at the Crawford Path Trailhead on U.S. Route 302. Along the way it passes through the largest alpine zone east of the Rocky Mountains, while negotiating a series of prominent summits, all named after former U.S. presidents. Listed in order from north to south (the way in which the traverse is most commonly hiked), the peaks are as follows:

1. Mt. Madison – 1,636 m (5,367 ft)
2. Mt. Adams – 1,760 m (5,774 ft)
3. Mt. Jefferson – 1,741 m (5,712 ft)
4. Mt. Washington – 1,917 m (6,288 ft)
5. Mt. Monroe – 1,637 m (5,384 ft)
6. Mt. Eisenhower – 1,457 m (4,780 ft)
7. Mt. Pierce – 1,314 m (4,310 ft)

Although widely known for its bald, windswept summits, the Presidential Traverse is bookended by steep approach trails that ascend through a series of fascinating ecozones before reaching tree line. The hike begins in northern hardwood forest, featuring deciduous trees such as red oak, maple, and birch. Winding its way past babbling brooks and gorgeous waterfalls, it then reaches the boreal (or spruce-fir) zone at around 762 m (2,500 ft), which is marked by "softwood" evergreens and a fern- and moss-covered forest floor.

Continuing to climb to approximately 1,219 m (4,000 ft), the path arrives at the *krummholz* (crooked wood) zone, a surreal landscape of gnarled, twisted, weather-beaten conifers. Finally, at 1,341 m (4,400 ft), the alpine zone is attained, at which point weary hikers will be greeted by one of America's most dire and blunt wilderness warning signs, courtesy of the White Mountain National Forest Service: "Stop: The area ahead has the worst weather in America. Many have died there from exposure, even in the summer. Turn back now if the weather is bad."

If you think this sign is a little over the top, consider that more than 150 people have died since 1849 while climbing Mount Washington, the highest point on the Presidential Traverse, and

↑ The Presidential Traverse can either be done as a long day hike or split over two or even three days.
→ A boardwalk winding through the enchanting forest.

every year unprepared hikers have to be rescued from the high country of the White Mountains. Still need more convincing? On April 12, 1934, a wind speed of 372 km/h (231 mph) was recorded on the summit of Mount Washington, the highest velocity ever registered at the time. This mark stood unsurpassed until 1996, when a wind gust of 407 km/h (253 mph) was measured on Western Australia's remote Barrow Island.

The Presidential Traverse can either be done as a long day hike or split over two or even three days. Whichever the case, you should be fit, properly equipped, and aware of bail-out points in case the weather takes a turn for the worse. Note that

↑ An ethereal blanket of snow covers the treetops during winter in the White Mountains.
→ The sun rises and the clouds linger.

"One of the premier backpacking adventures east of the Continental Divide, this classic 40 km (25 mi) trail has an elevation gain and loss of almost 6,096 m (20,000 ft) and has long been regarded as a rite of passage among New England hikers."

← Before reaching the alpine zone, the Presidential Traverse ascends through northern hardwood forests, which feature babbling brooks and roaring waterfalls.
↓ The Christmas-red berries of the evergreen yew tree.

experienced ramblers in good shape generally take between 12 and 14 hours to complete the entire trail, so if you want to knock it off in a single day, a pre-dawn start is recommended. For those who would prefer a slightly less strenuous approach, a multi-day schedule will give you more time to soak in the (hopefully) dramatic vistas, as well as the option to overnight in the White Mountains' famous huts, which offer filling meals and bunk bed accommodation (see info box).

When it comes to trekking across New England's rooftop, it's worth remembering that Mother Nature doesn't have a copy of your itinerary. No matter how prepared you may be, there will be times when, meteorologically speaking, it simply isn't possible. In such circumstances, there isn't much you can do except shrug your shoulders and adapt. That may translate to sitting tight in a campsite below tree line, waiting it out in one of the cozy mountain refuges, or even canceling your hike and trying again another day. The White Mountains aren't going anywhere, and by any criteria, a traverse of the Presidential Range is an adventure worth the wait.

↑↑ The Presidential Traverse passes through the largest alpine zone east of the Rocky Mountains.
↑ Lakeside accommodation high in the White Mountains.

GOOD TO KNOW

START / FINISH
Northern Terminus
Appalachia Trailhead (U.S. Route 2)
Southern Terminus
Crawford Path Trailhead (U.S. Route 302)

TOTAL ELEVATION GAIN & LOSS
Almost 6,096 m (20,000 ft)

SEASON
June to October

HELPFUL HINTS

ACCOMMODATION
It is possible to split the Presidential
Traverse into an overnight trip by staying
at one or more of the following places
along the route. From north to south,
accommodation options are as follows:

1. **Valley Way Campsite**
   Platform-style options for tents
2. **Madison Springs Hut**
   *Meals and coed bunk room
   accommodation*
3. **Lakes of the Clouds Hut**
   *Meals and coed bunk room
   accommodation*
4. **Mizpah Spring Hut**
   *Meals and coed bunk room
   accommodation*
5. **Naumann Campsite**
   Platform-style options for tents

FLORA & FAUNA

A TOUGH PLACE TO GROW
The Presidential Range contains more
than 20 sq km (8 sq mi) of alpine zone,
the largest area of alpine tundra east
of the Rocky Mountains. Defined as an
area in which trees are eight feet tall
or less, the Alpine Zone is an exposed
and inhospitable place, which, despite
the harsh conditions, is home to a rich
array of fragile arctic-alpine flora such
as the Pincushion Plant (*Diapensia
Lapponica*) and Labrador Tea (*Ledum
Groenlandicum*). When hiking through
the Alpine Zone, hikers are advised to

stay on marked trails in order to avoid
trampling the plants, which once trodden
on may never recover. As it says on the
trails signs which greet hikers heading
above tree line, "The Alpine Zone ... It's
a tough place to grow."

BACKGROUND

FIVE FACTS ABOUT MOUNT WASHINGTON

1. On April 12, 1934, a wind speed of
   372 km/h (231 mph) was recorded
   on the summit of Mount Washington,
   the highest velocity ever recorded at
   the time.
2. The average wind speed on top of
   Mount Washington is 56.3 km/h
   (35 mph).
3. The summit is covered in cloud
   55 percent of the time.
4. Traditionally it snows every month
   of the year on Mount Washington.
5. For less energetic souls, there is a
   cog railway which takes customers
   to the summit of Mount Washington,
   where a warm and cozy cafeteria
   and an impressive panorama awaits.

BONUS TRACK

For those looking for an easier way of
reaching the top of New Hampshire's
Mount Washington, it is possible to take
a train to the summit. Yes, you read that
correctly. Opened in 1869, the Mount
Washington Cog railway—affectionately
known as the "Cog"—was the world's
first mountain-climbing cog railway
(and still ranks as the second-steepest
after the Pilatus Railway in Switzerland).
150 years later, tourists continue to ride
the rails to the apex of the northeast's
highest peak, but now they have the
choice of taking either a biodiesel train
or the vintage steam locomotive.

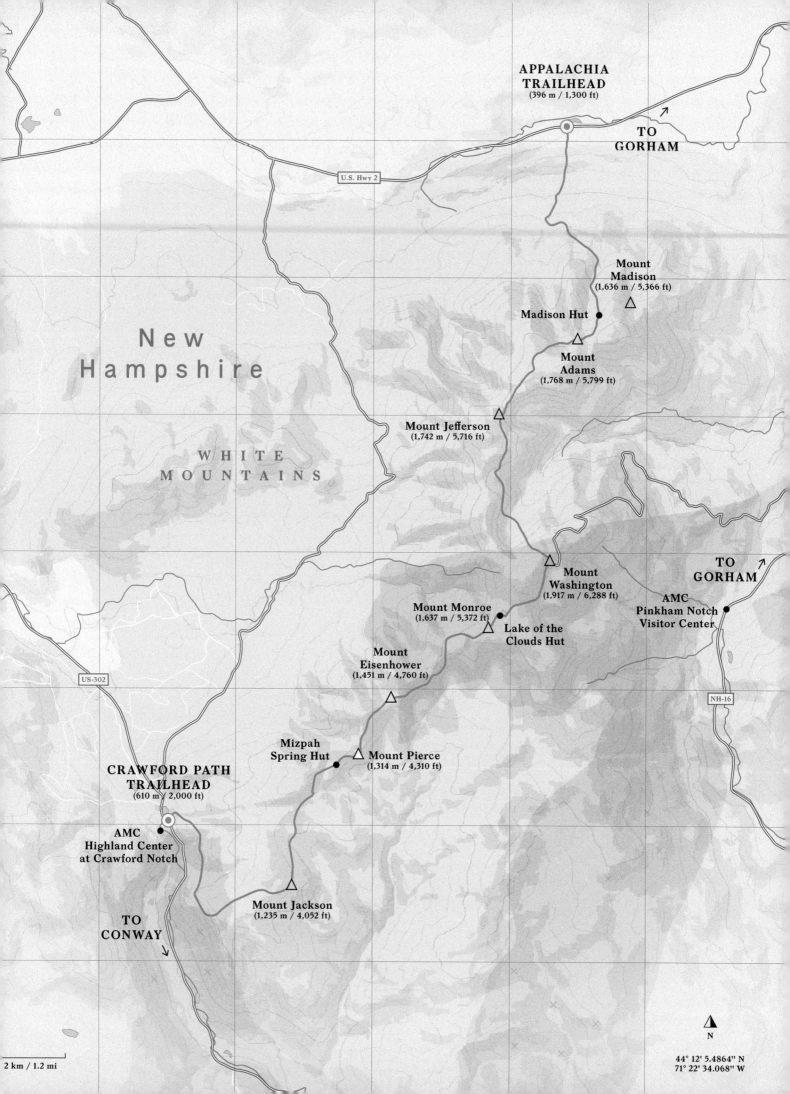

APPALACHIA
TRAILHEAD
(396 m / 1,300 ft)

TO
GORHAM

U.S. Hwy 2

New
Hampshire

WHITE
MOUNTAINS

Mount Madison
(1,636 m / 5,366 ft)

Madison Hut

Mount
Adams
(1,768 m / 5,799 ft)

Mount Jefferson
(1,742 m / 5,716 ft)

Mount
Washington
(1,917 m / 6,288 ft)

TO
GORHAM

Mount Monroe
(1,637 m / 5,372 ft)

Lake of the
Clouds Hut

AMC
Pinkham Notch
Visitor Center

Mount
Eisenhower
(1,451 m / 4,760 ft)

US-302

NH-16

Mizpah
Spring Hut

Mount Pierce
(1,314 m / 4,310 ft)

CRAWFORD PATH
TRAILHEAD
(610 m / 2,000 ft)

AMC
Highland Center
at Crawford Notch

TO
CONWAY

Mount Jackson
(1,235 m / 4,052 ft)

2 km / 1.2 mi

N

44° 12' 5.4864" N
71° 22' 34.068" W

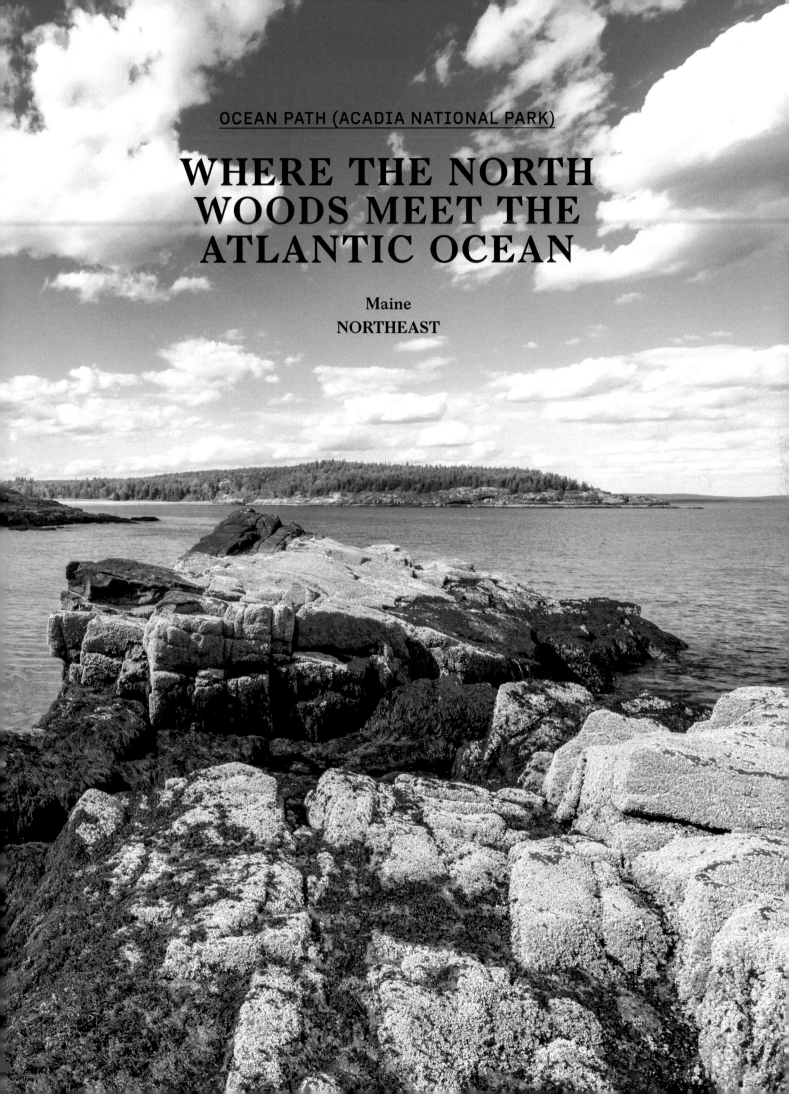

WHERE THE NORTH WOODS MEET THE ATLANTIC OCEAN

Maine
NORTHEAST

"Not only is Acadia the easternmost national park in the United States, it's also one of the first places in the country from which you can take in the sunrise over the Atlantic Ocean."

↑ The Beehive Trail connects with the Gorham
  Mountain Trail and Ocean Path to form an excellent
  9.4 km (5.8 mi) loop.
→ The sunrise over the Atlantic Ocean as seen from
  Cadillac Mountain.
↗ Bass Harbor Head Lighthouse.

ABOUT THE TRAIL

→ <u>DISTANCE</u> 7.1 km (4.4 mi); *add 2.3 km (1.4 mi) if you return via Gorham Mountain and the Beehive Trail*

→ <u>DURATION</u> 2 to 3 hours; *4 to 5 hours if you add Gorham Mountain and the Beehive Trail*

→ <u>LEVEL</u> Easy to moderate

Acadia National Park is Maine in a nutshell. With its spectacular coastline, dense forest, granite-topped peaks, and picture-postcard lakes, it embodies all of the natural wonders for which the Pine Tree State is renowned. Open to explore all year round, it's a park that can be enjoyed by outdoor lovers of all ages and fitness levels, but it's especially suited to early risers. Why? Because not only is Arcadia the easternmost national park in the United States, it's also one of the first places in the country from which you can take in the sunrise over the Atlantic Ocean.

Established in 1916, Acadia National Park occupies approximately 190.2 sq km (47,000 acres) of real estate across Maine's Mount Desert Island and the Schoodic Peninsula. As one of America's most beloved national parks, it has long been a magnet for generations of outdoor-loving New Englanders looking to escape the hustle and bustle of urban life. From a hiker's perspective, Arcadia contains more than 193 km (120 mi) of well-maintained trails within its ocean-rimmed boundaries. There is something for everyone, from family-friendly lakeside strolls and coast-hugging meanders to steep and exposed scrambles. And what sets Acadia's trail system apart from many of the country's larger national parks is that its natural wonders are easily accessible within one to six hours of walking—no need to carry heavy packs laden with tents, sleeping bags, and multiple days of food supply. Acadia may well be the day-hiking capital of America's National Park System.

One of the most scenic of Arcadia's wayfaring options is the Ocean Path. An out-and-back affair between Sand Beach and Otter Point, it measures 7.1 km (4.4 mi) in total and showcases

"What sets Acadia's trail system apart from many of the country's larger national parks is that its natural wonders are easily accessible within one to six hours of walking—no need to carry a heavy pack laden with a tent, sleeping bag, and multiple days of food supply."

← The precipitous climb to the Beehive.
→ Coastal vistas along the Ocean Path.
↘ The view from the Gorham Mountain Trail, overlooking Sand Beach, Old Soaker Island, and the Ocean Path.

a coastal medley of sheer cliffs, a sandy beach, wave-sculpted sea stacks, and pink-granite coastline. Along the way there are plenty of side trails by which you can explore the shore, and perhaps find a solitary spot to take in the grandeur of the Atlantic Ocean. Some of the hike's standout features include Monument Cove and Thunder Hole, a small but dramatic inlet where the surf booms as it crashes into the rocks.

With mellow treadway and gorgeous views, the Ocean Path is understandably one of Acadia's most popular trails. It's worth noting that the path can be particularly crowded between 9 a.m. and 3 p.m.; if you're aiming for a more peaceful experience, make an effort to begin your hike before dawn, and be sure to catch the sunrise from the Otter Cliff area. Illuminated by the rays of daybreak, the pink-granite headland, spruce forest, and shimmering waters make for a sublime maritime amalgam. You may find yourself pondering, "Why don't I wake up this early every day?!"

For those looking for something a little longer and more challenging, consider returning to Sand Beach via the Gorham

Mountain Trail (see map). The views from the top of its name-sake peak (158 m [520 ft]) are outstanding, with a bird's-eye perspective of the entire Ocean Path. (Note: From late July to mid-September you can also snack on blueberries from the summit's many bushes.) On the final leg back to the starting point, there is one more possibility to extend the loop even further by descending via the classic Beehive Trail. One of the park's most challenging hikes, the Beehive Trail includes a cheek-puckering climb down a cliff face with the aid of steep granite steps, handrails, and iron-rung ladders (see photo). This option is not recommended for those with a fear of heights, or in inclement conditions.

There is no more satisfying way to experience Acadia's multitude of natural wonders than on foot and at sunrise. No specialized gear is required, nor is a high level of fitness or hiking experience a prerequisite. All you really need is a reliable alarm and perhaps a strong pot of coffee to kick-start your day. After all, how often do you get a chance to be among the first people in America to greet the dawn?

GOOD TO KNOW

START / FINISH
Sand Beach parking area

SEASON
Year round

PERMITS
No backcountry permits are required to hike in Acadia National Park. However, all visitors are required to pay an entrance fee during the peak season of May to October.

HELPFUL HINTS

MAINE LOBSTER
The picturesque village of Bar Harbor is the hub of Acadia National Park, where there's no shortage of great seafood restaurants to sample Maine's world-famous lobster. Some excellent dining choices include Thurston's, Beal's, Trenton Bridge, Travelin' Lobster, Side Street Cafe, and the Thirsty Whale.

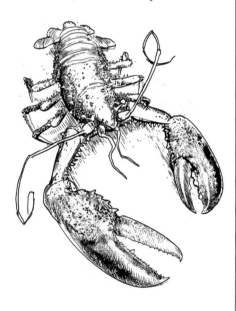

AVOIDING THE CROWDS
More than 85 percent of Acadia National Park's annual visitors come between June and September. If you want to steer clear of the hordes, ideally plan your visit during the spring, autumn (the foliage is amazing), or even the chilly winter months. If work and/or family commitments mean that summer is your only option, you can still mitigate the crowds by avoiding weekends and public holidays, and by making the effort to hit the trail at dawn.

OTHER HIKING OPTIONS IN ACADIA
1. Precipice Trail
2. Jordan Pond Loop
3. Penobscot Mountain (via the Spring Trail)
4. Cadillac Mountain Summit Loop
5. Bubble Rock Trail
6. Bass Harbor Head Light (lighthouse)

FLORA & FAUNA

THE RETURN OF PEREGRINE FALCONS
In recent years, some of Acadia's cliffs and paths have been periodically off-limits to the public in order to protect nesting peregrine falcons. These include Precipice Trail, Jordan Cliffs Trail, and Valley Cove Trail. (the Ocean Path, Gorham Mountain, and Beehive Trail remain open.) The peregrine falcon is the fastest animal on the planet, able to reach speeds in excess of 322 km/h (200 mph) when diving toward its prey. These incredible birds are native to the eastern United States, but by the mid-1960s they were no longer a breeding species and therefore deemed endangered. Scientists attributed this to human impact—pesticides, pollutants, nest robbing, and shooting. In recent decades, Acadia has played an important role in the Peregrine Falcon Reintroduction Program's goal of restoring a self-sustaining population of peregrines to the eastern United States. Such has been the success of Acadia's nesting program that the park's superintendent described it as one of their great conservation stories.

BACKGROUND

ROCKEFELLER'S CARRIAGE ROADS
In addition to its more than 193 km (120 mi) of hiking trails, Acadia boasts 72 km (45 mi) of motor vehicle–free carriage roads within its boundaries. Built between 1913 and 1940, this system of immaculately constructed "broken stone" roads and equally exquisite stone bridges was financed by philanthropist John D. Rockefeller. The roads are used exclusively by hikers, bikers, equestrians, and horse-drawn carriages.

NEARBY: THE 100 MILE WILDERNESS

Just over a two-hour drive northwest of Acadia National Park lies Maine's most famous footpath. Stretching between Monson in the south and Baxter State Park in the north, the 100 Mile Wilderness is both the northernmost section of the world-famous Appalachian Trail (AT), as well as a classic hiking journey in its own right. Arduous, remote, and usually muddy, it passes by countless streams, waterfalls, ponds, and lakes during its course, while periodically emerging onto lofty summits perfect for soaking in wide-ranging panoramas. The northern terminus of the 100 Mile Wilderness is the legendary Mount Katahdin, the state's highest peak (1,605 m [5,267 ft]), whose name comes from the native Penobscot people and means "the Greatest Mountain." The climb to Katahdin's summit is perhaps the most testing of the entire trail; during the ascent it's necessary to negotiate huge boulders while ascending over 1,219 m (4,000 ft) in the space of just 8.4 km (5.2 mi). But your efforts will ultimately be rewarded, as the views from the top are among the most beautiful in all of New England. A more fitting finale to a challenging hike is hard to imagine.

Eagle Lake

Cadillac Mountain
(466 m / 1,528 ft)
△

Champlain Mountain
(323 m / 1,059 ft)
△

BAR
HARBOR

Precipice
Trailhead ●

Bubble Pond

Entrance
Station ●

The Bowl

Acadia
National Park

Pemetic Mountain
(380 m / 1,246 ft)
△

The Beehive
(158 m / 518 ft)
△

SAND
BEACH

Gorham Mountain
(160 m / 524 ft)
△

Great
Head ⚑

M a i n e

Gorham Mountain Trail

Jordan Pond
House ●

OTTER
CREEK

Thunder Hole ●

Monument
Cove ●

Boulder Beach ●

Otter
Cove

Otter Cliff ⚑

Blackwoods
Campground △

Otter
Point ⚑

SEAL
HARBOR

Hunter's
Head ⚑

Atlantic
Ocean

△
N

600 m / 0.5 mi

44° 19' 14.7036" N
68° 11' 29.9868" W

SOUTHEAST

Hiking in the Southeast is not done for spectacular vistas. Its beauty is usually subtle and meditative, rather than dramatic—babbling brooks in lieu of raging rivers, rolling hills in place of towering peaks, or tranquil ponds instead of alpine lakes.

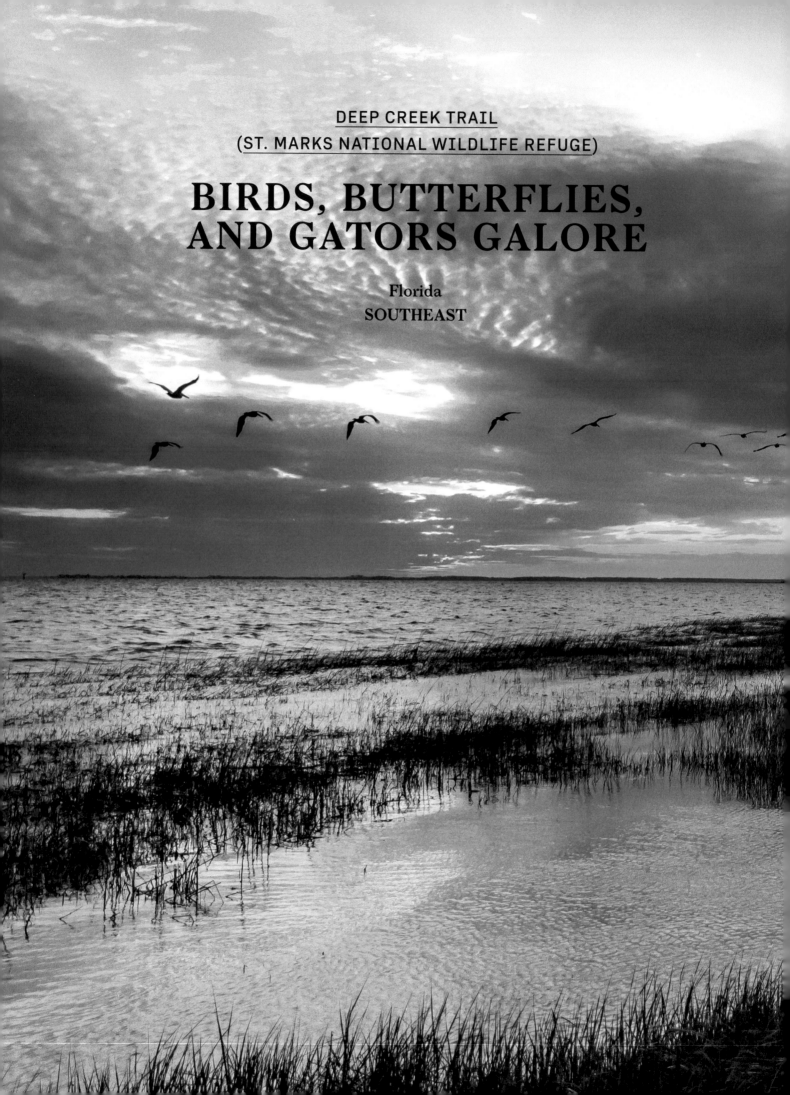

DEEP CREEK TRAIL
(ST. MARKS NATIONAL WILDLIFE REFUGE)

BIRDS, BUTTERFLIES, AND GATORS GALORE

Florida
SOUTHEAST

ABOUT THE TRAIL

→ <u>DISTANCE</u> 19.8 km (12.3 mi)

→ <u>DURATION</u> 5 to 7 hours

→ <u>LEVEL</u> Easy

E stablished in 1931, St. Marks National Wildlife Refuge (NWR) on the northwest coast of Florida is one of the oldest wildlife refuges in the United States. It's a quiet place for most of the year, where you can expect to encounter more alligators than people, and more ribbiting frogs than purring car engines. Encompassing 275 sq km (68,000 acres) of marshes, islands, beaches, and tidal creeks, St. Marks's estuarine environment boasts a small but well-maintained trail system. You can find a peaceful hiking experience here, exploring in solitude among a diverse range of flora and fauna.

Beginning and ending a few minutes' drive southeast of the visitor center, the Deep Creek Trail is the premier pathway in St. Marks NWR. Measuring 19.8 km (12.3 mi) in length, it's marked with white signposts and follows a combination of old logging roads and pool-skirting levees. The scenic loop passes through multiple ecosystems, including pine flatwoods, cypress swamp, and open marsh. Opportunities to view wildlife abound on the trail, and the birdlife and American alligators are of particular note.

St. Marks was originally founded as a sanctuary for migrating birds, and 300 species of feathered creatures have been documented inside its boundaries. This ornithological paradise is home to many different types of waterfowl, raptors, shore-birds, and wading birds. A more delicate winged animal, the monarch

"It's a quiet place for most of the year, where you can expect to encounter more alligators than people, and more ribbiting frogs than purring car engines."

← The Ring Levee Campsite area.
↓ Monarch butterflies stopping by St. Marks on their way to Central Mexico.
↓↓ A fiddler crab (*Uca*).

butterfly, can also be observed in the NWR every October and November. During their annual migration south, thousands of monarchs stop to feed on the abundant milkweeds before continuing a 3,219 km (2,000 mi) journey across the gulf to the highlands of central Mexico. Every autumn, St. Marks plays host to a Monarch Butterfly Festival, which includes educational demos, wildlife exhibitions, live music, and good food.

Besides the many birds and butterflies, St. Marks features a year-round population of alligators. These prehistoric marvels count among Mother Nature's ultimate survivors, having been around for more than 150 million years. Unlike their contemporaries, the dinosaurs, gators managed to stave off the Cretaceous-Tertiary mass extinction that occurred some 65 million years ago (as did sharks, sea turtles, platypus, bees, snakes, and, perhaps unfortunately, cockroaches).

↑ Looking south toward Florida's Big Bend Coast, one of America's most pristine wetland areas.
↓ Great blue heron (*Ardea herodias*).

Adult male American alligators measure between 3.4 and 4.6 m (11 and 15 ft) in length and tip the scales at over 453 kg (1,000 lb); females can measure up to 2.4 m (8 ft). While hiking along the levees of the Deep Creek Trail, you will likely see many alligators lurking in the swampy waters or sunning on the banks. Although they are carnivorous predators, they are naturally shy creatures. As long as you use common sense (no feeding, keep a distance of at least 20 m [66 ft] at all times), you have a better chance of being hit by lightning or winning the lottery than of being attacked by an alligator.

A complete loop of the Deep Creek Trail takes between five and seven hours. Before or after your hike, be sure to make the short drive down to the refuge's most famous man-made feature, St. Marks Lighthouse. Built in 1842, it ranks as the second-oldest lighthouse in Florida. Seeing the maritime beacon's silhouette at sunrise or sunset is an immersive experience—and a perfect accompaniment to a day spent appreciating the rich ecology of St. Marks National Wildlife Refuge, one of America's true coastal gems.

↑ An alligator patrolling the bayous of St Marks.
↓ A boardwalk through the swamps.

GOOD TO KNOW

START/FINISH
Deep Creek Trailhead, Lighthouse Road (limited parking available)

SEASON
October to May

PERMITS
A permit is not required to hike the Deep Creek Trail, though you will need to pay a small entrance fee for the wildlife refuge. Note that the trail is also open to bicycle and equestrian traffic.

HELPFUL HINTS

TIPS FOR THE TRAIL
- Both birds and mammals are at their most active early and late in the day. Plan on hitting the trail accordingly to increase your wildlife viewing possibilities.
- With the abundance of fauna to be found in St. Marks, this is one hike where binoculars are highly recommended. If you don't own any, you can pick up a pair on loan from the visitor center.
- A field guide to the flora and fauna of St. Marks is also available at the visitor center.
- Bring plenty of water, as there is no potable H_2O on the trail. Three to four liters is recommended.

FLORA & FAUNA

FIVE FACTS ABOUT ALLIGATORS
1. Alligators have between 74 and 80 teeth. As their teeth wear down, new ones come in. It's estimated that a gator can go through over 2,000 teeth during their lives.

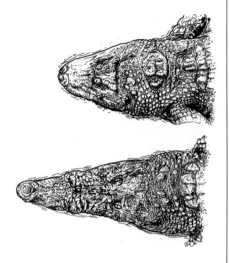

2. There are a few different ways to tell the difference between a gator and a crocodile, but the easiest is by the shape of their snout. An alligator snout has a broader, U-shaped front end, while a crocodile snout is V-shaped and pointier.
3. Unlike crocodiles, alligators are primarily freshwater animals, living in marshes, lakes, rivers, and swamps. *Note: They can tolerate saltwater environs for up to a few days.*
4. Alligators can hear underwater.
5. The average life expectancy of an alligator is 50 years.

BACKGROUND

THE FLORIDA TRAIL
For almost half of its length, the Deep Creek Trail runs concurrently with the Florida National Scenic Trail (FNST). Extending between 1,770 km (1,100 mi) and 2,092 km (1,300 mi), depending on route choice, the FNST stretches between Pensacola Beach in the north and Big Cypress National Preserve in the south. Well marked with orange blazes, it passes through swamplands, scrub, pine forests, hardwood hammocks, and palmetto prairies. It may well be the flattest long-distance hiking trail in the world, with a high point of only 82.3 m (270 ft) above sea level.

Varied environments on the FNST play host to an equally diverse range of fauna. Along the way you may spot black bears, gopher tortoises, wild pigs, cottonmouth snakes, alligators, and a large array of birdlife. If you are extremely lucky, you may even see the iconic Florida panther. This reclusive subspecies of cougar lives in the swamps and forests of southwestern Florida, and is one of the most endangered large mammals in the United States. During the 1970s it was estimated that only 20 Florida panthers remained in the wild; however, in recent decades they have made a comeback, and as of 2018 it's said that their number has grown to over 200.

AUTHOR'S ANECDOTE

PREHISTORIC BEDFELLOWS
In the winter of 2011/12, I hiked the Florida National Scenic Trail from Pensacola Beach to Big Cypress National Preserve. My favorite camping spot during the hike was the Ring Levee Campsite on the southern section of the Deep Creek Trail. Perched on the estuary's edge and surrounded by marshes and lakes, it affords an incredible sweep of northern Florida's famed Big Bend Coast. In addition to the view, my fondest memory of the night I spent in St. Marks National Wildlife Refuge was of my camping companions.

Before arriving at Ring Levee on an overcast December afternoon, I had counted no less than 17 alligators in the brackish waters and along the banks of St. Marks. I was mesmerized by these prehistoric creatures. They, on the other hand, seemingly couldn't care less about my presence—which was completely fine by me. Once I had set up my tarp, I spotted yet another gator (#18) not too far from where I was camped. Soon after the light faded and darkness ensued, I remember musing to myself, "I wonder if folks in Florida count alligators rather than sheep in order to fall asleep?"

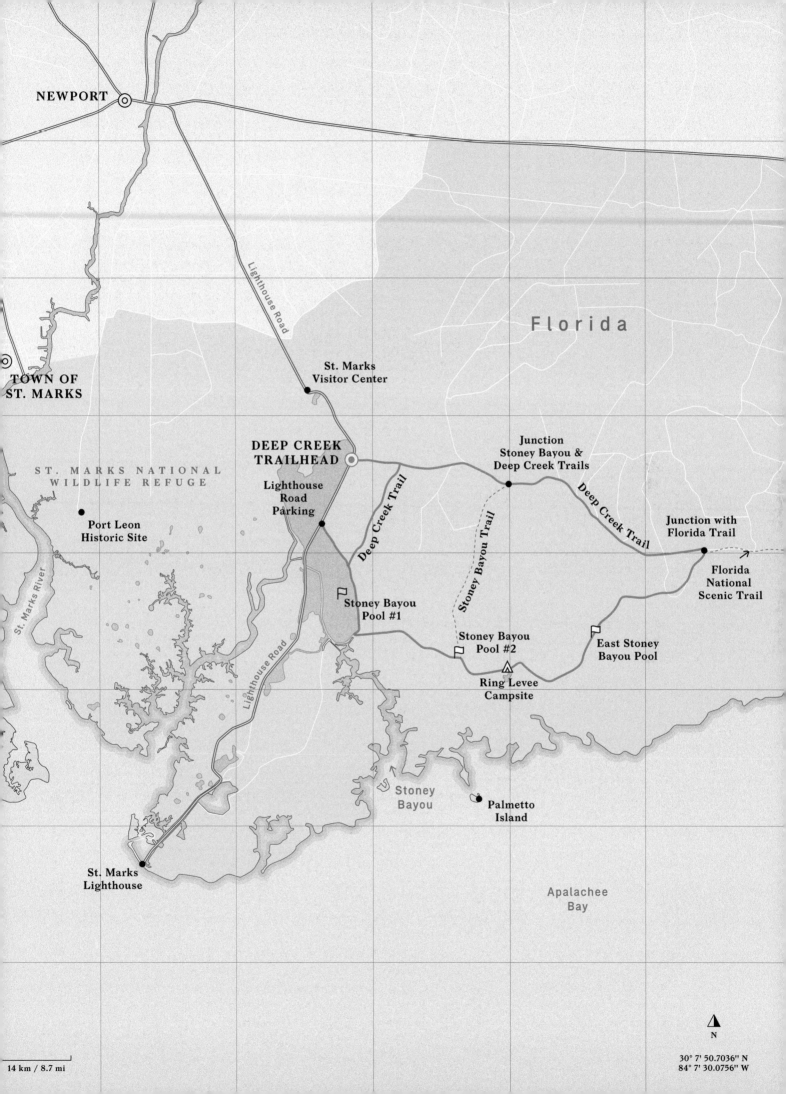

NEWPORT

TOWN OF
ST. MARKS

St. Marks
Visitor Center

Lighthouse Road

F l o r i d a

ST. MARKS NATIONAL
WILDLIFE REFUGE

DEEP CREEK
TRAILHEAD

Lighthouse
Road
Parking

Junction
Stoney Bayou &
Deep Creek Trails

Deep Creek Trail

Deep Creek Trail

Junction with
Florida Trail

Port Leon
Historic Site

Deep Creek Trail

Stoney Bayou Trail

Florida
National
Scenic Trail

Stoney Bayou
Pool #1

Stoney Bayou
Pool #2

East Stoney
Bayou Pool

St. Marks River

Ring Levee
Campsite

Lighthouse Road

Stoney
Bayou

Palmetto
Island

St. Marks
Lighthouse

Apalachee
Bay

14 km / 8.7 mi

N

30° 7' 50.7036'' N
84° 7' 30.0756'' W

CEDAR RUN — WHITEOAK CANYON LOOP
(SHENANDOAH NATIONAL PARK)

CHASING WATERFALLS IN THE BLUE RIDGE MOUNTAINS

Virginia
SOUTHEAST

ABOUT THE TRAIL
→ <u>DISTANCE</u> 21 km (13 mi)
→ <u>DURATION</u> 6 to 9 hours
→ <u>LEVEL</u> Moderate

Located 120 km (75 mi) west of Washington, DC, Shenandoah National Park (SNP) is the Chile of America's National Park System—long, narrow, and mountainous. Bestriding the crest of Virginia's Blue Ridge Mountains, the park is a mecca for hikers and backpackers living on the East Coast of the United States, offering more than 805 km (500 mi) of pathways within its boundaries. Notable among these is one of America's most beautiful waterfall trails: the Cedar Run–Whiteoak Canyon Loop.

Linking two of Shenandoah's deepest ravines, the loop measures 21 km (13 mi) in length and has a total elevation gain and loss of 1,260 m (4,150 ft). The trail is well marked and straightforward to follow, but far from easy due to its rocky terrain and steep gradients. Most hikers take between six and nine hours to complete the circuit, though it can also be made into an excellent overnight excursion, with great camping options along the way (see info box).

There are multiple points from which to begin or end the Cedar Run–Whiteoak Canyon Loop; however, the best is arguably from Weakley Hollow Fire Road on the park's eastern boundary. Hiking in a clockwise direction allows you to get the toughest climbing out of the way early in the day while you're still fresh. Ascending the Cedar Run Trail, the going is uniformly steep and impressive; you'll pass a continuous series of tumbling cascades and inviting pools set against a lush backdrop of seeps, mosses, and ferns. Keep your ears and eyes open for the many birds living in the canyon, including nesting warblers and pileated woodpeckers.

About halfway up Cedar Run Canyon, be sure to stop at the "big falls" and admire Halfmile Cliff. It's here that you can take the plunge down a long rock slide into a deep and chilly pool—not to be missed on a hot day! It may look sketchy, but everybody seems to get down safe and sound. (Tip: Don't forget to check out the smaller cascades along the trail too. While the bigger falls get all the attention [and the crowds], a short side trip off the beaten path can reward you with a waterfall and accompanying pool all to yourself.)

Not long after passing the cascades, the gradient lessens as the trail approaches Skyline Drive—a well-known 169 km (105 mi) road that traces the crest of the Blue Ridge Mountains for the entire length of SNP. From here, the trail climbs a further 215 vertical meters (700 ft) to reach the summit of Hawksbill Mountain (1,230 m [4,050 ft]), the geographic high point of the national park. The panorama is spectacular, with sweeping views of the Shenandoah Valley to the west and the rolling hills of Virginia's Piedmont region to the east. If you're lucky, you may even spot one of the majestic peregrine falcons that nest on the cliffs below the summit.

← A great spot for lunch or contemplation, Upper Falls is the highest cascade (26 m [86 ft]) in Whiteoak Canyon.
↑ The steep and rocky treadway of Whiteoak Canyon.

> **"Don't forget to check out the smaller cascades along the trail too. While the bigger falls get all the attention (and the crowds), a short side trip off the beaten path can reward you with a waterfall and accompanying pool all to yourself."**

"The park is a mecca for hikers and backpackers living on the East Coast of the United States, offering more than 805 km (500 mi) of pathways within its boundaries."

↑ The Summit of Hawksbill Mountain (1,235 m [4,050 ft]), looking down on the Shenandoah Valley below.
← Pink azaleas (*Rhododendron periclymenoides*).
↗ Red-spotted purple butterfly (*Limenitis arthemis*).
→ Crossing the Robinson River just above the upper falls in Whiteoak Canyon.

Descend from Hawksbill Mountain and head west on the Salamander Trail, named after the endangered Shenandoah salamander (see info box), to join the world-famous Appalachian Trail (AT). There are more great views from along the AT, and a short side trip to Betty's Rock is well worth your time. Continue northwards until you reach the junction with the Whiteoak Canyon Trail just before Skyland. At this point, descend gradually southeast until you arrive at the impressive upper falls, the tallest of the six major cascades in Whiteoak Canyon. This is an idyllic spot to grab a snack and enjoy the airy views from cliffs high above the cataract.

After the upper falls, the trail descends precipitously to the lower falls, some of the sections steep enough to warrant steps. The lower falls may be the most beautiful of the entire hike if you consider their broad sweep of rock, spit flow, and huge plunge pool below—jump right in for another swim. While hanging out and enjoying the views, you'll be serenaded by the rushing waters of the Robinson River, the watercourse responsible for carving Whiteoak Canyon. The path becomes more gradual from here as it winds its way back to the trailhead on Weakley Hollow Road.

The Cedar Run–Whiteoak Canyon Loop is one of the highlights of Shenandoah National Park. Along with stunning views of the Blue Ridge Mountains, an abundance of cascades, and a wide array of wildlife, what makes this hike impressive is its proximity to Washington, DC, the sixth largest metropolitan area in the United States. If you find yourself in and around the city, it takes less than two hours to drive into the park—a perfect weekend getaway to recharge your batteries.

GOOD TO KNOW

START / FINISH
Lower Whiteoak Canyon Trailhead on Weakley Hollow Fire Road (day use fee)

Alternatives:
- Hawksbill Gap parking area, mile 45.6 on Skyline Drive (park entrance fee)
- Upper Whiteoak Canyon parking area, mile 42.6 on Skyline Drive (park entrance fee)

HIGHEST / LOWEST POINT
Hawksbill Mountain
(1,235 m [4,052 ft])
Lower Whiteoak Canyon Trailhead
(350 m [1,120 ft])

SEASON
Year round. The spring sees wildflowers, dogwood, redbud, and mountain laurel in bloom. During the fall, the dense deciduous forests come alive in a blaze of orange, red, and yellow. For those who don't mind below-freezing temperatures, winter is incredible, with frozen waterfalls and enhanced views from the ridges thanks to autumnal leaf drop. High summer can be hot and humid, but it makes a swim in one of the canyon's pools even more refreshing!

HIGHLIGHTS
1. The six major cascades in Whiteoak Canyon that range from 10.7 m (35 ft) to 26.2 m (86 ft) in height
2. Spotting a Shenandoah salamander
3. The view from the top of Hawksbill Mountain, the highest point of the loop and in all of Shenandoah National Park
4. Hiking a section of the world-famous Appalachian Trail
5. Sliding down a waterfall on Cedar Run, followed by a swim in the cooling waters

HELPFUL HINTS

SUNRISE FROM THE SUMMIT
If you have the time, consider camping near the base of Hawksbill Mountain, and ascending the following morning to catch the sunrise from the summit. There are a number of good tent sites situated near Rock Spring Hut, a 2 km (1.2 mi) round-trip detour west on the Appalachian Trail.

FLORA & FAUNA

Considering its proximity to Washington, DC, much of Shenandoah National Park has an exceptionally wild feel to it. In regard to flora, the lower reaches of the canyons are rainforest-like with an abundance of ferns, mosses, and seeps.

Along the trail, hikers will pass through stands of white, red, and chestnut oaks, as well as hickories, hemlock, and omnipresent red maples.

As for wildlife, there is a healthy black bear population, as well as bobcats, coyotes, otters, deer, peregrine falcons, ravens, and Shenandoah salamanders.

SHENANDOAH SALAMANDER
Endemic to Shenandoah National Park, the endangered Shenandoah salamander is a member of the family *Plethodontidae*, a lungless species of salamander that breathes through its skin. Ranging in length from 7.5 to 11 cm (3.0 to 4.3 in), they can occur in two color phases: one with a thin yellow or red stripe down its back, and the other unstriped and dark with brass-colored flecks.

BONUS TRACK

The Blue Ridge Mountains have long been celebrated both in hiking, as well as in musical circles. In regard to the latter, over the decades many folk and country music artists have dedicated songs and even entire albums to this storied subrange of the Appalachians. Among the most notable tunes have been Alan Jackson's "Blue Ridge Mountain Song," and Dolly Parton's, "My Blue Ridge Mountain Boy."

Banjo aficionados will enjoy Flatt & Scruggs's 1957 classic, "Blue Ridge Cabin Home," and for those interested in going back even further in history, there is "The Trail of the Lonesome Pine." Published in 1913, this popular ballad featured in the 1937 Laurel & Hardy film, *Way out West*, and describes the singer's longing to go back to the Blue Ridge Mountains, in order to be reunited with the girl that he loves.

This theme of "returning home" can be found in many songs about the Blue Ridge Mountains. It is a range that inspires a sense of belonging and shared experience in those that hail from the region. In the words of North Carolina native and legendary country music performer, Ronnie Milsap:

Blue Ridge Mountains turning green/I wanna go home again to see my mountain friends/Springtime opens up my heart/Makes me want to share that good ole mountain air

Life's so young and free for all/For those who answer the Blue Ridge Mountains call/Blue Ridge Mountains turning green/I wanna go home again to see my mountain friends.

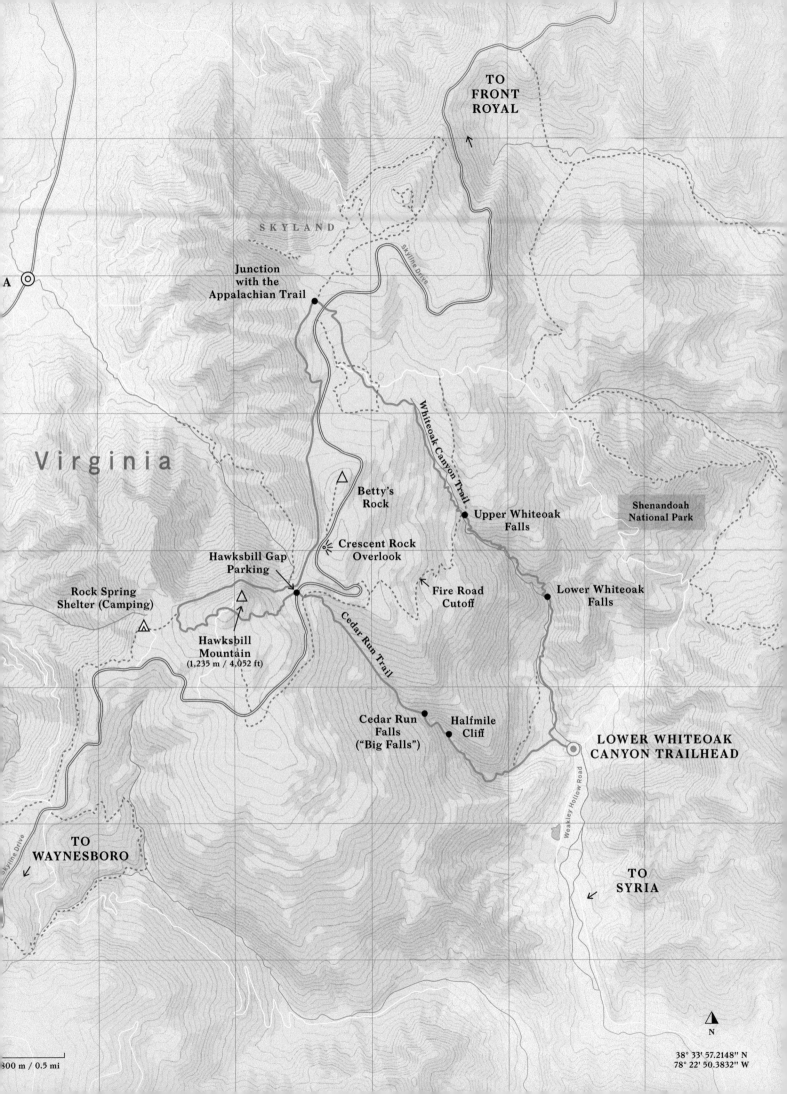

TO FRONT ROYAL

SKYLAND

Skyline Drive

Junction with the Appalachian Trail

Virginia

A

Betty's Rock

Whiteoak Canyon Trail

Upper Whiteoak Falls

Shenandoah National Park

Crescent Rock Overlook

Hawksbill Gap Parking

Fire Road Cutoff

Lower Whiteoak Falls

Rock Spring Shelter (Camping)

Cedar Run Trail

Hawksbill Mountain (1,235 m / 4,052 ft)

Cedar Run Falls ("Big Falls")

Halfmile Cliff

LOWER WHITEOAK CANYON TRAILHEAD

Weakley Hollow Road

Skyline Drive

TO WAYNESBORO

TO SYRIA

N

38° 33' 57.2148" N
78° 22' 50.3832" W

300 m / 0.5 mi

BARTRAM TRAIL

IN THE FOOTSTEPS OF
THE FLOWER HUNTER

Georgia and North Carolina
SOUTHEAST

ABOUT THE TRAIL

→ <u>DISTANCE</u> 187 km (116 mi)
→ <u>DURATION</u> 5 to 7 days
→ <u>LEVEL</u> Moderate

The Bartram Trail (BT) is a little-known ambulatory gem of the southern Appalachian Mountains. Meandering its way for 187 km (116 mi) through the peaceful woodlands of Georgia and North Carolina, the BT offers a glimpse of what the world-famous Appalachian Trail used to be. Same mountains, same flora and fauna, yet with only a fraction of the foot traffic and far more in the way of tranquility for solitude-seeking hikers and backpackers.

The trail is named after William Bartram, an eighteenth-century botanist, artist, writer, and all-around outdoorsman. Described by historian Judith Magee as "the most influential single figure in natural history in pre-revolutionary America," Bartram traveled widely throughout the country's Southeast between 1773 and 1777, manifesting his observations in the form of extensive notes and drawings on the region's flora, fauna, and native tribes. His collective works were published in 1791, and *Bartram's Travels* was soon recognized for both its enlightened impressions of the area's indigenous population—with whom the author encouraged mutually respectful interaction—and its profound botanical contributions to the scientific community.

The impact of Bartram's work was also apparent in the artistic world, most notably among British Romantic poet Samuel Taylor Coleridge and his friend and collaborator William Wordsworth. Parts of Coleridge's "The Rime of the Ancient Mariner" and "Kubla Khan" drew inspiration from Bartram, as did Wordsworth's "Ruth" from the *Lyrical Ballads* collection.

As one might expect from a pathway named for a botanist, there's an impressive array of plant life along the trail. You might see—and in some cases sample—wild strawberries, sweetshrub, fraser magnolias, ginseng,

↖ Engraved stone trail signs mark the Georgia section of the Bartram Trail.
↑ Rays of light pierce through the foliage.

mountain laurel, flame azaleas, and thickets of rhododendron. As it creeps over forested hills and descends into fog-laden dales, the trail also showcases cascading waterfalls and babbling brooks. When it comes to backpacking the BT, the senses of smell, touch, hearing, and taste rate right alongside that of sight in regard to one's overall wilderness experience.

From a navigational perspective, the Bartram Trail is well marked with diamond-shaped yellow blazes in Georgia and rectangular yellow blazes in North Carolina. The former segment is also distinguished by a series of beautifully engraved stone markers, which many veteran hikers have deemed their all-time favorite trail signs due to their classic font and weather-beaten appearance. The other notable man-made elements on the trail are the stone towers perched atop Rabun Bald and Wayah Bald. On a clear day, the 360-degree panoramic views from these topographic high points are magnificent—try to time your arrival for either sunrise or sunset.

Apart from the occasional hilltop lookout, most of the Bartram Trail is set along forested corridors in which sweeping views are few and far between. And that's okay. There are many types of beauty, and the allure of the BT is usually subtle rather than dramatic, intimate rather than distant. This is exactly the way it should be for a trail dedicated to William Bartram, a man who spent much of his life documenting botanical minutiae, and who was affectionately known among the Seminole tribe of the southeastern United States as "the flower hunter."

↑ Bartram's Ixia (*Calydorea coelestina*)
↓ Rectangular yellow blazes mark the way during the North Carolina section of the Bartram Trail.

"Apart from the occasional hilltop lookout, most of the Bartram Trail is set along forested corridors in which sweeping views are few and far between. And that's okay. There are many types of beauty, and the allure of the BT is usually subtle rather than dramatic, intimate rather than distant."

↑ Hilltops peek out from a sea of low-lying clouds.
← A leaf-strewn waterfall during an autumn hike of the Bartram Trail.

GOOD TO KNOW

START / FINISH
Northern Terminus
Cheoah Bald, North Carolina
Southern Terminus
Russell Bridge, Georgia

HIGHEST / LOWEST POINT
Wayah Bald (1,641 m [5,385 ft])
Chattooga River (460 m [1,500 ft])

SEASON
April to November. Spring and autumn
are ideal, the former representing peak
wildflower season, and the latter seeing
the forests ablaze with a kaleidoscope
of fall colors.

HIGHLIGHTS
1. Engraved stone trail markers
   throughout the Georgia section
2. The 360-degree panorama from
   Wayah Bald at sunrise
3. Solitude
4. Babbling brooks and creaky
   wooden bridges
5. Tumbling waterfalls and
   emerald pools

HELPFUL HINTS

FRANKLIN'S PUMPKINFEST
The Bartram Trail passes through only
one town during its 187 km (116 mi)
course: Franklin, North Carolina. Widely
known as one of the premier outdoor
towns in the Appalachian Mountains,
Franklin offers the perfect opportunity
to stock up on supplies, have a hearty
restaurant meal (or two), and treat
yourself to a night of comparative luxury
in one of its many hotels.

For those who happen to visit
Franklin during October, it also
represents a chance to compete
in the world's foremost (only?)
pumpkin rolling competition, which
takes place during the town's annual
pumpkin festival. Established in 1983,
Pumpkinfest features street performers,
mountain arts and crafts, and, if you
happen to miss out on the rolling event,
you can always try your luck in the
pumpkin pie-eating contest.

BACKGROUND

THE MYSTERY OF
THE BARTRAM TRAIL
In the early 2000s, the Bartram Trail was
voted the No. 1 long-distance trail in the
United States for solitude by readers of
Backpacker magazine. And sure enough,
when hiking the BT it's highly unlikely
that you'll encounter many (if any) other
thru-hikers. However, this presents a
conundrum: if the trail was selected
No.1 for solitude, but hardly anyone ever
hikes it, then who voted for it?

BONUS TRACK

Located near Franklin, North Carolina,
Wayah Bald Lookout is the highest point
of the Bartram Trail at 1,641 m (5,345 ft)

above sea level. Built as a fire lookout
by the Civilian Conservation Corps in
1937, its name "Waya" is the Cherokee
word for "wolf," so-called because of
the red wolves which once roamed
the surrounding hills and valleys. This
scenic viewpoint is one of the highlights
of the BT, and on a clear day you can see
Cheoah and the Great Smoky Mountains
to the north, and the Little Tennessee
River Valley and Southern Nantahala
Wilderness to the south.

AUTHOR'S ANECDOTE

THE SOUTHEASTERN SERPENTINE
TRAIL
The Bartram Trail constitutes part
of a 938 km (583 mi) trek through the
Appalachian Mountains called the
Southeastern Serpentine Trail (SST).
The SST combines four separate
pathways—the Foothills, Bartram, and
Benton MacKaye Trails, along with the
Great Smoky Mountains National Park
section of the Appalachian Trail (AT)—
to form a continuous long-distance
hiking route through some of the less
frequented parts of southern Appalachia.

Beginning at Table Rock State Park
in South Carolina and finishing at
Springer Mountain, Georgia, the SST
passes through four states (the other
two are North Carolina and Tennessee)
and will take most hikers around
30 to 35 days to complete. With the
exception of the Smokies and Foothills
segments, you will have the trail almost
all to yourself for most of the way
(approximately 70 percent of the total
distance). And that is a rarity in the
busy Appalachian Mountains.

Hiking the SST is like walking back in
time, reminiscent of what the AT would
have been like 50 years ago. Same
mountains, less development, and far
fewer people. I hiked its length in the
fall of 2011, and my principal memories
from the trek remain the moments of
peace and tranquility I experienced,
along with the sound of my footsteps
crunching their way through the sea
of fallen leaves that cover much of the
Appalachians every November.

WEST

America's West has long been a source of inspiration for lovers of the outdoors. From pristine coastline to towering volcanoes, unforgiving desert to the majestic Sierra Nevada, it is a region in which triple-take views are commonplace and the only constant is that of change.

HALF DOME (YOSEMITE NATIONAL PARK)

A VAST EDIFICE OF STONE AND SPACE

California
WEST

ABOUT THE TRAIL

→ <u>DISTANCE</u> 27.4 km (17 mi)
→ <u>DURATION</u> 10 to 12 hours
→ <u>LEVEL</u> Challenging

Half Dome is among the world's most famous rocks. A granite monolith that towers more than 1,466 m (4,809 ft) above Yosemite Valley, its hulking presence has inspired wonder in generations of visitors. And for those who not only gaze up in awe, but also undertake the journey to its rounded summit, the reward is one of the most breathtaking and heart-soaring vistas imaginable.

Ascending Half Dome is as logistically and physically challenging as it is aesthetically pleasing. Due to its popularity,

hikers will first need to run the gauntlet of red tape that is the permit application process (see info box). If awarded a place, what awaits is a round trip to the top of Yosemite National Park's most iconic landmark, entailing an arduous 2,932 m (9,619 ft) of total elevation gain and loss—all within the space of 27.4 km (17 mi).

The hike begins at Happy Isles Trailhead (Tip: Aim to start an hour or two before dawn if you want to avoid the inevitable midday summit crowds.) The trail initially lopes through a forest of giant Sequoias before ascending past two of Yosemite's most renowned cascades, Vernal and Nevada Falls. There are a couple of different options for tackling this section: the Mist Trail or the John Muir Trail. Taking the latter path up and the former trail back down (on the return journey) is a good way to do it. This will allow for a wonderful, anticipatory perspective of Half Dome at daybreak, and then

"Yosemite Valley, to me, is always a sunrise, a glitter of green and golden wonder in a vast edifice of stone and space. I know of no sculpture, painting, or music that exceeds the compelling spiritual command of the soaring shape of the granite cliff and dome, of patina of light on rock and forest, and of the thunder and whispering of the flowing waters."

—

ANSEL ADAMS

← From the top of the subdome, hikers will get their first close-up view of the legendary ascent to Half Dome's summit.
↓ Metal cables and wooden slats assist hikers on the final push to the top.

dramatic, up-close-and-personal views of Vernal Falls as the sun sets.

Above the cascades, there will be a brief altitudinal respite in the form of Little Yosemite Valley. Enjoy the flat terrain while it lasts, because the path soon turns north, where it ascends through more Sequoias to arrive at a place called "the sub-dome." This steep and exposed precursor to the final climb is made via a switch-backing, stair-climbing section of trail that ascends approximately 200 m (656 ft) in elevation in a mere 20 to 30 minutes. Upon topping out, hikers will find themselves face to rock face with the legendary summit of Half Dome.

Due to its intimidating, 45-degree slope, the final push to the monolith's apex is done with the assistance of metal cables and wooden slats. Nonetheless, its vertiginous character has caused many a hiker's knees to shake and will to waver (just momentarily!). Don't worry too much; most people find

Half Dome, Tenaya Canyon, and Yosemite Valley, as seen from the top of Clouds Rest.

↑ Alpine Lily (*Lilium parvum*).
→ Secluded waterfalls and giant granite monoliths.
↓ The Ahwahnee Bridge.

that when they actually get started and realize that the cables and slats are solid—dare I say it—as a rock, the climb is not as challenging as it looks. This last stretch will take as little as 15 minutes if the cables are uncrowded, and as much as 45 minutes if they are not. This is where your pre-dawn start will really pay off, as hiking up and down Half Dome is a lot more enjoyable if you can do so at your own pace, minus the crowds.

Once you arrive at the summit, take a deep breath (or 20) and soak in the panorama. You've made it! Among myriad amazing features in view are Clouds Rest (see info box), Mount Starr King, Unicorn Peak, and, of course, the valley floor, where you started your hike four to six hours earlier. Before descending, take some time to walk around Half Dome's expansive 52,609 sq m (13 acre) crown. Find a solitary spot and let your mind drift to wherever the breeze and the clouds may take you.

Yosemite National Park is one of Mother Nature's most astonishing creations, a place that has moved many legendary figures to wax poetic, including landscape photographer Ansel Adams: "Yosemite Valley, to me, is always a sunrise, a glitter of green and golden wonder in a vast edifice of stone and space. I know of no sculpture, painting, or music that exceeds the compelling spiritual command of the soaring shape of the granite cliff and dome, of patina of light on rock and forest, and of the thunder and whispering of the falling, flowing waters. At first the colossal aspect may dominate; then we perceive and respond to the delicate and persuasive complex of nature."

GOOD TO KNOW

START/FINISH

Happy Isles, Yosemite Valley
Out-and-back to the summit of Half
Dome via a combination of the Mist and
John Muir Trails.

TOTAL ELEVATION GAIN

1,466 m (4,809 ft)

SEASON

Late May to early October. Due to the
steepness of the final 122 m (400 ft)
ascent to the summit, the National
Park Service installs metal cables and
wooden slats on this section around
Memorial Day (the last Monday in May)
and takes them down again around
Columbus Day (i.e., the second Monday
in October). These dates can vary from
year to year depending on conditions.

PERMITS

During hiking season, a permit is
required for Half Dome (via the
Yosemite National Park Service).
As of 2019, a maximum of 300 permits
are issued per day; 225 for day hikers
and 75 for backpackers. The majority
of permits are awarded through a
pre-season lottery that takes place
each March, though there are also
a limited number of places available
a couple of days in advance. To
increase your odds of success, try
to avoid applying for a permit on
weekends or public holidays.

HELPFUL HINTS

CAMPING

Obtaining a day-hike permit for Half
Dome can be difficult, but a backpacking permit is even harder to
procure. For this reason, the majority
of those who hike up Half Dome
do so in one long day. If you are
adamant about trying your luck at
an overnighting permit, the main
camping option along the trail is
Little Yosemite Valley Campground,
situated 7 km (4.2 mi) from the
Happy Isles Trailhead.

GEAR

Trail running shoes; headlamp; gloves
(for the cables); day pack; insulation
garment for the often chilly summit; rain
jacket; and sufficient food for a full day
of hiking.

WATER

The only place to obtain potable water
on the trail is at a drinking fountain
at the Vernal Fall Footbridge, which
is only a 20–30-minute walk from the
Happy Isles Trailhead. After that, it is
possible to get H_2O from the Merced
River up until Little Yosemite Valley, but
the water will need to be purified with
either a filter or chemicals.

BACKGROUND

CLOUDS REST

For those looking for a less crowded
but equally spectacular Yosemite
hiking experience, consider heading
to the summit of nearby Clouds Rest
(3,025 m [9,926 ft]). You do not need
a permit for this 22.5 km (14 mi)
round-trip hike, which begins and
ends at Sunrise Trailhead. The ascent
involves 701 m (2,300 ft) of elevation
gain, and it takes most ramblers 8–10
hours to complete the round trip. The
360-degree panorama from the summit
is a jaw-dropper, with a bird's-eye
perspective of Tenaya Canyon, Sentinel
Dome, Mount Hoffmann, and the cable
side of Half Dome. Upon completing
the hike, be sure to reward yourself
with a cooling swim in the crystal-clear
waters of Tenaya Lake.

BONUS TRACK

Hiking season in Yosemite National Park
generally runs from late May to the start
of October. Depending on the season's
snowfall and the altitude at which you
are hiking (elevations in Yosemite range
from 600 m [2,000 ft] to above 4,000 m
[13,000 ft]), each month brings with it
different pros and cons:

June: Conditions in the valley are
usually ideal, but if you wish to venture
into the higher parts of the park, expect
to encounter a great deal of lingering
snow. Nighttime temperatures are often
still below freezing.

July: Snowmelt is at its peak, so
those hiking at loftier elevations should
expect to encounter raging rivers that
may be difficult to ford. Temperatures
are warming up, with an average range
of between 13–32°C (55–90°F).

August: Generally the weather is
ideal, but this is when Yosemite's famed
mosquitos are at their worst. A head net
and bug repellant can be sanity-savers.

September: The pick of the bunch.
The school holiday crowds have abated
along with the bugs, and although the
nights are becoming cooler again, the
temperatures are usually mild. Plus, you
may experience the beautiful hues of fall
foliage. The nights are getting shorter,
and by the end of the month, the chances
of early snowfall become greater.

ACTIVITIES

Apart from being a hiker's paradise,
Yosemite has long been known as a
haven for rock climbers. Each and
every year mountaineers from around
the world migrate to the valley, drawn
by iconic granite behemoths such as
El Capitan and Half Dome.

For less seasoned climbers looking
to scale new heights, perhaps the
best place to start is at the Yosemite
Mountaineering School & Guide Service,
which holds classes in Half Dome Village
and Tuolumne Meadows. Founded in
1969, the school offers group classes
(limited to six students per instructor)

or private lessons. Beyond climbing, they also offer guided overnight backpacking trips and cross-country ski classes during the winter months.

BASE CAMP TALES

Mountains have historically been seen as male-dominated terrain. The women who clambered up Yosemite's peaks in the late nineteenth century—wearing heavy and uncomfortable bloomers, leggings, long-sleeved blouses, and wide-brimmed hats—blithely dismantled this perception in a series of climbs executed with stoicism and flair.

Sarah Louisa Dutcher, an assistant to the famed western photographer Carleton Watkins, was the first woman to climb Half Dome in 1875. Twenty years later, a fearless foursome—sisters Stella, Bertha, and Mabel Sweet, and friend Maybel Davis—summited Mt. Lyell, the park's highest peak. Though they were the third group of women who had accomplished the ascent, they were the first to make their descent through Tuolumne Canyon—and certainly the first to quicken the descent by sliding down the glacier on the seat of their bloomers!

But perhaps the most famous of the park's early female adventurers was Kitty Tatch. A waitress at the nearby Sentinel Hotel, Tatch was captured in a famous photograph by George Fiske performing high kicks 914 m (3,000 ft) above the valley on the edge of Overhanging Rock. She was joined in this iconic image by her good friend and fellow waitress, Katherine Hazelston.

POINT OF VIEW

By any criterion, Yosemite is one of the world's most beautiful national parks. Therefore, it's no surprise that there are a multitude of spectacular viewpoints from which visitors can take in the scenery. Some of the most notable and easily accessible of these lookouts include Tunnel View, El Capitan Meadow, Glacier Point, and Olmstead

Point. The catch: these scenic spots are very much on the "beaten track," and therefore you'll invariably have to share your views with hordes of other tourists.

That said, it's possible to find quiet and peaceful vistas in even the most popular corners of Yosemite if you put in a little extra effort. In the case of Olmstead Point, that means making a 10–15-minute climb to the top of the dome located across the road from the parking lot. Less than 800 m (0.5 mi) later, you'll find yourself on the mini summit with jaw-dropping views of Half Dome, Clouds Rest, Mount Hoffman, and Lake Tenaya as your reward.

NEARBY: THE JOHN MUIR TRAIL

"Climb the mountains and get their good tidings. Nature's peace will flow into you as sunshine flows into trees. The winds will blow their own freshness into you, and the storms their energy, while cares will drop off like autumn leaves." —John Muir from *Our National Parks* (1901)

The trail to Half Dome coincides, in part, with the northernmost section of the John Muir Trail (JMT). One of America's most renowned long-distance pathways, the JMT runs 340 km (211 mi) from Happy Isles in Yosemite Valley to the summit of Mount Whitney, the highest point in the contiguous United States. Along the way it passes through three national parks (Yosemite, Kings Canyon, and Sequoia) and two designated wilderness areas (John Muir and Ansel Adams), while showcasing an alpine arcadia of jagged granite peaks, sweeping glacial valleys, thunderous waterfalls, and hundreds of sapphire-colored lakes.

The JMT is named in honor of the famous nineteenth-century Scottish-American naturalist and conservationist. John Muir was at the forefront of the fight to preserve America's wilderness, and was instrumental in the establishment of the country's National Park System. The construction of the path that bears his name began after his death in 1915,

and was eventually finished in 1938, which commemorated the 100th anniversary of Muir's birth.

DEEP ROOTED

A short walk from the Yosemite Museum lies the reconstructed Miwok Village of Ahwahnee. Located in Yosemite Valley on the very same spot that the original existed in the 1870s, it consists of a ceremonial roundhouse, a sweat lodge, acorn silos, bark teepees, and a chief's cabin. Ahwahnee is the name the Miwok tribe gave to Yosemite Valley, and the residents of this majestic area referred to themselves as the Ahwahneechee.

Before foreign prospectors upended their way of life, the Ahwahneechee lived in and around the High Sierra. They gathered from the earth—berries, bulbs, seeds, and acorns—hunted deer, and fished the mountain waters for trout. The Ahwahneechee also utilized leaves, flowers, and wood for natural medicines, household items, weapons, and special dishes like manzanita berry cider, which is still occasionally prepared at ceremonial gatherings today.

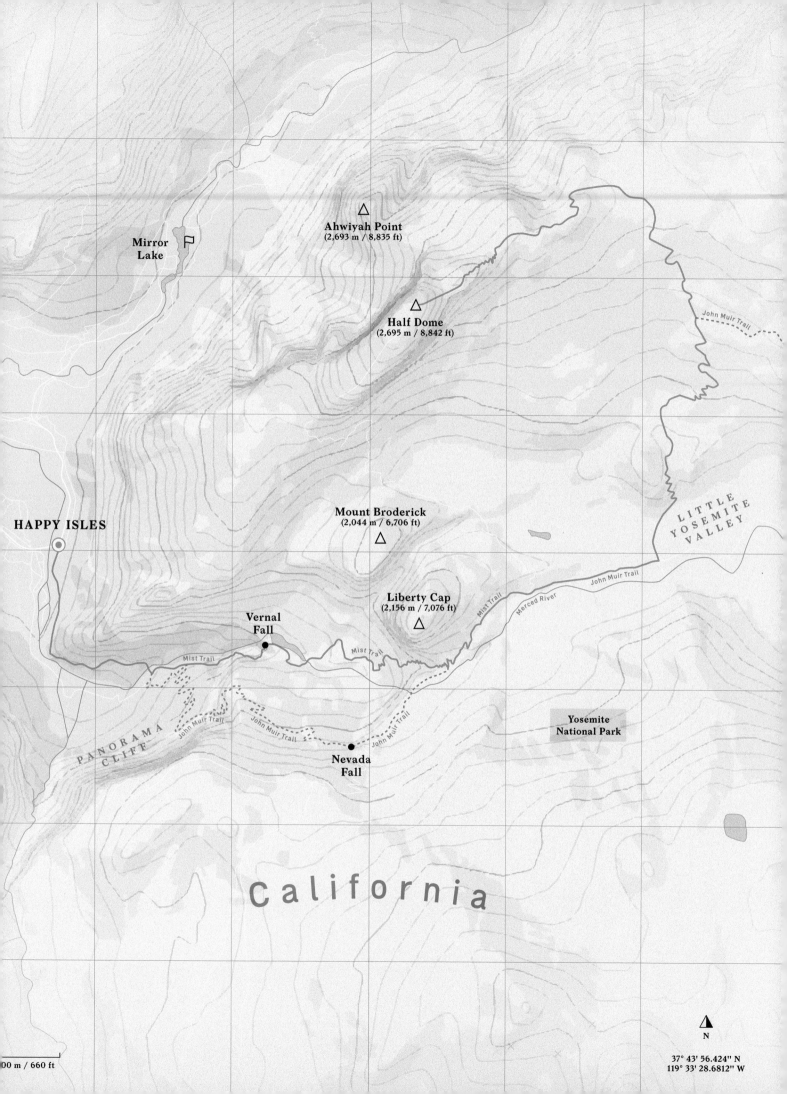

Mirror Lake

Ahwiyah Point
(2,693 m / 8,835 ft)

Half Dome
(2,695 m / 8,842 ft)

John Muir Trail

HAPPY ISLES

Mount Broderick
(2,044 m / 6,706 ft)

LITTLE
YOSEMITE
VALLEY

John Muir Trail

Liberty Cap
(2,156 m / 7,076 ft)

Mist Trail

Merced River

**Vernal
Fall**

Mist Trail

Mist Trail

John Muir Trail

**Yosemite
National Park**

John Muir Trail

John Muir Trail

John Muir Trail

P A N O R A M A
C L I F F

**Nevada
Fall**

C a l i f o r n i a

N

00 m / 660 ft

37° 43' 56.424" N
119° 33' 28.6812" W

DESERT DREAMS IN SOUTHERN CALIFORNIA

California

WEST

ABOUT THE TRAIL
→ <u>DISTANCE</u> 11.1 km (6.9 mi)
→ <u>DURATION</u> 3 to 4 hours
→ <u>LEVEL</u> Easy

L egend has it that Mormon settlers gave Joshua trees their name, the sprawling branches reminding them of the biblical prophet, Joshua, with his arms raised toward the sky in prayer. The veracity of this tale may be debatable, but what is not is the fact that these distinctive desert plants and the surreal arid landscape that surrounds them have long provided inspiration for pioneers, writers, musicians, and hikers alike.

From an environmental perspective, Joshua Tree National Park is a tale of two intersecting deserts. Located approximately 210 km (130 mi) west of Los Angeles, you've got the low and arid Colorado Desert, and the higher, more vegetated Mojave Desert. The former lies in the western part of the park, and is hotter, drier, and distinguished by plants such as the cholla and ocotillo. The latter is found in the eastern and southern sections, and features the eponymous Joshua trees, as well as myriad billion-year-old rock formations.

Until visiting the park in person, many people are unaware that Joshua trees are not actually trees at all. Part of the yucca plant family, they're water-storing succulents with extensive root systems designed by Mother Nature to soak in the maximum amount of moisture possible. Growing up to 12.2 m (40 ft) high, their average life expectancy is 150 years, though some have been known to live between 300 and 500 years. Fun fact: The fibrous trunks of Joshua "trees" don't form annual growth rings. Botanists estimate their age according to other indicators such as their shape and height.

The Willow Hole Trail is one of the national park's classic rambles, an easy 11.1 km (6.9 mi) out-and-back hike that can be enjoyed by people of all ages and experience levels. Starting from the Boy Scout Trailhead, the flat and well-maintained pathway initially heads northeast through a wide expanse of Joshua trees. After 1.9 km (1.2 mi) it diverges from the Boy Scout Trail, and heads toward one of Joshua Tree's most iconic features, the Wonderland of Rocks. An appropriately named 31 sq km (12 sq mi) collection of house-sized boulders, massive rock piles, granite domes, and monoliths, this section's treadway transforms from hard pack to soft sand, and traverses multiple maze-like washes and side canyons, where you'll need to pay attention in order to stay on track. As you delve further into the Wonderland, the formations grow larger and more fantastical, until the main wash widens and the trail finally arrives at the turnaround point—the oasis of Willow Hole.

A seasonal waterhole set among an abundance of luxuriant greenery, Willow Hole is a hydrological lifeline for many of the park's bird species, as well as bigger animals like the iconic bighorn sheep (see info box). It makes for a perfect mid-hike picnic spot, with plenty of places to find shady sanctuary. Note that Willow Hole is for day use only; camping is not permitted here.

↑ Sunlight piercing through the Joshua trees.
→ The high desert floor takes on a golden hue.

"These distinctive desert plants and the surreal arid landscape that surrounds them have long provided inspiration for pioneers, writers, musicians, and hikers alike."

The Colorado Desert section is hotter and drier than the Mojave Desert areas, and is distinguished by plants such as the cholla and ocotillo.

Once you've rested, there's nothing left to do but make the two-hour return journey. On the way back, consider exploring some of the many side canyons that the trail passes to discover even more amazing formations, and possibly other ancient treasures as well. Before the arrival of Europeans in the late 1700s, the Joshua Tree National Park area was used seasonally by the Cahuilla, Chemehuevi, and Serrano peoples. Traces of their former presence can be found within the Wonderland of Rocks complex in the form of pictographs and petroglyphs. A small, but significant site lies in Hidden Valley, just south of the Willow Hole Trail near Barker Dam.

As much as any other national park in the United States, Joshua Tree is a place best appreciated at sunrise and sunset. Apart from these times offering cooler temperatures and enhanced wildlife viewing, they're also the times during which the park's namesake "trees" truly come alive. Silhouetted against a vibrant orange sky, the zigzagging branches spread their largess toward the heavens as if asking for direction, making one believe that the theory of the Mormon settlers wasn't so far from the truth after all.

"Silhouetted against a vibrant orange sky, the zigzagging branches spread their largess toward the heavens as if asking for direction, making one believe that the theory of the Mormon settlers wasn't so far from the truth after all."

← The Mojave Desert section of the national park features the eponymous Joshua trees, as well as myriad billion-year-old rock formations.
↙ Cholla cactus (*Cylindropuntia fulgida*).
→ Wildflower blooms in Joshua Tree are not an annual event. They only occur after sufficient rain has fallen during the winter.
↓ Approaching the Wonderland of Rocks.

↑↑ Walking among the Cholla Cactus Garden.
↑ The night sky over Joshua Tree National Park.

GOOD TO KNOW

START/FINISH
Boy Scout Trailhead

SEASON
Hiking season in Joshua Tree National Park is from late September to mid-June. Daytime temperatures during the winter are pleasant, but during the evenings it can drop to freezing or below. Summer can be scorching, with temperatures often exceeding 38°C (100°F).

PERMITS
No permits are needed for day hiking in Joshua Tree National Park. For all overnight excursions, hikers must register (it's free) at one of the 13 backcountry registration boards around the park.

SKULL ROCK
One of the most recognizable landmarks in Joshua Tree National Park, Skull Rock is a distinctive pointed-head rock with two hollowed-out eye sockets. Situated just off Park Boulevard, it's the geological highlight of a 2.7 km (1.7 mi) nature trail that begins and ends at Jumbo Rocks Campground.

OTHER RECOMMENDED HIKING OPTIONS IN JOSHUA TREE NP
1. Ryan Mountain (4.8 km [3 mi])
2. Pine City (7.1 km [4.4 mi])
3. The Maze Loop (8.1 km [5 mi])
4. Warren Peak (9.4 km [5.8 mi])
5. Summit Springs (18.3 km [11.4 mi])

HELPFUL HINTS

WHAT TO BRING?
Hat; sunblock; sunglasses; lightweight running or trail running shoes; two to three liters of water.

TRAIL RUNNING SHOES VS. HIKING BOOTS
When hiking in arid environments such as Joshua Tree National Park, leave the heavy, waterproof boots at home and go with lightweight, breathable trail running shoes. Your feet will thank you. Why? First, they're generally more comfortable and less cumbersome than boots. Second, stability in hiking footwear is largely derived from a sturdy sole unit and a solid heel counter (not the actual height of the model), both of which are provided by high-quality trail running shoes. And third, when hiking in arid environs, less breathable, waterproof boots greatly increase the chance of blisters and fungal infections due to the fact that they cause your feet to sweat more.

Need more convincing? Each and every year hundreds of successful thru-hikers trek the length of multi-thousand kilometer pathways such as the Pacific Crest Trail and Continental Divide Trail—both of which include extended desert sections—while happily wearing either trail running shoes or running shoes with good grip. *From a personal perspective: After 30+ years and more than 100,000 km (62,137 mi) of hiking around the world (the first decade of which this author almost exclusively wore leather boots), he now only ever wears waterproof boots during extreme winter trips in snowbound, sub-freezing conditions, in which having waterproof footwear is essential in order to avoid the risk of frostbite.*

TRAFFIC

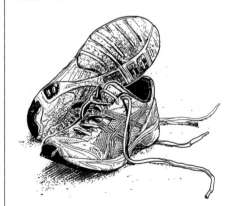

If driving to the park from Los Angeles, be sure to time your trip to avoid rush-hour traffic. If you make the mistake of leaving while commuters are heading to and from work on the freeways, it can make all the difference. What should be a 2 to 3 hour drive can instead take 5 or 6 hours.

FLORA & FAUNA

NOCTURNAL WILDLIFE
As a way of adapting to the region's extreme temperatures and lack of water sources, many of Joshua Tree's animals are mostly nocturnal, including desert bighorn sheep, coyotes, lynx, kangaroo rats, and snakes. From a viewing perspective, the best time to spot these creatures is either at dawn or dusk, when they're either just waking up or calling it a day.

DESERT BIGHORN SHEEP
Native to the arid regions of southeastern California, Nevada, northwestern Arizona, and southern Utah, desert bighorn sheep (*Ovis canadensis nelsoni*) are similar in virtually every respect to other species of bighorn sheep, except that they can go longer periods of time without drinking water. According to the U.S. Fish and Wildlife Service: "Unlike most mammals, desert bighorn sheep have the ability to lose up to 30 percent of their body weight in water (more than a camel) and still survive. Bighorn may go without drinking for weeks or months during the cooler parts of the year. ... During the hot, dry summer months, bighorn often go three to seven days without drinking, sustaining their body moisture from their food alone." The desert bighorn sheep is the flagship species of Joshua Tree National Park, and the Willow Hole oasis offers an excellent possibility of spotting one of the 200–300 that roam the park.

BACKGROUND

FROM IRELAND WITH LOVE
Since the late 1980s, Joshua Tree National Park has experienced a surge in visitors thanks to one of the best-selling rock albums of all time, U2's *The Joshua Tree*. What many of these visitors don't realize is that the Joshua tree that graces the album cover is not from its namesake national park. In actual fact, the featured yucca plant was located at Zabriskie Point in Death

Valley National Park, more than 322 km (200 mi) north of Joshua Tree NP. *Note: It was felled by extreme winds in 1980.*

INDIAN CANYONS

A worthy side trip located an hour west of Joshua Tree is Indian Canyons in Palm Springs. The site of North America's largest natural fan palm oasis, the Indian Canyons are the ancestral home of the Agua Caliente Band of Cahuilla people, who have thrived in the lushly vegetated area for thousands of years. Indian Canyons includes about 100 km (62 mi) of hiking trails of varied levels of difficulty. Some of the more popular hiking options include Murray Canyon, Andreas Canyon, East Fork, and the challenging Hahn Buena Vista.

AUTHOR'S ANECDOTE

RATTLE AND HUM

From a hiker's perspective, the best thing about rattlesnakes is that they rattle. Basically, it's the snake's way of saying, "Dude, you're crowding my space." Coming from a country, namely Australia, in which the snakes are generally far more stealthy (and venomous), I've come to appreciate this reptilian heads-up during the thousands of kilometers I've hiked in America's Southwest and northern Mexico.

Among these journeys, I've made three separate hiking trips to Joshua Tree National Park. The second, in June 2011, included one of the closest snake encounters I've had during my outdoor career. While venturing off-trail in the Wonderland of Rocks area, I was negotiating some technical terrain, when, upon leaping onto a large boulder, there it was. The rattlesnake had reared itself up not more than a meter from where I landed, and there was no mistaking the distinctive buzzing noise for which they are famous. Instinctively, I bounced over to the next large rock as if propelled by an internal pogo stick. At a safe distance, I observed my new friend with adrenaline pumping and sphincter contracted as the snake continued to keep an equally watchful

eye on my movements. With a big smile of relief on my face, I continued on my way, much more watchful than I had been not more than a couple of minutes before.

BASE CAMP TALES

THE SOUNDS OF JOSHUA TREE

Joshua Tree National Park vibrates on a frequency all its own—and we're not just alluding to the unique energy that comes with walking through its surreal desert landscapes. For many years, artists and musicians alike have flocked to the park and its surrounding areas to draw inspiration. Since 2003, it has also played host to the biannual Joshua Tree Music Festival, which takes place over four days every May and October. In addition to an eclectic mix of musicians, the event boasts a variety of personal growth workshops such as yoga and movement, and it even includes activities for kids, making it one of the premier family-friendly festivals in the country.

Desert Stars is another yearly festival hosted in downtown Joshua Tree, started by local musicians with a reverence for psych rock, shoegaze, and their high-desert home. Since 2007, stellar lineups have included Moon Duo, The Dandy Warhols, Luna, Spindrift, The Raveonettes, Swervedriver, and Dinosaur Jr., and the festival has grown to include a 100 percent local vendor marketplace.

In addition to festivals, there is always something in the way of live music happening in the area year round. Local venues include the famous Pappy and Harriet's, which has been graced by luminaries such as Paul McCartney, Eric Burdon, and Robert Plant. If you're looking for something a little more low-key, try the acoustic sounds of the Frontier Cafe or the psychedelic tunes of the Beatnik Lounge. Finally, there is Landers Brew Company, which not only offers a stage for up-and-coming musicians, but also a cold one for thirsty visitors after a long day of hiking in the park.

PIONEERTOWN

The aforementioned Pappy & Harriet's is located in a quirky place by the name of Pioneertown. Situated on the northern outskirts of Joshua Tree, Pioneertown was built in the 1940s to resemble a Wild-West movie set, and over the ensuing decades scores of cowboy films and TV shows were filmed there, including *Judge Roy Bean* and *The Cisco Kid*. These days Pioneertown continues to play its part in Hollywood productions, but also hosts a handful of boutiques, hotels, and bars, making it a popular side trip for visitors to the park.

PALM SPRINGS

About a 40-minute drive south of Pioneertown is the desert resort city of Palm Springs. During the 1930s it became a retreat for Hollywood celebrities, and over the decades it has developed into a popular tourist hub with a multitude of resorts, boutique hotels, golf courses, upscale restaurants, and seemingly endless shopping possibilities. Palm Springs is also a mecca for retirees and "snowbirds," people who come here solely during the winter months to escape the freezing temperatures of the northern states.

From an architectural perspective, Palm Springs is widely renowned for its mid-century modern architecture (1933–1965). Each and every February, it hosts Modernism Week, a celebration of architecture, design, fashion, art, and culture. The 11-day festival draws around 100,000 visitors and encompasses more than 350 events including films, lectures, live music, and modern garden and architectural tours. Some of the most notable mid-century modern sites in Palm Springs include the Tramway Gas Station, House of Tomorrow, Del Marcos Hotel, and the Kaufmann Desert House.

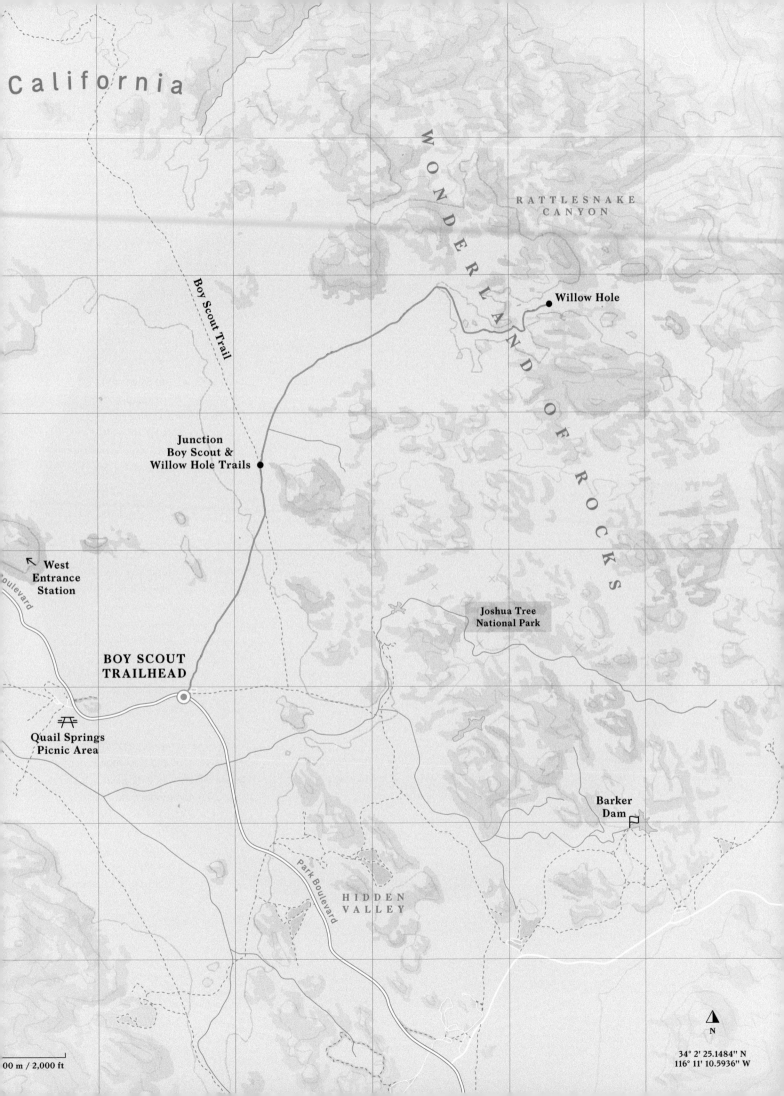

California

RATTLESNAKE
CANYON

Boy Scout Trail

● Willow Hole

W O N D E R L A N D   O F   R O C K S

Junction
Boy Scout &
Willow Hole Trails ●

↖ West
Entrance
Station

Joshua Tree
National Park

BOY SCOUT
TRAILHEAD

Quail Springs
Picnic Area

Barker
Dam ⚑

Park Boulevard

HIDDEN
VALLEY

▲
N

00 m / 2,000 ft

34° 2' 25.1484" N
116° 11' 10.5936" W

THE REBIRTH OF FIRE MOUNTAIN

Washington
WEST

ABOUT THE TRAIL
→ <u>DISTANCE</u> 45 km (28 mi) (*not including approach trails*)
→ <u>DURATION</u> 3 days
→ <u>LEVEL</u> Challenging

Mount St. Helens is an active stratovolcano located in Washington's Cascade Range. In centuries past, the indigenous peoples of the region referred to it as the "smoking" or "fire" mountain due to its tempestuous character. In more recent decades, it has been almost exclusively associated with its 1980 eruption, the most destructive natural disaster in U.S. history. Today, Mount St. Helens stands as a stark reminder of both the power of Mother Nature and her remarkable resilience in the face of devastation. To experience this hauntingly beautiful volcano up close and personal, you can hike around its base via the challenging Loowit Trail.

Measuring 45 km (28 mi) in length, the Loowit Trail circumnavigates Mount St. Helens's undulating flanks by way of deep gullies, lava boulder fields, and flower-laced pumice plains. The trail is marked with rock cairns, colorful tape, and wooden posts, and re-routes are common due to frequent washouts and landslides. The only constant on the Loowit Trail is that of change, and due to the rugged nature of the terrain, it's a trail best suited to experienced backpackers with good route-finding skills.

The Loowit Trail is as hydrationally challenging as it is topographically demanding. Unlike most other hikes in the Pacific Northwest, potable water sources on the Loowit are scarce; by mid-summer, seasonal streams are often dry, and more permanent watercourses are often silty. (Tip: Water filters can easily clog on the Loowit Trail. It is recommended to bring purifying tablets or drops instead.) Thankfully, there are some year-round sources where you can fill up with clear and great-tasting H_2O (see info box). The parched terrain, combined with hot summer days (mid 30s °C [mid 90s °F]) and a dearth of shade on the volcano's denuded slopes, means that you should plan on drinking at least 4 liters of water per day throughout the trek.

Apart from water, the primary consideration when planning for the Loowit Trail is campsite selection. There is a 16 km (10 mi) stretch of trail on the volcano's north side between South Fork Toutle River and Windy Pass where staying overnight is prohibited. This segment coincides with the blast zone, and it's here that you can gain an insider's understanding as to the magnitude of Mount St. Helens's cataclysmic eruption of May 18, 1980.

"Walking the Loowit Trail, there is an unmistakable sense of renewal permeating the stark volcanic landscape. Despite the massive scale of past devastation, Mother Nature has made a comeback."

← Heading toward Spirit Lake.
↑ Mount St. Helens Crater contains one of the world's newest glaciers.
← Indian Paintbrush (*Castilleja miniata*).

179

Wildflower-laden ridges afford majestic views of the volcano.

On that fateful spring day—after a couple of months of small earthquakes and minor volcanic activity—the entire north side of Mount St. Helens was blown away, reducing its 2,950 m (9,677 ft) peak to a horseshoe-shaped crater with a maximum elevation of 2,549 m (8,363 ft). The result was the largest landslide in recorded history, which ended in the deaths of 57 people, thousands of animals, and the entombment of approximately 518 sq km (200 sq mi) of pristine forest under the weight of millions of tons of volcanic debris. At the time of the eruption, Charlie Crisafulli, a U.S. Forest Service ecologist and one of the first scientists on the scene, recalled: "The initial impression was that nothing or few things would survive. It looked like everything had been destroyed, that all vestiges of life had been snuffed out."

Fast forward almost four decades. While traversing the blast zone section of the Loowit Trail, you may spot sure-footed mountain goats and herds of roaming elk, while the pumice plains around the rocky path are laden with wildflowers. Just a few kilometers north of this section is Spirit Lake, one of Washington's most famous wilderness landmarks. It is perhaps the most striking example of natural regeneration in the impacted area. In the aftermath of the landslide, it was thought to have been forever extinguished, with the level of its lake bed being raised approximately 70 m (200 ft). But thanks to runoff from rain and snowmelt, Spirit Lake soon began to reinvent itself, and almost 40 years later it's actually larger in area (though significantly more shallow) and full of thriving aquatic life.

Walking the Loowit Trail, there is an unmistakable sense of renewal permeating the stark volcanic landscape. Despite the massive scale of past devastation, Mother Nature has made a comeback. And while the still-active Mount St. Helens may forever be the "smoking mountain," it is now a far cry from the wasteland that many believed it to be post-1980, proving once again that when left to its own devices, life will find a way.

"The only constant on the Loowit Trail is that of change, and due to the rugged nature of the terrain, it's a trail best suited to experienced backpackers with good route-finding skills."

← Lupines bloom at Mount St. Helens.
↓ Negotiating lava boulder fields.
→ Descending one of the Loowit Trail's many gullies in the shadow of the "smoking mountain."

GOOD TO KNOW

START/FINISH
The Loowit Trail is a loop hike around Mount St. Helens. There are multiple places from which you can start/finish your trek including:

1. **Climber's Bivouac/Ptarmigan Trailhead** (3.2 km [2 mi])
2. **June Lake Trailhead** (2.6 km [1.6 mi])
3. **Windy Ridge Trailhead** (6.4 km [4 mi])

June Lake is not only the shortest approach trail, but arguably the most picturesque as well *Note: Measurements in parenthesis denote distance from the trailhead to the Loowit Trail.*

TOTAL ELEVATION GAIN & LOSS
1,828 m (6,000 ft) approx.

SEASON
Late June to early October

PERMITS
You do not need a permit to backpack on the Loowit Trail, though you will need a Northwest Forest Pass (available online) to park at any of the trailheads.

CAMPING
Camping is possible throughout the Loowit Trail with the exception of the 16 km (10 mi) stretch between Windy Pass and the South Fork Toutle River.

HELPFUL HINTS

PERMANENT WATER SOURCE LOCATIONS
1. 800 m (0.5 mi) west of the Windy/Loowit Junction
2. 400 m (0.25 mi) from the Loowit/Toutle Junction on the Toutle Trail
3. 1,600 m (1 mi) from the Butte Camp/Loowit Junction on the Butte Camp Trail

SUMMITING MOUNT ST. HELENS
A side trip to the summit of Mount St. Helens is a perfect complement to any hike of the Loowit Trail. Accessed via Monitor Ridge on the volcano's southern side, the route begins at the junction of the Loowit and Ptarmigan Trail (Climber's Bivouac), then making its way steeply through boulder fields and loose pumice and ash before eventually arriving at the crater rim after 4.6 km (2.9 mi).

From the top, hikers are afforded incredible views not only of the impacted area around St. Helens but also of its nearby sister volcanoes Mount Hood, Mount Rainier, and Mount Adams. Additionally, you can take in the surreal site of one of the world's newest glaciers, which formed in the volcano's crater after the 1980 eruption.

BACKGROUND

FOUR FACTS ABOUT MOUNT ST. HELENS
1. **An Explosive History**
   Over the past 4,000 years, Mount St. Helens has erupted more than any other volcano in the Cascade Range. Approximately 3,600 years ago, it was devastated by an eruption that was an estimated four times larger than the May 18, 1980 event.
2. **Blowing Its Top**
   The May 18, 1980 eruption reduced the height of Mount St. Helens by 401 m (1,316 ft).
3. **Financial Cost**
   In addition to the massive loss of life (human, animal, flora), the 1980 eruption was the most economically destructive volcanic event in American history, costing over 1 billion dollars (3.3 billion today).
4. **The Ash Cloud**
   In the space of three days, the massive volcanic ash cloud that resulted from the 1980 eruption drifted across the United States, and within 15 days it had encircled the earth.

BONUS TRACK

Founded in 1879, the United States Geological Survey (USGS) is in charge of overseeing all studies and measurements of volcanoes in the country (approximately 169 volcanoes are currently considered to be active). Their nationwide staff monitors seismic, geodetic, hydrological, and geochemical data and assesses any significant fluctuations.

In 2018, the USGS compiled and published a review based on the threat levels of the lava-spewing mountains, scoring them on a 24-factor hazard model that resulted in a threat ranking. The volcanoes were placed into five different categories: very low, low, moderate, high, and very high. According to the extensive report, a total of 18 volcanoes were considered to have a "very high" rating. Coming in first on this list of threatening volcanoes was Hawaii's Kilauea volcano, which erupted in the summer of 2018, and caused the evacuation of some 1,700 nearby residents. At number two was Mount St. Helens, which isn't expected to erupt anytime soon, but scientists continue to observe it daily from the Cascades Volcano Observatory (CVO), located in Vancouver, Washington.

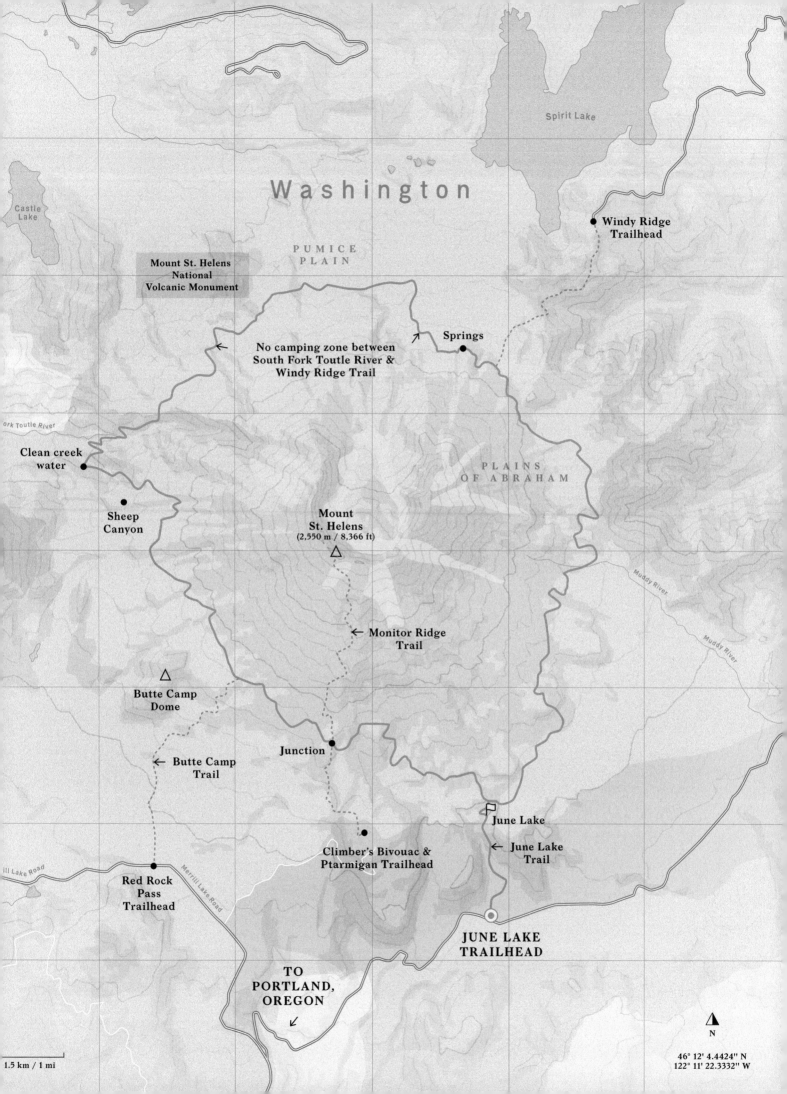

Spirit Lake

W a s h i n g t o n

● Windy Ridge
Trailhead

Castle
Lake

P U M I C E
P L A I N

Mount St. Helens
National
Volcanic Monument

No camping zone between
South Fork Toutle River &
Windy Ridge Trail

← Springs ●

ork Toutle River

Clean creek
water ●

P L A I N S
O F   A B R A H A M

Muddy River

Sheep
Canyon ●

Mount
St. Helens
(2,550 m / 8,366 ft)
△

Muddy River

△
Butte Camp
Dome

← Monitor Ridge
Trail

← Butte Camp
Trail

Junction ●

⚑
June Lake

← June Lake
Trail

● Climber's Bivouac &
Ptarmigan Trailhead

ill Lake Road

● Red Rock
Pass
Trailhead

Merrill Lake Road

◎

JUNE LAKE
TRAILHEAD

TO
PORTLAND,
OREGON
↙

△
N

1.5 km / 1 mi

46° 12' 4.4424'' N
122° 11' 22.3332'' W

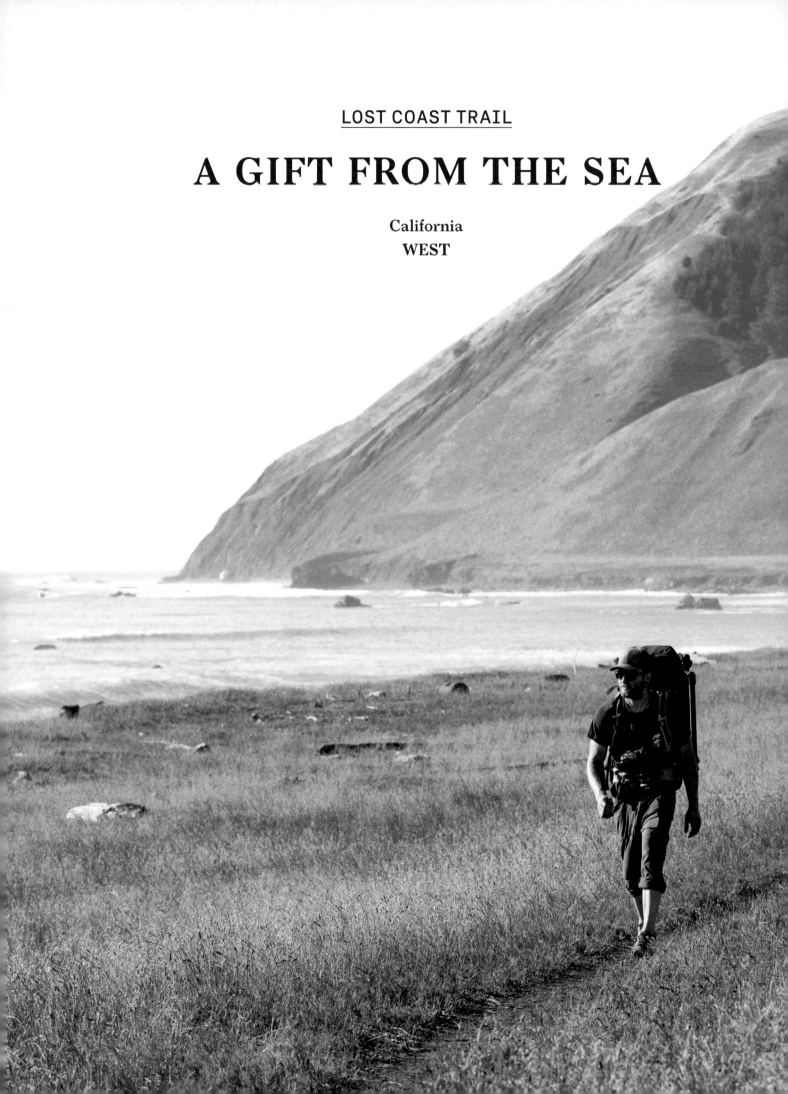

A GIFT FROM THE SEA

California
WEST

ABOUT THE TRAIL
→ <u>DISTANCE</u> 40 km (25 mi)
→ <u>DURATION</u> 3 to 4 days
→ <u>LEVEL</u> MODERATE

The Lost Coast is California's most pristine stretch of coastline—no roads, no cell phone reception, no cliff-hanging mansions. Just 129 km (80 mi) of undeveloped shoreline marked by towering cliffs, secluded beaches, and pounding surf. Thanks to its rugged, inaccessible character, the possibility of building any state or county highways across its terrain has always remained too costly, leaving this oceanfront sanctuary closed to everyone except those who are willing to explore its untamed beauty on foot. And the premier way in which to do so is via the Lost Coast Trail (LCT).

Located entirely within the King Range National Conservation Area (about a 5-hour drive north from San Francisco), the LCT extends 40 km (25 mi) from Mattole Beach in the north to Shelter Cove in the south. Taking most ramblers three or four days to complete, it's generally trekked in a southbound direction in order to keep the prevailing winds at your back. Along the way, the trail passes through a diverse coastal environment of rocky headlands, rolling sand dunes, flower-laden prairies, and black sand beaches dotted with driftwood and seashells.

Though the LCT is suitable for hikers of almost all experience levels, it's not without its challenges—principally the tides. When you hike the Lost Coast Trail, you will literally be on the Pacific Ocean's timetable from start to finish. Approximately 30 to 40 percent of the LCT's total length is impassable at high tide, which means that twice daily a large chunk of the "trail" actually disappears under water. If you happen to get caught out in one of these intertidal zones, particularly in rough conditions, you may not have anywhere to go except west.

Fortunately, tide troubles are almost entirely avoidable as long as you carry a current copy of the tide timetable and plan accordingly. When mapping out your LCT trip itinerary, try to factor in as much flexibility as possible. There are plenty of campsite options along the way if you find yourself a little behind (or ahead of) schedule.

Negotiating the ocean's highs and lows isn't the only obstacle on the Lost Coast Trail. There's also the terrain. For much of its duration, you will be walking over soft sand, loose pebbles, and slippery rocks and ledges. This lack of terrestrial firmness means that twists, strains, and tweaks are commonplace on the LCT. But the following tips should help keep your ankles and knees in good shape throughout the hike:

1. Keep your pack weight as light as possible.
2. Trekking poles can help with balance.
3. Regardless of how fast your companions may be going, always walk at a pace that feels comfortable for you.
4. When hiking over wet rocks, focus on your footfall. Whenever possible, aim to land with your whole foot at once, rather than heel-to-toe.

← The infrequently trodden southern section of the Lost Coast Trail passes through forested valleys and along scenic ridges.
↑ Footsteps in the sand.

"Coastal hiking means accepting the natural world on its own terms. It's about calibrating your internal compass with that of the environment and adopting a pace that's in step with the Pacific Ocean's ebb and flow."

189

↑ The Lost Coast is California's most pristine
   stretch of coastline—no roads, no cell phone
   reception, no cliff-hanging mansions.
→ Sea lions soaking in the sun.

5. If you want to take in the scenery while negotiating the slick segments, stop walking. The number one reason hikers injure themselves on the Lost Coast Trail—along with rushing—is that they become distracted by a beautiful vista and end up slipping.

For those longing for terra firma, the Lost Coast Trail also traverses the wildflower-filled Spanish and Miller Flats. Not only is the treadway solid through these gorgeous coastal meadows, but the blooming grasslands will also afford you the opportunity to observe some of the trail's wildlife, including deer, elk, and perhaps even mountain lions and black bears. The roster of terrestrial fauna living along the LCT is impressive.

But if forced to pick just one standout from the animal kingdom, it would have to be the charismatic sea lions that frequent the trail's shoreline. With their distinctive barks and growls, these "dogs of the sea" are among the most playful and vocal of all mammals. You'll likely catch them bobbing up and down in the waves, waddling along the beach, or casually draping themselves on a rock formation to soak up the sunshine.

In her classic text, *Gift from the Sea*, Anne Morrow Lindbergh wrote, "The sea does not reward those who are too anxious, too greedy, or too impatient. ... Patience, patience, patience, is what the sea teaches." And that, in a nutshell—or should we say seashell—is what the Lost Coast Trail is all about. Whether it's the tides or the terrain, coastal hiking means accepting the natural world on its own terms. It's about calibrating your internal compass with that of the environment and adopting a pace that's in step with the Pacific Ocean's ebb and flow.

↗ The California poppy (*Eschscholzia californica*) is the state flower and can be found along the trail's coastal prairie sections.
↓ At high tide, hikers may be forced to scramble across wet and slippery rocks.

GOOD TO KNOW

START / FINISH
Northern Terminus
Mattole Beach
Southern Terminus
Black Sands Beach (Shelter Cove)

SEASON
Year round. May to October is ideal; during this period, temperatures are usually mild, and the chance of heavy rains and high winds diminishes.

PERMITS
A free-of-charge, walk-in license is required for all overnight trips in the King Range National Conservation Area. You can self-register at the trailheads.

BEAR CANISTER
You are officially required to carry a bear canister when backpacking in the King Range National Conservation Area. If you don't own one, you can rent it from local BLM offices (Bureau of Land Management), REI stores, or the General Stores in Shelter Cove and Petrolia (near Mattole).

CAMPING
There are abundant camping options along the Lost Coast Trail. Most sites are situated near the trail's many creeks, where water is readily accessible.

HELPFUL HINTS

TIDES
Approximately 30 to 40 percent of the Lost Coast Trail is impassable at high tide. You should carry a digital and/or paper copy of the tide times during your hike. See the NOAA Tides & Currents website for details.

THE SOUTHERN LOST COAST TRAIL
If you're looking for a trek that's a little longer, consider adding on the LCT's infrequently trodden southern section. Extending approximately 45 km (28 mi) from the Hidden Valley Trailhead in the north (6.4 km [4 mi] from Shelter Cove) to Usal Beach in the south, this segment stays mostly inland, passing through forested valleys and along scenic ridges.

FLORA & FAUNA

FEATHERED FRIENDS
Almost 300 species of native and migratory birds can be observed along the Lost Coast. Among the most prominent are cormorants, seagulls, brown pelicans, peregrine falcons, murres, ospreys, and turkey vultures.

GIANT REDWOODS
Either before or after your hike, consider spending a couple of days exploring nearby Humboldt Redwoods State Park. Less than an hour's drive inland from the coast, Humboldt is home to the largest expanse of old-growth redwood forest in the world.

BACKGROUND

THE ALCATRAZ OF LIGHTHOUSES
Located just under 6.4 km (4 mi) from the northern terminus is the historic Punta Gorda Lighthouse. Until its construction in 1911, the waters just off the Lost Coast were treacherous for maritime traffic due to a combination of razor-sharp reefs, rock formations, and heavy fog. Coined the "Alcatraz of Lighthouses" because of its remote and difficult-to-access location, Punta Gorda remained in operation until 1951, when it was made redundant by advancements in navigational technology.

AUTHOR'S ANECDOTE

THE SUNSET COAST
Growing up on Australia's eastern seaboard, the Pacific Ocean has been a part of my life for as long as I can remember. Swimming, fishing, diving, and surfing. Walking and running along its shores. Falling out of bed in the wee hours of the morning, just so I could make it down to the beach to watch the sun rise over the distant horizon.

Fast forward to the spring of 2014, and the other side of the world's largest ocean. Some 12,000 km (7,456 mi) northeast of where I was raised. A place where the sun sets, rather than rises, over the water. During my time hiking along California's Lost Coast Trail, I never missed a single moment of the sun's daily goodbye. Despite the fact that I'd traveled far and wide since my formative years in Australia, the combination of the Earth's star and the Pacific still filled me with the same sense of wonder and possibility that it had all those years before.

BONUS TRACK

The Lost Coast Trail lies within the King Range National Conservation Area, a pristine 275 sq km (68,000 acre) coastal wilderness in Northern California. The entire area falls under the jurisdiction of the Bureau of Land Management (BLM), a governmental organization founded by President Harry S. Truman in 1946. Currently, the BLM oversees over one million sq km (nearly 250 million acres), or roughly 10 percent of the total area of the United States.

PACIFIC CREST TRAIL

MOTHER NATURE'S PACKAGE DEAL

California, Oregon, and Washington
WEST

ABOUT THE TRAIL
→ <u>DISTANCE</u> 4,281 km (2,660 mi)
→ <u>DURATION</u> 5 months
→ <u>LEVEL</u> Challenging

The Pacific Crest Trail (PCT) is one of the world's longest footpaths. It stretches for a mind-boggling, knee-wobbling 4,281 km (2,660 mi) between Mexico and Canada, via California, Oregon, and Washington. Along the way it passes through seven national parks, 24 national forests, and takes most hikers around five months and a sumo-esque 600,000 calories to complete. Beyond the statistics, the PCT is a wilderness journey par excellence. And for those wayfarers fortunate enough to hike its entirety, it represents a life experience they will carry far beyond the approximately six million steps it takes to walk from one border to the other.

One of the things that differentiates the Pacific Crest Trail from most other long-distance pathways is its incredible ecological diversity. According to the U.S. Forest Service, the PCT traverses six of North America's seven ecozones (see info box). From its southern terminus in the high desert of California, to its northern terminus among the dense forests of Manning Provincial Park in British Columbia, you'll find an all-star cast of Mother Nature's finest works.

There's America's most aptly named geological formation, Eagle Rock; the fantastically twisted Joshua trees of the Mojave Desert; the incomparable alpine landscape of the High Sierra; and the majestic stratovolcanoes of the Cascade Range, to name but a few. Nestled among the latter is Crater Lake, a giant caldera in southern Oregon that ranks as the deepest lake in the United States (594 m [1,949 ft]). Formed by the collapse of the massive Mazama volcano approximately 7,700 years ago, the rain- and snow-fed waters of Crater Lake are said to be among the world's cleanest. The effect of the lake's deep cobalt hue, combined with the steep cliffs that surround the lake, and the otherworldly Wizard Island—a volcano within a volcano—makes for one of the most awe-inspiring vistas imaginable. Upon seeing Crater Lake for the first time in 1911, famed adventure writer Jack London opined, "I thought I had gazed upon everything beautiful in nature as I have spent my years traveling thousands of miles to visit the beauty spots of the earth, but I have reached the climax. Crater Lake is above them all."

Aside from its smorgasbord of natural wonders, the Pacific Crest Trail is perhaps best known for its thru-hikers, those who traverse the entire trail in one calendar year. Among the most celebrated of these accomplished ramblers are Scott "Bink" Williamson and George "Billy Goat" Woodard.

Williamson has been a prominent figure on the PCT since the early 1990s. One of the pioneers of the ultralight backpacking movement, he has completed the trail at least 13 times, including multiple speed records. In 2006, he became the first person to achieve what was known as a "yo-yo" of the PCT—a staggering 8,500 km (5,300 mi) single-season journey from

← Hiking the Knife's Edge in the Goat Rocks Wilderness. That's Mount Rainier looming large in the distance.

↑ The northern terminus of the Pacific Crest Trail is on the U.S./Canada border in the Pasayten Wilderness next to Manning Provincial Park.

"The Pacific Crest Trail is a transformative experience. After spending months walking in the wilderness, hikers will find that their lung capacity has increased, their legs have become stronger, and their smile lines have grown deeper."

↑ Following the L.A. Aqueduct through the Mojave Desert.
→ Tunnel Falls on the Eagle Creek Alternate Route.

"Aside from its smorgasbord of natural wonders, the Pacific Crest Trail is perhaps best known for its thru-hikers, those who traverse the entire trail in one calendar year."

↑ The PCT may have more double-take views than any other long-distance hike in the world.

→ Desert wildflowers can be found in abundance during the southernmost 1,126 km (700 mi) of the PCT.

Mexico to Canada and back again. But even more remarkable than the countless miles Williamson has hiked is the sheer determination and perseverance of the man. On January 20, 1996, while working his shift at a convenience store in California, Williamson was shot in the face by an armed robber. He was rushed to the hospital, where doctors decided against removing the bullet, which was lodged near his spine, due to the risk of paralysis. Undeterred, Williamson was back hiking the PCT less than three months later, once again bound for Canada.

The second rambler of this notable duo is George Woodard, universally known in the backpacking world as "Billy Goat." A former train conductor from Maine who took up long-distance hiking upon retiring at the age of 49, he has been walking 150 days a year ever since. More than three decades and 80,467 km (50,000 mi) later, the spry octogenarian has become the Pacific Crest Trail's most venerated ambulator. With his floppy broad-brimmed hat, shaggy mane, and flowing beard that would put Santa Claus to shame, Billy Goat is to the PCT what Tom Bombadil is to Tolkien's Middle Earth: indivisible from the very woods he has long called home.

The Pacific Crest Trail is a transformative experience. After spending months walking in the wilderness, hikers will find that their lung capacity has increased, their legs have become stronger, and their smile lines have grown deeper. Along with the physical changes, they may also discover a peace of mind and clarity of thought previously unknown to them. Let's call it Mother Nature's PCT Package Deal—a six-million-step plan for bringing out the best in folks.

↑ Watchful deer.
↓ Washington's Glacier Peak Wilderness in the fall.

↑↑ Splitting the notch.
↑ A sapphire-blue lake in California's High Sierra; the favorite section of many PCT thru-hikers.

GOOD TO KNOW

START/FINISH
Northern Terminus:
U.S./Canada border near Manning Park, British Columbia, Canada
Southern Terminus:
U.S./Mexico border near Campo, California, USA

HIGHEST/LOWEST POINT
Forester Pass, California
(4,421 m [14,505 ft])
Columbia River, Oregon/Washington
(55 m [180 ft])

SEASON
Northbound:
April to early October
Southbound:
Mid-June to end of October

TOP 10 ON-TRAIL HIGHLIGHTS
1. Crater Lake, Oregon
2. Evolution Valley, California
3. The waterfalls along Eagle Creek, Oregon
4. Lake Chelan, Washington
5. Swimming in the invigorating waters of a High Sierra lake
6. Goat Rocks Wilderness, Washington
7. Rae Lakes, California
8. The silhouette of Joshua trees at sunset in the Mojave Desert, California
9. Eagle Rock, California
10. The feeling of joy when you reach the northern (or southern) terminus after completing 4,281 km (2,660 mi) of hiking

HELPFUL HINTS

TOP FIVE TOWNS ALONG THE TRAIL
1. Stehekin, Washington
2. Etna, California
3. Cascade Locks, Oregon
4. Ashland, Oregon
5. Idyllwild, California

TOP FIVE FOOD STOPS
1. Stehekin Pastry Company, Stehekin, Washington (perhaps the best bakery in America!)
2. Timberline Lodge, Government Camp, Oregon (breakfast or lunch buffet)
3. Paradise Cafe, Pines to Palms HWY, California (burgers)
4. Morning Glory Cafe, Ashland, Oregon (anything on the breakfast menu)
5. Caribou Crossroads Cafe, Belden, California (milkshakes)

FLORA & FAUNA

ECOLOGICAL DIVERSITY
Among myriad fantastic factoids, perhaps the most amazing thing about the PCT is that it passes through six of North America's seven ecozones. The U.S. Forest Service lists them as follows: "alpine tundra (above timberline); subalpine forest; upper montane forest; lower montane forest; upper Sonoran (oak woodland, chaparral/grassland); and lower Sonoran (Mojave/Sonoran Deserts)." In case you're wondering, the only ecozone that the PCT misses is subtropical.

FAUNA
Rattlesnakes, eagles, roadrunners, mountain lions, eagles, coyotes, marmots, woodpeckers, bears, elk, mountain goats, bobcats, and cougars are among the many species of wildlife that can be spotted on the PCT.

AUTHOR'S ANECDOTE

RON "TRAIN" ULRICH
I hiked the Pacific Crest Trail for the second time in 2012. While passing through California's scorching hot Mojave Desert, I heard a rumor of a fellow hiker by the name of Ron Ulrich. What set Ron apart from the hundreds of other wayfarers walking from Mexico to Canada was his taste in attire. Eschewing the traditional thru-hiker uniform of long sleeve shirt and lightweight shorts, Ron decided it would be fun to hike the entire 4,281 km (2,660 mi) of the PCT in a wedding dress. Not just one wedding dress mind you, but 26 of them; on average one for every 161 km (100 mi) of trail. Early on in his journey, Ron was given the trail name "Train," not because he hiked as fast as a locomotive, but because of the long back portion of the wedding gowns that flowed behind him as he glided his way north toward the threshold of Canada.

GEAR RECOMMENDATIONS

There is no universal blueprint as to how you should hike a long-distance trail such as the PCT. Each person has his or her own motivations, needs, and level of experience. That said, one thing upon which everyone can agree is that hiking is substantially easier and more enjoyable if your pack doesn't weigh the proverbial ton. The trick is finding functional, light, durable, and fairly priced gear options that suit both your individual needs, as well as the dictates of the environment(s) into which you are venturing.

Begin your gear search by focusing on what's called the "Big Three" of backpacking gear: your backpack, shelter, and sleeping bag. These will usually be the heaviest items that you carry, and it is here that the biggest weight savings can usually be achieved. Note that all recommendations below are for manufacturers that have long-established reputations for making high-quality backpacking gear suitable for thru-hikers.

BACKPACK

Pro Tip Heavy backpacks are designed to carry heavy loads. A pack that weighs less than 1.36 kg (3 lb) and has a carrying capacity of no more than 65 liters should suffice to get both you and your gear from Mexico to Canada. Anything bigger than that is overkill.

Recommended backpack manufacturers include (in no particular order): Granite Gear; Ultralight Adventure Equipment; Osprey; Mountain Laurel Designs; Hyperlite Mountain Gear; Six Moon Designs; and Gossamer Gear.

SHELTER

Pro Tip There are three things to look for when choosing your thru-hiking home: 1. Lightweight (no more than 1.36 kg [3 lb]); 2. Storm-worthy; 3. Meets your individual needs in regard to comfort. Four to five months is a long time to go backpacking, and about a third of that period will be spent in your shelter. You will want to have a tent you feel at home in.

Recommended lightweight tent makers include (in no particular order): Tarptent; Big Agnes; MSR; NEMO; Six Moon Designs; Mountain Laurel Designs; and Gossamer Gear.

SLEEPING BAG (OR QUILT)

Pro Tip The best durability and warmth-to-weight ratio in sleeping bags is provided by down models. Look for a bag that has at least 800 fill power and doesn't weigh more than 1.13 kg (2.5 lb). In regard to temperature ratings, your average male PCT hiker will be comfortable with a bag that

is accurately rated to -7°C (20°F), whereas your average female PCT hiker is usually fine with a -9°C (15°F) model. *Note: Women tend to sleep a little colder than guys.*

Recommended lightweight sleeping bag (and quilt) makers include (in no particular order): Western Mountaineering; Feathered Friends; Montbell; Marmot; Katabatic Gear (quilts); Nunatak (quilts).

PEAK PERFORMANCE: THE MENTAL SIDE OF THRU-HIKING

"Thru-hiking is 90 percent mental." This is one of the most commonly heard mantras in the U.S. long-distance hiking community. Over the years it has been repeated so often in articles, online forums, and books that it seems to be accepted as gospel by many, if not most thru-hikers. The thing is, it isn't true. Not even close. The "90 percent mental" theory is up there with other enduring backpacking myths like needing boots to go hiking, sleeping warmer when you are naked, and the notion that it is OK to use biodegradable soap in water sources.

In reality, the mental challenge of thru-hiking, though undeniably important, varies greatly from individual to individual and from hike to hike. To say it's 90 percent (or even 80 percent for that matter) across the board simply isn't accurate. The ratio of psychological to physical depends on two principal factors: 1. A hiker's experience level in relation to the environment(s) into which he or she is venturing, and; 2. The extent to which he or she enjoys/loves being out in the wilderness unconditionally.

EXPERIENCE

In a nutshell, the more field experience you have, the less the mental challenge of thru-hiking will likely become. Before a long-distance hike, you can scour online forums, read motivational books, do backpacking courses, gear shakedowns, and read scores of hiking

journals, but in the big picture none of it counts for squat if you don't like spending time in the woods. And how do you know if you will enjoy spending five continuous months hiking and camping? No drum roll. Before setting out on your journey, simply spend as much time as you can backpacking in different conditions. Overnighters, week-long excursions—whatever you can manage. Obviously this doesn't guarantee you will finish your thru-hike. However it does improve your chances of achieving your goal, and more importantly having a good time in the process. Think of it like a relationship with Mother Nature. The more dates you go on beforehand, the better the odds that things will work out well when you eventually get married (i.e. thru hiking).

UNCONDITIONAL ENJOYMENT

When you unconditionally enjoy (let's call it love) spending time in the wilderness, the inevitable challenges that one encounters during a thru-hike—boredom, loneliness, physical discomfort, inclement weather—are usually blips rather than potential reasons to quit your hike. In fact, let's go one step further and say that the hardships are more like stepping stones rather than stumbling blocks. Why? Because when you love something unconditionally, you are in for the long haul. The novelty doesn't wear off after a few weeks or a couple of months. As a result, you are always looking to improve and grow as a hiker. When problems arise, you accept them, learn what you can from them, and get on with things—just like in a healthy long-term relationship or friendship. And in doing so, potentially spending months hiking and camping becomes less of a psychological challenge and more of a confirmation or a celebration.

CANADA

MANNING PARK

• Stehekin
⚑ Lake Chelan

SEATTLE
⚓ Snoqualmie Pass

Washington

• Goat Rocks

Columbia River
(55 m / 180 ft)

△ Mount Hood
(3,429 m / 11,249 ft)

PORTLAND

△ Mount Jefferson
(3,199 m / 10,497 ft)

• Bend

Oregon

⚑ Crater Lake

Ashland •

Mount Shasta
△ (4,322 m / 14,179 ft)

• Old Station

Sierra City •

⚑ Lake Tahoe

} Sonora Pass

Yosemite
National Park   ╳ • Tuolumne Meadows

San Francisco

Forester Pass
(4,009 m / 13,153 ft)

Kings Canyon
National Park   } △ Mount Whitney
(4,421 m / 14,505 ft)

Sequoia
National Park   • Kennedy Meadows

California

• Agua Dulce

Pacific
Ocean

LOS ANGELES
• Idyllwild

• Warner Springs

SAN DIEGO

CAMPO

MEXICO

20 km / 75 mi

△ N

36° 22' 20.154" N
121° 2' 14.1324" W

THE WILD CHILD OF AMERICA'S NATIONAL SCENIC TRAILS

Washington, Idaho, Montana
WEST

ABOUT THE TRAIL

→ <u>DISTANCE</u> 1,931 km (1,200 mi)

→ <u>DURATION</u> 65 days

→ <u>LEVEL</u> Challenging

T he Pacific Northwest Trail (PNT) stretches from Montana's Rocky Mountains to Washington's Olympic Coast—two geographically distinct termini separated by three national parks, seven national forests, and 1,931 km (1,200 mi) of some of the finest mountain scenery in the United States. The wild child of America's long-distance hiking scene, the PNT is the wilderness equivalent of an exceptionally gifted artist who flies under the public radar. It's not a question of if, but when its extraordinary quality will be discovered by the world at large.

The idea for a border-hugging trail between the Continental Divide and the Pacific was conceived by conservationist Ron Strickland in 1970. Seven years later, the Pacific Northwest Trail Association was formed to develop, preserve, and protect the trail's wilderness corridor. In 2009, after decades of hard work and advocacy, the PNT was designated by Congress as one of America's 11 National Scenic Trails. But unlike some of its older and more established siblings such as the Pacific Crest Trail and Appalachian Trail, the PNT is still very much in its infancy in regards to infrastructure.

More of a backcountry route than a manicured pathway, the PNT is an amalgamation of beach walks, bushwhacks, forest roads, rock scrambles, paved roads, old railroad beds, and trails. Most of it isn't signed or blazed, large chunks are unmaintained, and some of it is overgrown. Suffice to say, the PNT is a trek best suited to experienced long-distance ramblers with a love of solitude, good navigation skills, and a sustained sense of adventure.

Although it's possible to do the PNT in either direction, most hikers go from east to west toward the setting sun. Highlights of the trail are many, but some of the standout sections include Washington's Mount Baker Wilderness, the rarely visited Selkirk Mountains of Idaho, and what may well be the most epic start and finish lines of any long-distance hiking trail in the world: Glacier National Park and Olympic National Park.

Covering more than one million acres in western Montana, Glacier National Park was described by George Bird Grinnell, one of the fathers of the American conservation movement, as "the crown of the continent." It is wilderness on a grand scale, an ice-age-sculpted wonderland of jagged granite peaks, sweeping valleys, dramatic cirques, and serene alpine meadows. And Glacier's majestic landscapes are home to a similarly impressive array of big-ticket wildlife including mountain goats, moose, bison, Canadian lynx, wolves, cougars, wolverines, and black and grizzly bears. From a hiker's perspective, it's hard to think of a better place to start or finish a long distance trek—unless maybe you are talking about its PNT bookend, Olympic National Park.

↑ Montana's majestic Glacier National Park.
↘ Curious marmots observing hikers.

"Glacier National Park was described by George Bird Grinnell, one of the fathers of the American conservation movement, as "the crown of the continent."

→ A tumbling cascade in Montana's Glacier National Park.
↑ Crossing the Baker River in Washington's Mount Baker Wilderness.

"The final 100 km (62 mi) traces a pristine coastline marked by wave-sculpted sea stacks, tidal pools filled with starfish and sea anemones, soaring bald eagles, and some of the best ocean views you are likely to ever see."

↑ Trekking through the Pasayten Wilderness of eastern Washington.
← Web-spinning caterpillars.

Located across the Puget Sound from Seattle, Olympic National Park is arguably the most ecologically diverse park in the United States. Within its almost one-million-acre boundaries (nearly the same size as Glacier), it showcases four distinct environments: temperate rainforest, lowland (drier) forest, alpine, and coastal. Each has its own unique feel, and within a couple of days, PNT hikers can go from navigating spooky primeval rainforests (the Twilight books and movies were set here), to taking a bracing dip in a snow-ringed mountain lake, to shuffling along a lonely beach, accompanied only by the meditative sound of rolling waves. If you're someone who tends to get bored on long hikes seeing the same scenery day after day, look no further. Olympic National Park is to natural diversity what Martin Scorsese is to gangster movies.

One of the coolest things about hiking the PNT from east to west is finishing at Cape Alava, the westernmost point in the lower 48 states. The final 100 km (62 mi) before you arrive, trace a pristine coastline marked by wave-sculpted sea stacks, tidal pools filled with starfish and sea anemones, soaring bald eagles, and some of the best ocean views you are likely to ever see. And the clincher? You get to finish your last days by taking in the sunset from the comfort of your shoreline campsites—a more than commensurate reward for a challenging 1,931 km (1,200 mi) hike from the Rockies to the Pacific.

↑ A secret inlet on Washington's rugged Olympic Coast.
↓ Sea stacks, driftwood, and the Pacific Ocean.

GOOD TO KNOW

START/FINISH
Western Terminus
Cape Alava, Olympic National Park, Washington
Eastern Terminus
Chief Mountain, Glacier National Park, Montana

HIGHEST/LOWEST POINT
Cathedral Pass, Washington
(2,310 m [7,580 ft])
Olympic Coast, Washington (sea level)

SEASON
Early July to late September

PERMITS
No trail-wide permit is required to hike the PNT, though backcountry camping permits are required for Glacier National Park, North Cascades National Park Complex, and Olympic National Park.

CULINARY HIGHLIGHTS
Bob's Chowder Bar in Anacortes, Washington, and the iconic bakery of Polebridge Mercantile, located on the outskirts of Glacier National Park in Montana. Established in 1914, the Mercantile is also a grocery store and gas station. However, it's the legendary baked goods that draw visitors here from far and wide. Try the huckleberry bear claws, chocolate scones, and macaroons.

HELPFUL HINTS

ALTERNATE ROUTES
The PNT is a hike in which ramblers have many different route options available to them. Two of the best are as follows:
1. **Selkirk Crest–Lion's Head alternate in Idaho's Selkirk Mountains**
   This crest-tracing high route is superior to the official PNT, which stays low along Lion's Creek.
2. **Kintla Lake in Glacier National Park**
   This is the original PNT route designed by trail founder Ron Strickland, and it is significantly more scenic (though more prone to snowy conditions) than the official route via Bowman Lake.

FLORA & FAUNA

BERRY CAPITAL OF AMERICA?
The Pacific Northwest is a top contender for wild berry capital of the United States; there is no better way to sample your fill than by hiking the PNT during the summer months. Along the trail corridor, hikers will find blueberries, blackberries, huckleberries, raspberries, thimbleberries, and

salmonberries. *Tip: The lush Chuckanut Mountains just south of Bellingham, Washington, are renowned for their abundance of salmonberries.*

BIGFOOT ON THE PNT
The Pacific Northwest Trail passes by Chopaka Lake in North Central Washington. The area's primary claim to fame is that on May 26, 1996, it was the site of one of the most famous Bigfoot (Sasquatch) videos ever filmed. The controversial recording shows a grainy figure resembling the description of a giant, ape-like creature running and walking near the lake.

BACKGROUND

THE VANISHING GLACIERS OF GLACIER NATIONAL PARK

In 1850 there were an estimated 150 glaciers in Glacier National Park, the eastern terminus of the PNT. Virtually all of these still existed in 1910, when the park was established by U.S. Congress. Largely due to the effects of global warming, there are fewer than 40 today. Dr. Dan Fagre from the U.S. Geological Survey explains, "There are variations in the climate, but it is humans that have made all those variations warmer. The glaciers have been here for 7,000 years and will be gone in decades. This is not part of the natural cycle."

AUTHOR'S ANECDOTE

THE 12 LONG WALKS
On July 2, 2011, I stood at the western terminus of the Pacific Northwest Trail—Cape Alava. It's a place that will always be dear to my heart, as it marked the beginning point of the longest journey of my hiking life, a 23,081 km (14,342 mi) series of treks I called the "12 Long Walks."

As the name suggests, the trip consisted of a dozen consecutive thru-hikes ranging in length from 322 km (200 mi) to 4,345 km (2,700 mi). During the 545 day peregrination, I passed through 29 U.S. states, 4 Canadian provinces, and wore out 28 pairs of trail running shoes (and most of what was left of my knee cartilage). Along the way I even set some records, including the fastest ever calendar year completion of America's Triple Crown of hiking—the Pacific Crest, Continental Divide, and Appalachian Trail (236 days).

From a gastronomical perspective, I burned an average of 6,000–7,000 calories per hiking day, and in so doing consumed 56.1 kg (123.7 lb) of dehydrated beans and 620 snickers bars (losing one tooth in the process). On the wildlife front, I saw 1 wolf, 2 mountain lions, 17 moose, and 48 bears (including 22 grizzlies).

After almost 18 months of continuous hiking, I finished the 12 Long Walks on December 28, 2012, at the summit of Springer Mountain, Georgia—the southern terminus of the Appalachian Trail.

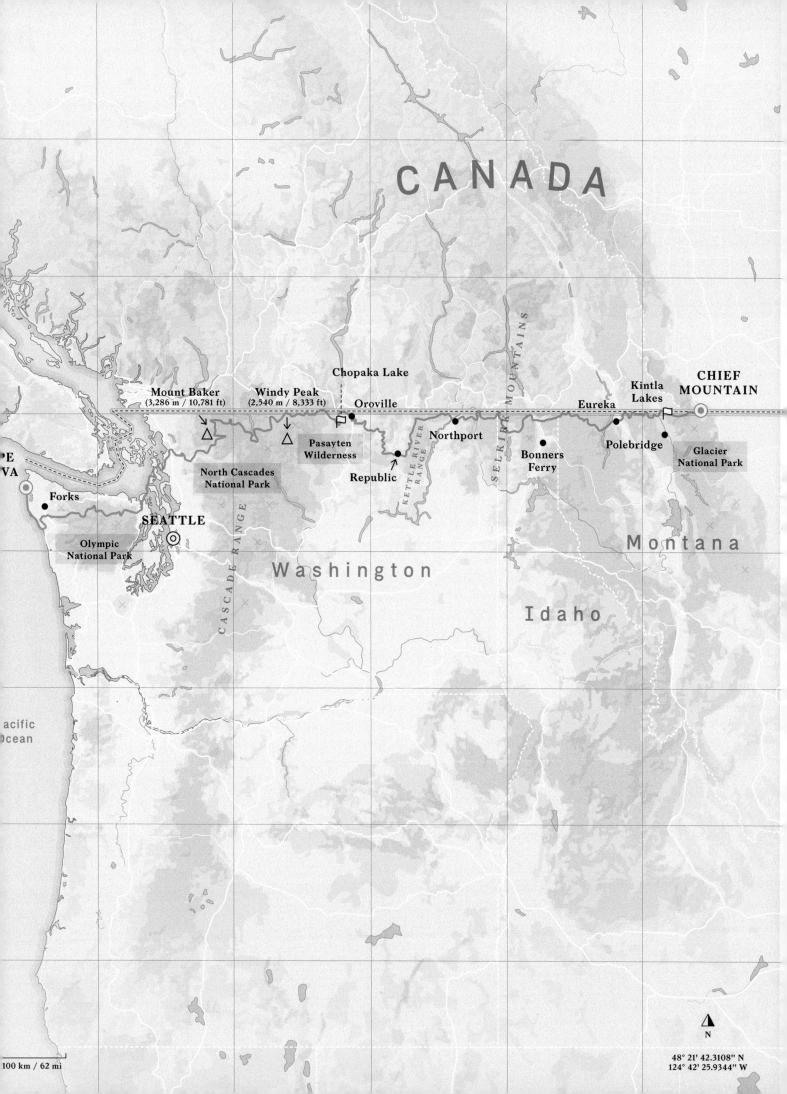

CANADA

Chopaka Lake

CHIEF
MOUNTAIN

Mount Baker
(3,286 m / 10,781 ft)

Windy Peak
(2,540 m / 8,333 ft)

Kintla
Lakes

Oroville

Eureka

Pasayten
Wilderness

Northport

Polebridge

North Cascades
National Park

Republic

Glacier
National Park

'E
'A

Bonners
Ferry

Forks

Montana

SEATTLE

Olympic
National Park

Washington

Idaho

acific
Ocean

100 km / 62 mi

N

48° 21' 42.3108" N
124° 42' 25.9344" W

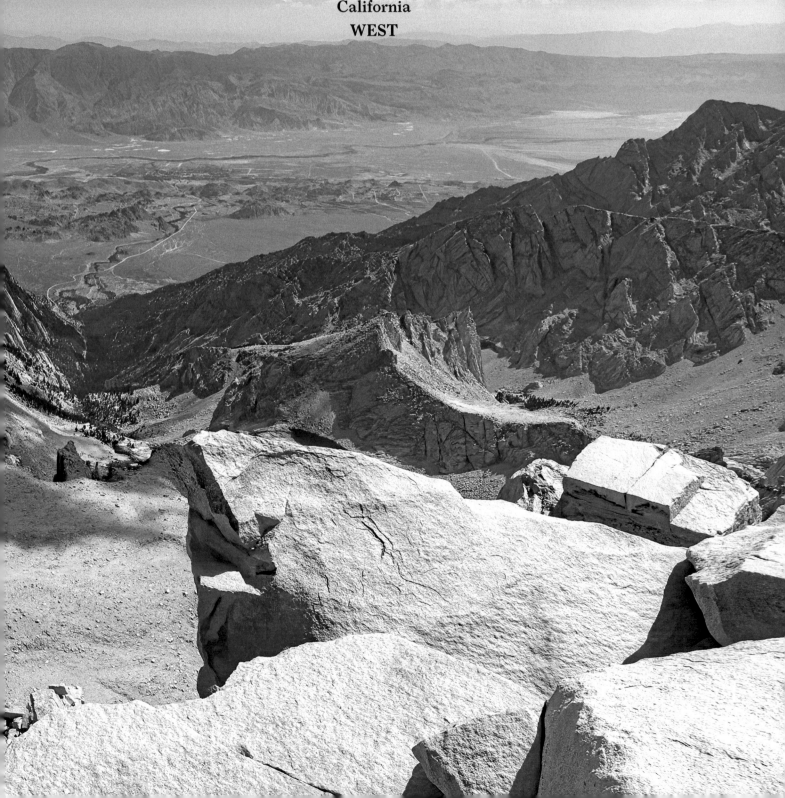

WHEN THE SUN CLOCKS OUT, AND THE MOON CLOCKS IN

California
WEST

ABOUT THE TRAIL
→ <u>DISTANCE</u> 314 km (195 mi) approx.
→ <u>DURATION</u> 15 to 20 days
→ <u>LEVEL</u> Very Challenging

The views you work the hardest for are invariably the ones that resonate the most. When it comes to long-distance hikes in the United States, rarely do those words ring truer than on California's Sierra High Route (SHR). In the course of approximately 314 lung-busting kilometers (195 mi), it negotiates more than 30 high-altitude passes, many of which include Class 2 or 3 scrambles (non-technical climbing sometimes requiring the use of your hands). The payoff for all the huffing and puffing comes in the form of an alpine Shangri-La of glacier-sculpted valleys, sapphire-blue lakes, and serrated granite peaks; it's quite possibly the most scenic multi-week trek in the lower 48 states.

The Sierra High Route was conceived by veteran mountaineer Steve Roper in the late 1970s. Roper's goal was to put together a route for experienced hikers that offered an off-the-beaten-track adventure, stayed mostly above tree line, and avoided well-marked trails whenever possible. By any criteria, he succeeded, and then some. The SHR passes through some of the most pristine and rarely visited wilderness in the contiguous United States. In the words of Jim Gorman and Robert Earle Howells for National Geographic magazine, "If the Sierra's original pathbreaker and solitude lover, John Muir, were alive today, it's a fair bet he'd hike the Sierra High Route instead of the trail that bears his name."

While we are on the topic of the world-famous John Muir Trail (340 km [211 mi]), one of the first questions that many hikers have about the SHR is how does it compare to its much more frequented neighbor? The comparison breaks down as follows:

Both the JMT and SHR are stunning hikes that are similar in length and travel in a north/south direction through the High Sierra mountains that Muir famously dubbed the "Range of Light." Despite the geographic proximity of the two walks, they are quite distinct in character. The JMT is a well-marked and well-maintained pathway from start to finish, and spends considerable time traversing valley floors. After the Appalachian Trail, it may well be the most popular long-distance trail in the United States. In contrast, the aptly named Sierra High Route stays between 2,743 m (9,000 ft) and 3,658 m (12,000 ft) for almost

↖ John Muir Hut on the pass of the same name.
↑ Descending from Frozen Lake Pass.

"The payoff for all the huffing and puffing comes in the form of an alpine Shangri-La of glacier-sculpted valleys, sapphire-blue lakes, and serrated granite peaks; it's quite possibly the most scenic multi-week trek in the lower 48 states."

↑ Dawn views of Mount Whitney (4,421 m [14,505 ft]), the highest point in the contiguous United States.

← Opportunistic marmots can often be spotted on the Sierra High Route's many passes. Be sure to keep an eye on your food!

↗ Storm clouds approaching.

→ Russell Carillon Col on the Southern Sierra High Route.

all of its duration, and more than half of its total distance involves cross-country travel; that is, it's a route rather than a clear, established trail. Additionally, the SHR receives little in the way of hiker traffic. As of 2019, it's estimated that fewer than 50 people complete it per year, and it remains relatively unknown outside of the U.S. long-distance hiking community. In a nutshell, the SHR is a wilder, more difficult alternative to the JMT, and demands a higher level of backcountry expertise from those aspiring to hike its entire length.

Spanning the heart of the Sierra Nevada range through Sequoia and Kings Canyon National Parks, Inyo National Forest, and Yosemite National Park, the Sierra High Route takes most hikers between two and three weeks to complete. Distinguishing specific highlights along the way is like trying to pick the best spot to go for a vodka in Moscow—practically impossible (though good fun to research). Among an assortment of backcountry treasures, places such as the eminently swimmable Bear Lakes Basin, the difficult-to-reach Frozen Lake Pass, the cobalt-blue Marion Lake, and the organ-pipe basalt columns of Devils Postpile consistently rate highly among SHR alumni.

The Sierra High Route's combination of rugged terrain, untouched wilderness, and solitude can make you feel more in tune with both the natural world and your own spirit—a journey as outwardly challenging as it is inwardly illuminating. At route's end, many hikers find that their most treasured memories of the SHR haven't come in the form of breathtaking vistas, but in the moments of clarity they experienced along the way.

GOOD TO KNOW

START/FINISH
Northern Terminus
Mono Village, California
Southern Terminus
Road's End, Sequoia & Kings Canyon
National Parks, California

SEASON
July to September. Depending on the
snow year, mid-June and early October
may also be possible.

PERMITS
You'll need a backcountry permit for
the Sierra High Route. If beginning
at the southern terminus of Road's
End, you can pick one up at the park
office trailhead. Alternatively, you can
organize one in advance via the Sequoia
& Kings Canyon National Parks or
Yosemite National Park websites.

HELPFUL HINTS

ALTITUDE AWARENESS
From the southern terminus of Road's
End, the initial climb from the Copper
Creek Trailhead immediately takes the
hiker from 1,539 m (5,050 ft) to over
3,048 m (10,000 ft) above sea level.
The route then stays above that altitude
for almost all of its course. If you're
coming from sea level, this may prove
to be a head-spinning proposition.
To minimize the chances of Acute
Mountain Sickness (AMS), consider
making a late-afternoon start
and camping mid-climb at around
2,134–2,438 m (7,000–8,000 ft).

SWIMMING HEAVEN
If you happen to be a water lover, there
are enough swimming opportunities
on the Sierra High Route to satisfy your
average mermaid. At these altitudes, the
water temperature can be a little nippy
(guys, you may be singing soprano for
the next couple of hours). Don't let that
dissuade you from taking the plunge.
It's one of the most invigorating feelings
imaginable to swim in an alpine lake
with beautiful mountains on all sides!

TIPS FOR HIKING DOWNHILL
Hiking downhill takes its toll. Twists,
slips, and tumbles are most likely to
occur while descending, and no other
type of hiking causes more wear and
tear on the joints and muscles. This
especially holds true on demanding,
largely off-trail hikes such as the
Sierra High Route. By learning how to
hike downhill efficiently on all types
of terrain, you can minimize impact
on the body and decrease the
probability of falls and/or mishaps
occurring. Here are six tips to become
a better downhill hiker:

1. Center of Gravity: Don't lean forward.
Don't lean back. Your center of gravity
should be low and over your legs.
2. Minimize Stress: Keep your downhill
leg slightly bent on impact. This will help
minimize stress on the knees, as the
muscles rather than the joints take the
brunt of the strain.
3. Focus: Pay extra attention to foot
placement. Many slips occur on
downhill stretches that immediately
follow long ascents. After the exertion of
the climb, the tendency is to "let it all
hang out" on the descent, which can
subsequently lead to mistakes.
4. Shorter Steps: When the gradient is
steep, taking smaller steps will help to
keep your center of gravity over your
legs, thus promoting greater balance
and control.
5. Hip Belt: On steep, uneven descents it
can be helpful to tighten your hip belt.
This assists in minimizing pack
movement, which can impede your
balance if left unchecked.
6. Flow: Once you have the necessary
techniques down pat, stay as loose as
possible. Think flow. Move with the
terrain, rather than against it.

BACKGROUND

SOUTHERN SIERRA HIGH ROUTE (SSHR)
For those looking to extend their Sierra
backpacking experience, it's possible
to combine the SHR with a little-known
but equally spectacular route known
as the Southern Sierra High Route.

Conceived by Alan Dixon and Don
Wilson, the SSHR joins the SHR at
Dusy Basin and brings the total hiking
distance to approximately 435 km
(270 mi). Apart from gifting any rambler
more time in the Range of Light, this
additional section also makes things
easier on the logistical front, as its
southern terminus is at the transport-
friendly trailhead of Cottonwood Lakes,
as opposed to the difficult-to-access
Road's End.

AUTHOR'S ANECDOTE

THE YOSEMITE—
A SENTIMENTAL JOURNEY
As a longtime admirer of John Muir,
the Sierra High Route holds a special
place in my hiking heart. To my way of
thinking, its pristine, trailless nature
encapsulates the spirit of this great
man's writing in a way that other, more
frequented pathways in California's high
country never quite do.

To that end, I decided to carry a
well-leafed copy of Muir's *The Yosemite*
during my SHR thru-hike of 2011. At
the close of each hiking day, I would
find a place to camp, set up my shelter,
and spend at least half an hour reading
the classic text. As I did so, I would
regularly look up and gaze in wonder
at the surrounding peaks, soaking up
the alpenglow as the sun clocked out
and the moon clocked in. During one
of these moments, I thought back to
1986, when the 17-year-old version of
yours truly first discovered the writing
of John Muir. The memory made me
smile nostalgically—the book that got
me started was *The Yosemite*, the very
same copy I now held in my hands 25
years later on the SHR.

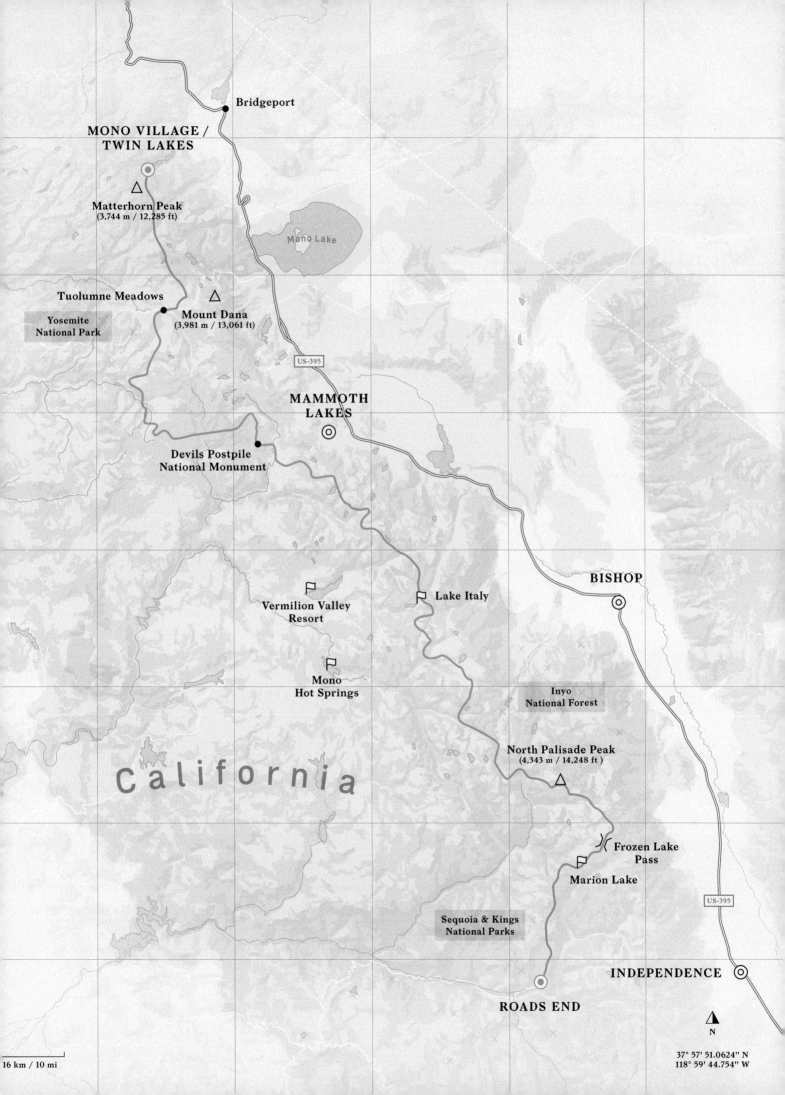

Bridgeport

MONO VILLAGE /
TWIN LAKES

Matterhorn Peak
(3,744 m / 12,285 ft)

Mono Lake

Tuolumne Meadows

Mount Dana
(3,981 m / 13,061 ft)

Yosemite
National Park

US-395

MAMMOTH
LAKES

Devils Postpile
National Monument

Vermilion Valley
Resort

Lake Italy

BISHOP

Mono
Hot Springs

Inyo
National Forest

C a l i f o r n i a

North Palisade Peak
(4,343 m / 14,248 ft)

Frozen Lake
Pass

Marion Lake

Sequoia & Kings
National Parks

US-395

INDEPENDENCE

ROADS END

N

16 km / 10 mi

37° 57' 51.0624" N
118° 59' 44.754" W

SOUTHWEST

From vast canyons to high deserts to the red rock delight that is the Colorado Plateau, America's Southwest is a geological wonderland wrapped in a storied history of ancient cliff dwellers, colorful outlaws, and never-say-die pioneers.

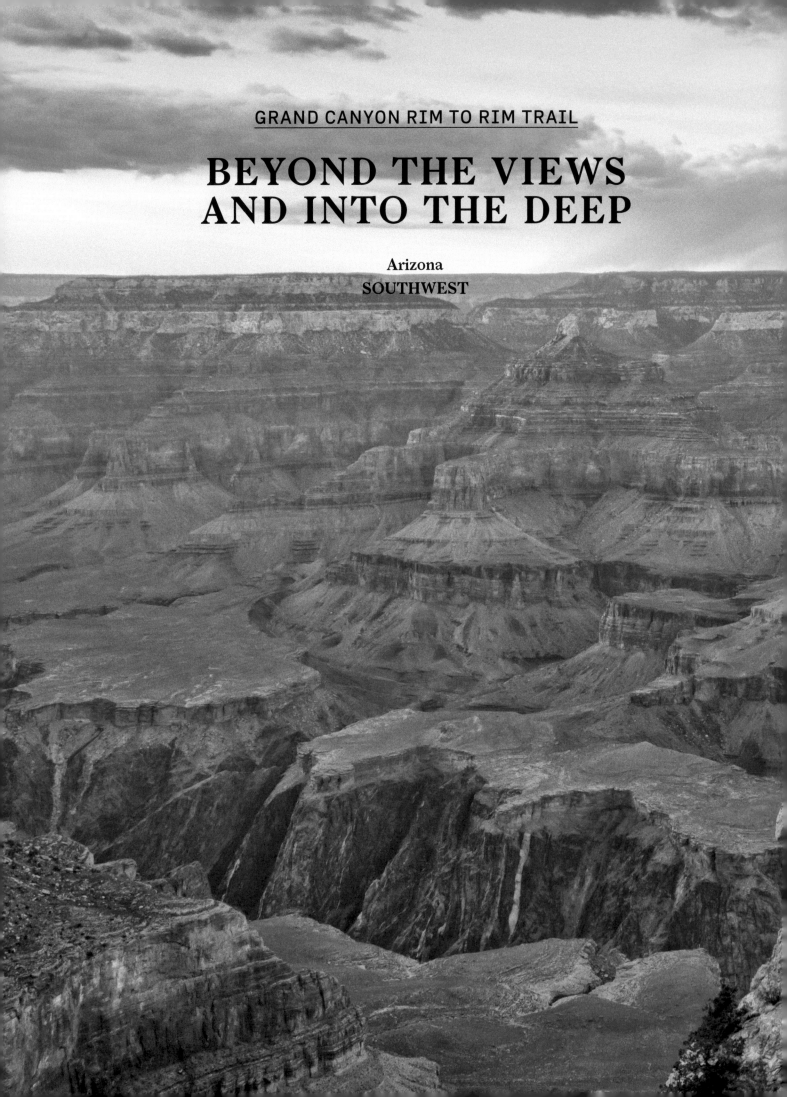

BEYOND THE VIEWS AND INTO THE DEEP

Arizona
SOUTHWEST

"You cannot see the Grand Canyon in one view, as if it were a changeless spectacle from which a curtain might be lifted, but to see it, you have to toil from month to month through its labyrinths."

—
JOHN WESLEY POWELL,
WHO NAMED THE GRAND CANYON.
FROM *THE EXPLORATIONS OF THE COLORADO RIVER
AND ITS CANYONS* (1874)

↑ Switchbacking on the Rim to Rim Trail.
→ Cooling down on the canyon floor.
↗ For much of the R2R there is very little in the way of shade.
  Be sure to bring along a broad-brimmed hat and sunscreen.

ABOUT THE TRAIL

→ <u>DISTANCE</u> 33.8 km (21 mi)

→ <u>DURATION</u> 10 to 12 hours

→ <u>LEVEL</u> Challenging

The Grand Canyon is visited by more than six million people per year. Of all these tourists, less than one percent venture into the canyon's depths on foot. And of this one percent, only a fraction hike the Rim to Rim Trail (R2R), a rollercoaster route connecting the canyon's North and South Rims via the Colorado River. Extending approximately 34 km (21 mi) (or 39 km [24 mi] depending on route choice), and with a total elevation gain and loss of 3,261 m (10,710 ft), the R2R is a great way to leave the crowds behind and experience one of America's most amazing natural treasures from the inside out, rather than the outside in.

Located in northern Arizona, the Grand Canyon measures 446 km (277 mi) long, up to 29 km (18 mi) wide, and at its deepest point 1,857 m (6,093 ft) from top to bottom. Its scale is breathtaking, and when seen at sunrise or sunset, its ancient terraced walls come alive in a sublime desert palette of crimson, orange,

and golden hues. Yet statistics and superlatives can never do the Grand Canyon justice. It's one of those places you need to see to believe. And for those who wish to go a step—or in this case 45,000 steps—beyond the views, there is the Rim to Rim Trail.

In a nutshell, the R2R is a hike in three parts. Beginning at the South Kaibab Trailhead (you can also go north to south, or start at Bright Angel Trailhead), you will descend into the canyon for 10.1 km (6.3 mi), hike briefly along its floor, and then ascend to its North Rim via the North Kaibab Trail (22.9 km [14.2 mi]). The entire path is well marked and maintained, and there are even drinking fountains (yes, fountains!) every 10 to 16 km (6.2 to 10 mi) to help you stay hydrated. Note that the spigots are only guaranteed to be turned on during the May to October hiking season, so if you happen to be hiking outside of this window, be sure to check with Park officials before setting out.

As for the scenery, from start to finish you will feel as if you have been transported (by your own two feet) into a rocky wonderland of cliffs, buttes, ravines, spires, and gorges. The trail traverses millions of years of geological history, and, thanks to the massive changes in elevation, it also passes through five distinct ecosystems: boreal forest, ponderosa forest, pinyon-juniper woodland, desert scrub, and riparian. The remarkable ecological range of the R2R is rivaled only by its climatic extremes.

Views over Skeleton Point from the South Kaibab Trail section of the R2R.

↑ The Black Suspension Bridge (134 m [440 ft]) over the Colorado River.
↓ Ribbon Falls.
→ North Kaibab Trail.

During the hiking season, it can be below freezing at the trailhead before dawn; yet by midday, it's not uncommon for the temperatures to exceed 40°C (104°F) on the canyon floor. Hiking the R2R is an exercise in adapting to perpetual change, and a strong set of quads and lungs will prove useful in meeting the challenge.

A great way to combat the heat of the Grand Canyon is to make the highly recommended side trip to the magical Ribbon Falls. Situated in a small, lush side canyon just south of Cottonwood Camp, Ribbon Falls tumbles 33 m (100 ft) over a velvety moss-covered rocky outcrop into an ice-cold pool below. The grotto has "an oasis in the Sahara" feel to it, and on a scorching-hot day, standing underneath the cascade may well feel like the best shower you have ever taken!

By any criterion, the Rim to Rim is one of America's finest trails. And it seems only fitting that such a trek should be capped with a memorable finale, which is best achieved by hiking from south to north. The section of the North Kaibab Trail between Cottonwood Campground and the North Rim is arguably the most spectacular of the trip. Additionally, the North Rim is far less developed and crowded than its southern bookend, and upon completing your hike you can enjoy a celebratory meal at the Grand Canyon North Rim Lodge. (Tip: reserve well in advance.) Perched on the canyon's edge, the setting is impossible to beat, as is taking in the sunset over one of the world's natural wonders with a celebratory beer in hand.

↑↑ "In the Grand Canyon, Arizona has a natural wonder which is in kind absolutely unparalleled throughout the rest of the world."—Teddy Roosevelt.
↑ North Kaibab Trail.

GOOD TO KNOW

START / FINISH
North Rim
North Kaibab Trailhead
South Rim
South Kaibab Trailhead

Alternatively, you can start or end this hike at the Bright Angel Trailhead on the South Rim. This option will add 4.8 km (3 mi) to the distance to total 38.6 km (24 mi); however, the gradient is notably more gentle than on the South Kaibab Trail.

HIGHEST / LOWEST POINT
North Rim (2,460 m [8,060 ft])
Colorado River (732 m [2,400 ft])

TOTAL ELEVATION GAIN & LOSS
3,261 m (10,710 ft)

SEASON
May to October

PERMITS
A permit is not required to hike the R2R as a day hike. For those wanting to overnight in the canyon, a permit is required (bookings should be made well in advance) via the Grand Canyon National Park Service website.

SHUTTLE
Between May 15 and October 15, the Trans-Canyon Shuttle has a twice-daily shuttle between the South and North Rims. It runs once daily between October 16 and November 15.

HELPFUL HINTS

NINE TIPS FOR HIKING THE R2R
1. Turn up in good shape.
2. Carry a light pack.
3. Begin your hike at dawn.
4. Stay hydrated. Know the location of water sources, and drink H_2O at regular intervals throughout the day.
5. Although the R2R is a difficult trail to get lost on, some folks still manage it. Take a basic map and GPS or compass.
6. Wear a broad-brimmed hat and use sunblock.
7. Wear comfortable, lightweight, breathable trail running shoes. Heavy leather "hiking" boots are an invitation for blisters in desert environments.
8. Pace yourself. Aim to finish as strongly as you start.
9. Bring plenty of high-energy snacks; your energy levels will stay more consistent if you eat small, lightly, and often (every 1.5 to 2 hours) rather than having two or three big meals during the course of the day.

FLORA & FAUNA

BLOOD-SHOOTING LIZARD
One of the most interesting of the 47 reptile species that reside in the Grand Canyon is the short-horned lizard (*Phrynosoma hernandesi*). When threatened, it can squirt blood from its eyes up to one meter (three feet) away in order to deter predators.

TIPS FOR HIKING IN SNAKE COUNTRY
Snakes aren't interested in biting hikers. Whether you're walking down the trail, taking a quick bathroom break behind a bush, or sleeping under the stars, snakes want to avoid a potential encounter just as much as you do. That being said, they will protect themselves if the need arises. Put yourself in their skin; if someone was about to step on you, wouldn't you do everything in your power to prevent it happening?

The Grand Canyon is home to 22 species of snakes, including 6 different types of rattlesnakes. While hiking in the park, especially during the hotter months when snakes are most active, it pays

to be aware of both the necessary precautions, as well as what to do in case of a worst-case scenario.

PRECAUTIONS
1. **Wide Berth.** Most snakes will slither off when they feel the vibrations of your footsteps. If you spot a snake on the trail, stop where you are and give it time to move on. In the event that this does not occur, let it be and go around it. Don't throw rocks, prod at it with a stick, or try to pick it up. This will only serve to agitate the snake, and possibly trigger a defensive response. If there is no way to bypass it, stomp your feet from a safe distance. Note that as a general rule, most snakes can strike a distance of half their body length; give yourself at least double or triple that, the goal being to encourage the snake to depart on its own terms, while doing everything you can to avoid being perceived as a threat.
2. **Watch your Step.** Without being paranoid, pay attention to the trail ahead of you. When crossing logs or blowdowns, step on, rather than over, obstacles whenever possible. A snake may be taking a siesta on the other side.
3. **Hand Placement.** As with your feet, try not to put your hands anywhere you cannot see (e.g. ledges, hollowed-out logs).
4. **Clothing.** The majority of snake bites are to the ankle/lower leg area, followed by the hands. If the path is overgrown or you are bushwhacking off-trail, it is a good idea to wear long, loose-fitting pants or gaiters. These items won't completely protect you from snake bite, but they can reduce the amount of venom that is injected.

TREATMENT
If, despite all your precautions, a worst-case scenario occurs and you are bitten by a snake:
1. **Stay calm.** People are more likely to go into shock from fear and agitation than they are from the actual bite itself.

2. **Do not try to capture the snake**. If the snake is still in view and you aren't sure of its species, make a mental note of any distinguishing characteristics, or take a photo of it for identification purposes.

3. **Do not use antiquated methods** such as cutting the area, sucking out the poison, or applying a tourniquet, all of which can potentially do more harm than good.

4. **Remove any jewelry** in case of swelling.

5. **Do not drink alcohol or caffeine**, which can speed up the rate at which your body absorbs venom.

6. **Limiting movement is vital**. If possible, immobilize the bitten limb with a splint; firmly, but not too tightly, as you need to allow for swelling.

7. **If you are close to a trailhead**, slowly walk out and then seek medical attention immediately.

8. **If you are a long distance** from civilization and have cell phone service, call emergency services and seek medical advice. If there is no phone service and you are hiking in a group, one of the members of your party should walk out and seek medical assistance ASAP.

9. **If you are hiking solo** and have no cell phone coverage, you are left with a decision to make. You either wait for help or walk out. If you are hiking on a popular trail such as the Rim to Rim, your best bet is the former option. On the other hand, if you are bitten in a place where the

odds of someone coming along are slim, your only alternative may be to walk out. If this is your decision, do not rush as it will only increase the rate in which the venom is spread. In such a scenario, it's

even more important that you splint the bitten limb in order to limit any unnecessary movement.

BASE CAMP TALES

Of the multiple governmental agencies that were involved in the construction of the park's trail system, the most notable is the Grand Canyon Civilian Conservation Corps. The CCC was a program created by President Franklin Delano Roosevelt in 1933 to bring young men—particularly those cast into unemployment by the throes of the Great Depression—out of poverty and imbue them with a sense of purpose. Under the supervision of the Departments of Agriculture and Interior, they were put to work on important conservation projects such as forest-fire fighting, building fire roads, tree planting, and state and national park development.

The CCC companies that landed in the Grand Canyon were assigned the task of improving the park for its visitors and increasing accessibility between the two rims. They built the stone wall along the South Rim, raised telephone lines, performed repairs on the steep switchbacks of the Bright Angel Trail, and erected visitor buildings. They also constructed pathways—some of which were built as mule trails, as these were the days when mules were still the preferred mode of transport into the canyon. The River Trail, Ribbon Falls Trail, and the Clear Creek Trail were all the labor of the CCC.

The CCC program ran between 1933 and 1942, by which time massive unemployment had ceased to be an issue, and the nation's focus had turned toward supporting the war effort. Many of the young men who had helped to shape the infrastructure of the Grand Canyon went on to serve honorably in the armed forces. The fruits of their labors, however, continue to be enjoyed decades later by the millions of tourists that visit the Grand Canyon each and every year.

POINT OF VIEW

The South Rim offers visitors dozens of incredible viewpoints over the Grand Canyon. Among the most notable are Hopi Point, Mather Point, Yavapai Point, Powell Viewpoint, Yaki Point, and, perhaps the most aptly named of all, Ooh Aah Point. The latter is 1.6 km (1 mi) down the South Kaibab Trail (part of the Rim to Rim Trail), and offers a respite from the crowds that often inundate the more easily accessible lookouts.

IN & OUT

The closest major airport to the Grand Canyon is Phoenix Sky Harbor International Airport (PHX), a 3.5-hour drive from the South Rim. Another alternative is Las Vegas's McCarran International Airport (LAS). The ninth busiest airport in the country, it offers plenty of direct flights from Europe and Asia, and is less than a 5-hour drive from the South Rim.

Once you've arrived in Arizona, a memorable way to make the final leg of the journey to the Grand Canyon is by train. Inaugurated in 1901, the Grand Canyon Railway starts its daily run from the town of Williams and heads north toward the South Rim— a trip of just over two hours and 103 km (64 mi). Along the way you'll pass through an enchanting landscape of Ponderosa pine, spruce, aspen, and Douglas fir forests, while having the chance to spot wildlife such as elk, mule deer, and if you're very fortunate, possibly even a mountain lion.

NORTH KAIBAB TRAILHEAD

● Supai Tunnel

North Rim ●

Roaring Springs
● Day Use

Manzanita
Rest Area

A r i z o n a

● Cottonwood

Ribbon Falls /
Ribbon Falls Route ●

North Kaibab Trail

**G R A N D
C A N Y O N**

Phantom Ranch ●

● Black Bridge

Silver
Bridge ●

Plateau ●
Point

Colorado River

Skeleton Point ●

Indian Garden ●

3 Mile
Resthouse

Cedar Ridge ●

1.5 Mile
Resthouse

Bright Angel ●
Trailhead

Yaki Point ●

**SOUTH KAIBAB
TRAILHEAD**

SOUTH RIM
VILLAGE

N

1.5 km / 1 mi

36° 5' 59.8128" N
112° 6' 40.6728" W

A ROUTE DESIGNED
AROUND THE JOURNEY

Arizona and New Mexico
SOUTHWEST

ABOUT THE TRAIL
→ <u>DISTANCE</u> 1,239 km (770 mi)
→ <u>DURATION</u> 45 to 50 days
→ <u>LEVEL</u> Challenging

The Grand Enchantment Trail (GET) is a 1,239 km (770 mi) backcountry route between Phoenix, Arizona, and Albuquerque, New Mexico. Conceived in 2003 by Brett Tucker, it has no official recognition, no affiliated trail association, and is little known outside of a small subsection of the American long-distance hiking community. Yet this unheralded traverse boasts a singular fusion of natural and historical elements that sets it apart from other long-distance hikes in the United States. Not only does it encompass one of the country's most ecologically diverse regions, but it also takes the hiker on a journey through the Southwest's fascinating past—from ancient cliff dwellings to Salinas Pueblo Missions to well-preserved Wild West–era ghost towns.

When most people think of Arizona and New Mexico, the desert is generally one of the first things that come to mind. There is no denying that both states contain more than their fair share of arid biomes, but geographically speaking, there is a lot more to this part of America's Southwest than many outsiders realize.

During its serpentine course, the GET showcases the enormous variety of flora, fauna, and terrain on offer. Via a combination of trails, cross-country terrain, and little-used 4WD tracks and dirt roads, the GET traverses 14 distinct mountain chains, passes up and over 10 summits measuring more than 3,048 m (10,000 ft), and constantly oscillates between desert (64 percent of the total path) and forested (36 percent of the total path) environments.

This ecological medley is encapsulated by the region's "sky islands," including the Pinaleño Mountains near Safford, Arizona. These high-altitude, forest-covered lone ranges are surrounded by swaths of desert lowlands. After thousands of years of geographic isolation, a degree of evolutionary speciation has occurred in the resident plant and animal populations of these areas—think the Southwest's version of Madagascar or Ecuador's fabled Galapagos Islands.

During the 45 to 50 days it takes on average to complete the GET, you will have a chance to see an array of fauna reminiscent of Noah's Ark. Among the assemblage are desert tortoises, javelinas, bobcats, roadrunners, rattlesnakes, elk, black bears,

↖ The view from the pass above Walnut Canyon in the White Canyon Wilderness.

and the reclusive Mexican wolf—count yourself lucky if you spot one (see info box). Another fascinating creature unique to this part of the world is the Gila monster (*Heloderma suspectum*). One of only a handful of venomous lizards in the world, this lizard is also the largest of those native to the United States.Gila monsters spend 95 percent of their lives underground, storing fat in their tails and going months between meals. Despite the intimidating moniker, they present little threat to hikers due to their sluggish demeanor. Easily recognizable, their black bodies have striking patterns of pink, orange, or yellow that call to mind an Australian Aboriginal painting come to life.

Gila Monsters take their name from the Gila River Basin of Arizona and New Mexico. This area is home to two of the Southwest's most compelling historical sites: the Gila Cliff Dwellings National Monument and the ghost town of Mogollon. The former is a group of well-preserved 700-year-old abodes from the area's Native American peoples of the Mogollon culture. Located in expansive caves above the Gila River (just 1.6 km [1 mi] round trip from the GET), the rock residences were only occupied for approximately two to three decades before their occupants deserted them for reasons still unknown to archeologists.

↑ Aravaipa Canyon.
↙ Siamese Pines in the West Fork Gila River drainage.

241

October is a great time to hike the GET. Temperatures are cooler, and the higher elevation areas are ablaze with autumnal colors.

The ghost town of Mogollon is a more recently abandoned site situated in the Gila National Forest. In the 1880s, this former mining center had a booming population of more than 5,000, and you can still explore its well-preserved houses, saloons, stores, theaters, and graveyards. Mogollon's wild reputation was such that it was widely known as a haven for gamblers, claim jumpers, and outlaws. According to legend, this included Butch Cassidy and the Wild Bunch.

As the crow flies, only 483 kilometers (300 mi) separate Phoenix and Albuquerque. Yet the serpentine Grand Enchantment Trail extends for a whopping 1,289 km (770 mi) in total. The principal reason for its winding course is simple: "it's a route designed around the journey." With these words, founder Brett Tucker encapsulates one of the hallmarks of any great long-distance trek—quality experiences rather than just getting from point A to B in the most expedient way possible. When it comes to extended walks in the wilderness, it's less about how far we hike or how quickly we finish, and more about the time we take to observe, explore, and appreciate along the way.

→ Jerusalem cricket (*Stenopelmatus*).
↓ Gila Cliff Dwellings National Monument.
→ GET pioneer, Brett "The Water Whisperer" Tucker, exploring the depths of Midnight Canyon.

"When it comes to extended walks in the wilderness, it's less about how far we hike or how quickly we finish, and more about the time we take to observe, explore, and appreciate along the way."

GOOD TO KNOW

START / FINISH
Western Terminus
First Water Trailhead, Superstition
Mountains, Arizona (near Phoenix)
Eastern Terminus
Tramway Trailhead, Albuquerque,
New Mexico

HIGHEST / LOWEST POINT
Mogollon Baldy, Mogollon Mountains,
New Mexico (3,283 m [10,770 ft])
Gila River, Sonoran Desert, Arizona
(533 m [1,750 ft])

SEASON
April to June and September to
November. Hiking the GET in summer
is not advisable. Temperatures can be
scorching, seasonal water sources may
be dry, and flash floods are possible
in certain canyon areas due to the
monsoon season.

PERMITS
GET thru-hikers will require two
permits—one for the Aravaipa Canyon
Wilderness, and the other to cross
Arizona state trust land.

CAMPING
Wild camping is permitted throughout
the trail.

HIGHLIGHTS
1. Aravaipa Canyon
2. Magdalena Mountains
3. Gila Cliff Dwellings National
   Monument
4. Santa Teresa Mountains
5. Potato Canyon
6. Mogollon ghost town
7. San Lorenzo Canyon
8. Homemade ice cream at Doc
   Campbell's Post
9. A night of luxury at D and D's Organic
   Haven B&B in Glenwood, New
   Mexico. Its hospitable owners, Dan
   and Deb, will even shuttle you to and
   from the trail.

HELPFUL HINTS

THE WATER WHISPERER
The GET traverses one of the driest
areas in the contiguous United States.
As a result, in formulating the route,
one of the principal challenges for Brett
Tucker was to make sure there were
sufficient water sources for hikers
along the way. He succeeded and then
some; the GET passes by more than 170
potential spots to fill up your bottles
during its sinuous course. Tucker's
uncanny ability to locate H_2O sources in
the middle of arid regions earned him
the nickname the "Water Whisperer"
by the U.S. long-distance hiking
community. *Note: GET hikers should
carry a water capacity of 5 to 7 liters
during their trek.*

FLORA & FAUNA

MEXICAN GRAY WOLF
The most endangered subspecies of wolf
in the world, the Mexican gray wolf (also
known as the Mexican wolf or lobo),
once roamed the land between Central
America in the south and Colorado in the
north. The smallest of North America's
gray wolves, they were hunted to the
point of extinction in the United States
by the mid-1970s due to the threat they
posed to livestock. In 1998, after more
than two decades of captive breeding
programs, 11 Mexican gray wolves were
reintroduced into the Apache and Gila
National Forests of Arizona and New
Mexico. As of 2018, there were at least
143 wolves living in the wild.

BACKGROUND

SALINAS PUEBLO MISSIONS
A short detour west of the GET, near the
town of Mountainair, New Mexico, lies
the fascinating Salinas Pueblo Missions
National Monument. Three separate
sites house the remains of ancient
Native American Pueblos (including
subterranean ceremonial chambers
used by the Puebloans called kivas) and
seventeenth-century Spanish missions.
Collectively, they stand as a reminder
of the early encounters between the
indigenous peoples and the Franciscan
missionaries.

AUTHOR'S ANECDOTE

SOUNDS OF ARAVAIPA CANYON
In April, 2012, I hiked the Grand
Enchantment Trail as part of a 2,867
km (1,782 mi) backcountry route
called the Southwestern Horseshoe.
My favorite section of the GET was the
20 km (12 mi) stretch through Arizona's
Aravaipa Canyon. An enchanting oasis
of willows, alders, and colorful cliffs
set among harsh desert environs,
the Canyon's hydrological lifeline is
Aravaipa Creek, one of only a handful
of perennial waterways in the region.
After splishing and splashing along its
course for multiple hours, I set up camp
on its banks just before the sun was
about to set. After enjoying a gourmet
meal of dehydrated beans and corn
chips, I was soon serenaded to sleep
by a soothing mix of crickets and gently
gurgling water. Seven hours of blissful
sleep later, I awoke to the dawn song
of a yellow warbler backed by the same
meditative babbling of Aravaipa Creek.
Is there any better way to start the day
than with Mother Nature's alarm clock?

TRAMWAY
TRAILHEAD

ALBUQUERQUE   Sandia
                     Crest

EL MALPAIS
NATIONAL
CONSERVVATION AREA

San Lorenzo
Canyon

Magdalena   Salinas Pueblo
                   Mission National
                   Monument
Arizona

Potato
Canyon

Gila
National Forest

FIRST WATER
TRAILHEAD

Mogollon

PHOENIX   New
                                       Mexico
        Winston

Mesa   Superior

                      Gila Cliff
        Aravaipa   Dwellings National
        Canyon   Monument

                Morenci

                      Silver City

        Safford

Pinaleño
Mountains

MEXICO

N

50 km / 30 mi   33° 41' 21.9912" N
                                       109° 1' 45.948" W

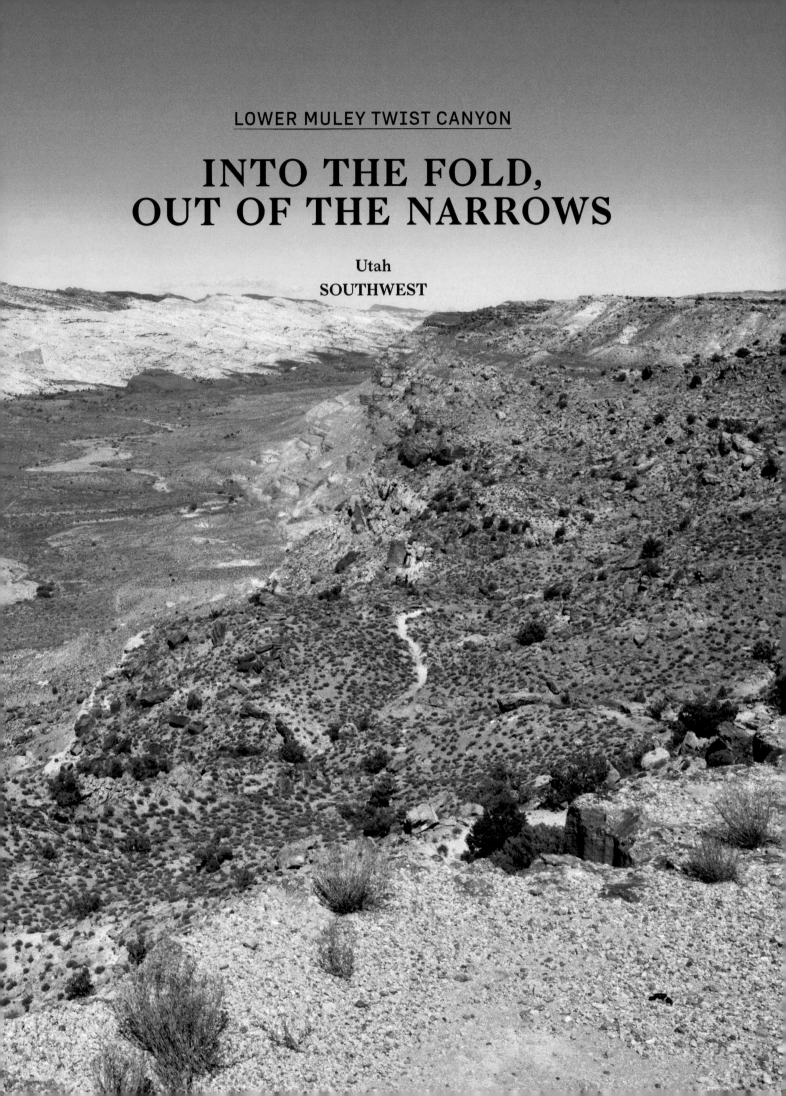

LOWER MULEY TWIST CANYON

INTO THE FOLD,
OUT OF THE NARROWS

Utah
SOUTHWEST

↑ Hamburger Rocks.
→ Turbid water flows along the canyon floor after heavy rain.

ABOUT THE TRAIL

→ <u>DISTANCE</u> 27.4 km (17 mi); *this includes the 3 km (2 mi) side trip to Hamburger Rocks*

→ <u>DURATION</u> 1 to 2 days

→ <u>LEVEL</u> Moderate

C apitol Reef may well be America's most underrated national park. For many visitors to Utah, it's a geographic footnote, a place to drive through on the way to the state's more famous national parks, including Zion, Bryce, and Arches. But for those who take the time to leave Highway 24—the only paved road that crosses the park—and explore the long and narrow Capitol Reef on foot, an uncrowded wonderland of red rock delights, ancient petroglyphs, and sweeping vistas awaits.

As with Utah's other protected wilderness areas, Capitol Reef hosts an enviable collection of geological marvels such as arches, slot canyons, hoodoos, buttes, domes, and monoliths. What sets it apart from its neighbors is the Waterpocket Fold, its signature landmark and the reason the park was created. Measuring almost 161 km (100 mi) in length, this classic monocline, or one-sided uplift in the Earth's crust, was created approximately 50 to 70 million years ago. The rock layers on the western side of the Fold have been lifted more than 2,134 m

(7,000 ft) higher than their equivalents on the eastern side, and when seen from above, it resembles a giant spine stretching out across a vast desert landscape. One of the best vantage points from which to take in the Waterpocket Fold is the Strike Valley Overlook, located just above Upper Muley Twist Canyon, a short distance from the starting point of our featured hike.

There are a few different options for trekking through the lower reaches of Muley Twist Canyon. The easiest from a logistical perspective is a loop hike beginning and ending at the Post Trailhead. Setting out from the eastern side of the Waterpocket Fold, the initial part of the 27.4 km (17 mi) rectangular-shaped route is the most difficult, consisting of a steep and trailless climb up and over the Fold (the way is marked by periodic cairns). Don't forget to look back during the ascent, as the views over Grand Gulch are spectacular. After about 1.5 hours of hiking, you'll reach the signposted junction with Lower Muley Twist Canyon.

For the next 11 km (7 mi), the route winds its way south past a series of dramatic undercut walls, deep alcoves, and increasingly high cliffs. Most of the walking is on loose sandy wash bottoms (Tip: shorten your stride to make the going easier), and during the hotter months of the year, much-appreciated shade can be found under small stands of cooling cottonwood trees. The geological highlight of this section are the alcoves—large, arched hollows in cliff walls that have been sculpted by water

Bunking down in Lower Muley Twist's giant rock amphitheater.

erosion. While exploring the inner reaches of these huge rock amphitheaters, take a moment to drink in the silence and ponder the fact that the immense place from which you are gazing out was literally millions of years in the making.

Not long after leaving the final alcove, the Lower Muley Twist Canyon turns eastward, cutting its way back through the Waterpocket Fold. At this point, the width of the canyon shrinks considerably (it measures less than 3 m [10 ft] wide at its narrowest), and the sandstone walls become significantly higher. Mormon pioneers brought their wagon trains through this winding rock corridor when heading south to San Juan County in the late nineteenth century, noting that the canyon was narrow enough to "twist a mule." Hence, the colorful moniker of Muley Twist was born. It's worth noting that this narrow section of canyon is not a place to linger during flash flood season, between July and September.

Once the narrows have been negotiated, the route continues east a little further before reaching another junction. At this point you can either return directly to the Post Trailhead, or head south and then east for a 3 km (1.86 mi) out-and-back side trip to the surreal Hamburger Rocks. Small and plump, these mushroom-shaped, coffee-colored hoodoos make for a striking juxtaposition with the white Navajo sandstone slope upon which they sit. Not to be missed!

Situated a few minutes' walk from Hamburger Rocks is a place called Muley Tanks, which may be the best chance you have of replenishing your H_2O supplies during the hike. The "tanks" are actually small rock basins that usually contain water (which you will need to purify). Take the opportunity to rehydrate and rest up before returning to the junction, and then head north for the final stretch along Grand Gulch, absorbing the fact that Capitol Reef National Park is a footnote no longer.

"Mormon pioneers brought their wagon trains through this winding rock corridor when heading south to San Juan County in the late nineteenth century, noting that the canyon was narrow enough to 'twist a mule.'"

← Emerging from the Narrows.
↑ Hiking along Grand Gulch.
→ Claret cup cactus (*Echinocereus Triglochidiatus*).

GOOD TO KNOW

START/FINISH
The Post Trailhead, located 800 m (0.5 mi) south of Burr Trail Road

SEASON
Year round. Milder conditions make the shoulder seasons of spring and fall ideal for hiking and backpacking. The summer months can be scorching, with temperatures reaching 37.8°C (100°F). July to September also coincides with monsoon season, which means that flash floods are a real possibility in the narrower sections of the canyon.

POST-HIKE FEAST?
If you are looking for somewhere to replenish all those calories you burned, consider Cafe Diablo in the nearby town of Torrey. Since opening its doors in 1994, it has established itself as one of Utah's best restaurants. Specializing in Southwestern cuisine, Cafe Diablo has plenty of vegetarian options and is open from April to October. Be sure to try the rattlesnake cakes!

FLORA & FAUNA

A TOWN CALLED FRUITA
Capitol Reef National Park boasts a number of orchards with approximately 3,000 fruit trees—a mix of cherry, apricot, peach, pear, apple, plum, mulberry, almond, and walnut (yes, almonds and walnuts are classified as fruit). The trees are all remnants of a former Mormon settlement called Fruita, which was established in 1880 and ultimately abandoned in the mid-1950s when it was acquired by the National Park Service. During harvesting season, visitors have sometimes been permitted to pick the ripe offerings, all of which can be paid for at self-pay stations near the orchard's entrances.

BACKGROUND

ANCIENT ROCK ART
Petroglyphs (images carved into rock) and pictographs (paintings on a rock's surface) can be found throughout Capitol Reef National Park. Most of this artwork was left by the Fremont people, who inhabited southern Utah from approximately 600–1300 AD. The figures depict humans, animals, and an array of other forms. Anthropologists suggest that the rock art recorded religious events, migrations, resource locations, hunting trips, and celestial information. The most well-preserved examples of petroglyphs in Capitol Reef are located 2.1 km (1.5 mi) east of the National Park Visitor Center on HWY 24.

BONUS TRACK

GEOLOGICAL DEFINITIONS
Slot canyon: A narrow canyon that is formed by the wear of water flowing through rock. Much deeper than it is wide, slot canyons typically consist of sandstone or limestone, though there are also examples in other rock types such as basalt and granite.

Hoodoo: Colloquially known as "fairy chimneys," these tall and thin pinnacles typically consist of hard rock sitting atop softer rock, and are most often found in arid, desert environments. Two of the most famous examples of hoodoos can be found in Bryce Canyon National Park in Utah, and Cappadocia in Turkey.

Butte: Flat-topped hills, which, unlike mesas, are taller than they are wide. In popular culture, they are perhaps most known for their appearance in classic Hollywood Westerns such as *Stagecoach* (1939) and *The Searchers* (1956), both of which were partly filmed in Monument Valley, Utah.

Monolith: Monoliths are single large rocks that typically consist of dense igneous or metamorphic rock. The world's largest monolith is Uluru (also known as Ayers Rock), which is located in the Northern Territory in Australia's Red Center.

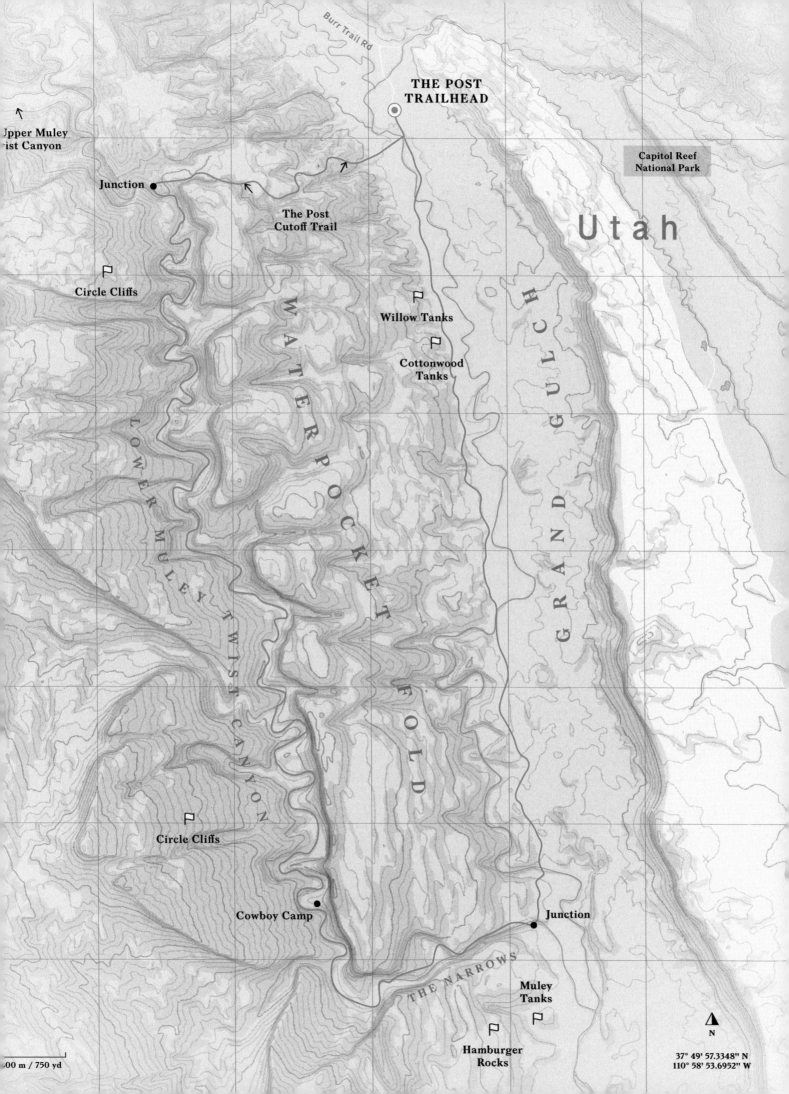

Burr Trail Rd

THE POST
TRAILHEAD

Upper Muley
Twist Canyon

Capitol Reef
National Park

Junction

The Post
Cutoff Trail

U t a h

Circle Cliffs

Willow Tanks

Cottonwood
Tanks

W A T E R P O C K E T   F O L D

G R A N D   G U L C H

L O W E R   M U L E Y   T W I S T   C A N Y O N

Circle Cliffs

Cowboy Camp

Junction

THE NARROWS

Muley
Tanks

N

Hamburger
Rocks

00 m / 750 yd

37° 49' 57.3348" N
110° 58' 53.6952" W

ALONG THE RIVER DIVIDE

Texas
SOUTHWEST

ABOUT THE TRAIL
→ <u>DISTANCE</u> 50 km (31 mi)
→ <u>DURATION</u> 3 days
→ <u>LEVEL</u> Challenging

For more than 1,600 km (1,000 mi), the Rio Grande forms the natural border between the U.S. state of Texas and Mexico. Along this river is a large elbow where the flow changes from southeast to northeast. This prominent curve gives its name to one of America's least-visited protected wilderness areas—Big Bend National Park.

Encompassing a total of 3,250 sq km (801,163 acres), Big Bend borders the Rio Grande, or the Río Bravo as it's known in Mexico, for approximately 190 km (118 mi). Within the park's vast boundaries there are three main ecosystems: mountain, desert, and river. The principal means to explore these diverse landscapes is via the park's 250 km (150 mi) of hiking trails. Among many different route options, the standout multi-day trek is the Outer Mountain Loop (OML).

Beginning and ending at Chisos Basin, the OML is a combination of the Pinnacles, Juniper Canyon, Dodson, Blue Creek, and Laguna Meadows trails. Measuring approximately 50 km (31 mi) in total, the treadway is well marked, and for much of its course, well maintained. However, this is far from an easy hike due to rough and undulating terrain, harsh weather conditions, and a lack of year-round water sources (see info box). The OML is a trip best suited to experienced backpackers, ideally those who are accustomed to hiking in arid environments.

If you had to pick just one word to describe Big Bend National Park it might well be "remote." The nearest commercial airport, Midland Odessa, is over 250 km (160 mi) away, contributing to the park's status as one of the least visited in the lower 48 states. Big Bend's "back of beyond" character makes it a favorite for solitude-seeking hikers and stargazers. Thanks to its geographic isolation, it has an International Dark Sky Park designation and is also one of just 13 parks in the world with a gold-tier certification from the International Dark Sky Association. If you've ever thought about ditching the tent and sleeping under the stars, Big Bend is definitely the place to do it! And for an experience you will never forget, try to time your visit to coincide with a meteor shower. (Tip: The best time to see a meteor shower is an hour or two before dawn.)

While the heavens may take center stage during the evenings, it's Big Bend's landscapes and wildlife that star during the daytime. Over its undulating course, the Outer Mountain Loop moves between the pine, juniper, and oak woodlands of the Chisos Mountains (see info box) to the semi-arid scrubland and bone-dry sandy washes of the surrounding desert lowlands.

> "One of just 13 parks in the world with a gold-tier certification from the International Dark Sky Association. If you've ever thought about ditching the tent and sleeping under the stars, Big Bend is definitely the place to do it!"

← The Rio Grande winds its way through Big Bend National Park.
↑ A moment of reflection in the Chisos Mountains.

The discrepancy in climate between these contrasting environments is equally marked, with a 10 to 20-degree variation in temperature between the Chisos and the desert floor. Roaming these multifarious biomes are mountain lions, black bears, javelinas, coyotes, and bobcats. For all you cartoon fans out there, also keep an eye out for roadrunners *(Geococcyx californianus)*—beep, beep!

Almost all of Big Bend's vast array of fauna and flora can be found on both sides of the Rio Grande. The region's biological lifeline has existed since a time before record, and this environmental connection between countries has long been recognized by both the U.S. and Mexican governments. The notion of an International Peace Park bridging the shared ecosystem was first proposed by U.S. President Franklin Roosevelt in 1944, and the idea has never entirely disappeared. As recently as 2011 under the Obama administration, both governments announced a working plan for proceeding with "the next steps for the continued coordination between the two countries in the protection and preservation of the transnational Big Bend/Rio Bravo region—North America's largest and most diverse desert ecosystem." No one can predict the future, but in an ideal world not separated by contentious political boundaries, perhaps the "seamless flow of nature" will again unite us all.

↑ Grazing horses and towering cliffs.
→ Big Bend's impressive rock formations are best enjoyed as the sun is either rising or setting.
↓ Heading towards the Chisos mMountains, the only range in America to be fully contained within the boundaries of a national park.

GOOD TO KNOW

START / FINISH
Chisos Basin Trailhead
(near the Chisos Basin Visitor Center)

HIGHEST / LOWEST POINT
The base of Emory Peak
(2,133 m [7,100 ft]); *or, for those who make the recommended ascent, the summit (2,385 m [7,825 ft])*
Chihuahuan Desert
(1,160 m [3,800 ft])

SEASON
October through April is ideal. Hiking in Big Bend during the summer months is not recommended, with temperatures on the desert floor regularly topping 38°C (100°F).

PERMITS
Backcountry permits are only issued in person at the park and can be obtained up to 24 hours in advance of your trip. Note that the more popular campsites tend to fill up quickly during the peak holiday season of December and January.

HELPFUL HINTS

CACHING WATER
Big Bend is one of the hottest and driest national parks in America. Hydration is of the utmost importance during any backpacking trip in the park. Drinking at least four liters of water per day is recommended, and due to the dearth of reliable H_2O sources, the National Park Service suggests that hikers cache water at the dedicated storage boxes before beginning the OML, located at Wilson Ranch (Blue Creek) and the end of Juniper Canyon Road.

SIDE TRIP
The loop can be extended by 8 km (5 mi) by making the recommended side trips to the South Rim and the summit of Emory Peak. At 2,385 m (7,825 ft), the summit is both the geographic and scenic high point of Big Bend National Park.

BORDER CROSSING
A great way to finish your OML hike is to visit the former mining village of Boquillas del Carmen (population: 275), situated on the Mexican side of the border. Visitors can take a short rowboat ferry ride from the Boquillas Crossing parking lot to enjoy a meal at one of the restaurants or check out the impressive local handicrafts on offer. Don't forget your passport.

FLORA & FAUNA

WILDLIFE IN BIG BEND
The national park boasts a remarkable collection of wildlife, including 450 species of birds, 75 species of mammals, 56 species of reptiles, and 11 species of amphibians.

CHISOS MOUNTAINS
The southernmost mountain chain in the United States, the Chisos are also the only range in the country to be completely contained within a single national park. Among its diverse range of flora is America's southernmost stand of Quaking Aspens, residing on the southwest flanks of Emory Peak. *Note: Aspens are North America's most widely distributed tree.*

BONUS TRACK

SIX FACTS ABOUT THE RIO GRANDE

1. The Rio Grande (from Spanish for "Big River") is the fifth longest river in North America (3,051 km [1,885 mi]), and the twentieth longest in the world. It extends from its source high up in Colorado's Rocky Mountains (3,700 m [13,000 ft]) through to the Gulf of Mexico.

2. In the United States, the Rio Grande passes through three states: Colorado, New Mexico, and Texas. In Mexico, it winds along the border states of Durango, Chihuahua, Coahuila, Nuevo León, and Tamaulipas.

3. The Rio Grande has marked the border between the United States and Mexico since 1848.

4. During the nineteenth century, the Rio Grande was plied by more than 200 steamboats, which ran regularly between Rio Grande City and the mouth of the river close to Brownsville (both of which are in Texas).

5. In Mexico, they refer to the river as the Rio Bravo, which means "furious" or "agitated" river.

6. During its course, the river passes alongside many major population centers; more than 6 million people in total live on the banks of the Rio Grande. Some of the principal cities on the U.S. side are Santa Fe, Albuquerque, Las Cruces, El Paso, McAllen, and Brownsville. On the Mexican side of the border, cities include Ciudad Juarez, Piedras Negras, Nuevo Laredo, Reynosa, and Matamoros.

THE WALL EFFECT
In recent times, the Rio Grande has been appearing a lot more in the national media because of Donald Trump's proposed border wall. From a wildlife perspective, the effects could potentially be devastating. According to peer-reviewed data published in BioScience: "The border wall threatens some populations by degrading landscape connectivity. Physical barriers prevent or discourage animals from accessing food, water, mates, and other critical resources by disrupting annual or seasonal migration and dispersal routes." By the numbers, a wall would disconnect about a third of 346 native species from 50 percent (or more) of their range that lies south of the border.

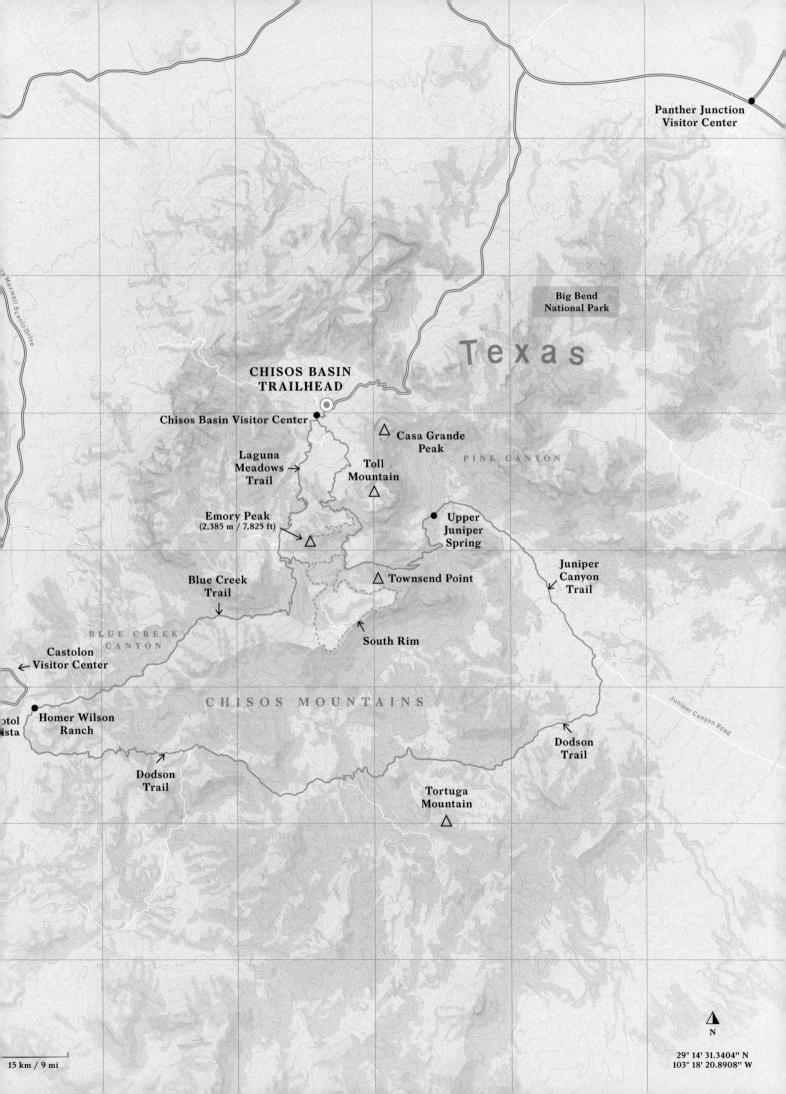

Panther Junction
Visitor Center

Big Bend
National Park

T e x a s

**CHISOS BASIN
TRAILHEAD**

Chisos Basin Visitor Center

△ Casa Grande
Peak

PINE CANYON

Laguna
Meadows
Trail →

Toll
Mountain
△

Emory Peak
(2,385 m / 7,825 ft)
△

● Upper
Juniper
Spring

Juniper
Canyon
Trail

△ Townsend Point

Blue Creek
Trail
↓

South Rim
↓

BLUE CREEK
CANYON

Castolon
Visitor Center
←

C H I S O S   M O U N T A I N S

Juniper Canyon Road

tol
sta

● Homer Wilson
Ranch

Dodson
Trail
↗

Dodson
Trail
↖

Tortuga
Mountain
△

's Maxwell Scenic Drive

△
N

15 km / 9 mi

29° 14' 31.3404" N
103° 18' 20.8908" W

GRAND GULCH – BULLET CANYON LOOP
(CEDAR MESA)

WALKING THE ANCIENT PATHS

Utah
SOUTHWEST

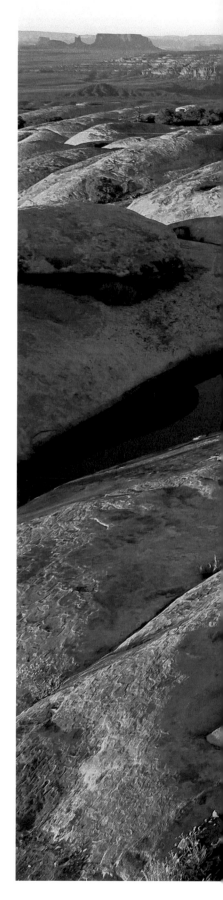

ABOUT THE TRAIL
→ <u>DISTANCE</u> 40 km (25 mi)
→ <u>DURATION</u> 2 to 4 days
→ <u>LEVEL</u> Moderate

Located in a remote corner of southeastern Utah, Cedar Mesa ranks among the most fascinating places in the American West. An uninhabited 1,000 sq km (400 sq mi) plateau, its sheer-walled canyons, Ancestral Puebloan dwellings, and captivating rock art make for a unique experience. Due to its isolated, rugged setting, Cedar Mesa's wonders are by no means easily accessible; do not expect to be greeted by manicured pathways, informative trail signs, or a state-of-the-art visitor center. Instead, one of the country's premier archeological treasures is its own reward for curious souls who make the trek out to this ornament of the ancient world.

Cedar Mesa's network of storied canyons can only be explored on foot. There are many hiking options throughout the area, but one of the more accessible introductions is the Grand Gulch and Bullet Canyon Loop. The route is approximately 40 km (25 mi) in length, generally easy to follow, and, most importantly from a practical perspective, has reliable water sources during the prime backpacking seasons of spring and fall. From start to finish, the canyon scenery is exquisite, including natural bridges, alcoves, spires, hoodoos, and vertiginous cliffs. Though seasoned backpackers could easily hike this route over two days, with so many geological and historical nooks and crannies to explore, many find that three or four days is a more appropriate timeframe.

Geologically speaking, Cedar Mesa has been around just a wee bit shy of forever. It's estimated that the rock layers in its canyons date back some 300 million years, and sharp-eyed observers might even find fossils in these natural chronometers that pre-date mammals. However, Cedar Mesa is no rock mausoleum—much vibrant flora and fauna can also be found within its walls. An explosion of wildflowers awaits in the spring, while the fall brings a brilliant yellow blaze of cottonwood trees. Gobbling turkeys and wandering deer abound, and for those inclined to look toward the heavens, the occasional bald eagle or peregrine falcon might be seen patrolling the deep blue sky.

↖ Seven miles to Grand Gulch.
↑ Expansive views of Cedar Mesa on the Grand Gulch and Bullet Canyon Loop.

↑ Exploring the Pueblo cliff dwellings.
→ Hiking the trailless canyons of Cedar Mesa.

The outstanding landscape speaks for itself, but what sets Cedar Mesa apart from the other red-rock wonderlands of Utah is its archeological sites. More specifically, you will find a history lesson in the Ancestral Puebloan people, those who lived here from the late centuries BC to the late 1200s AD. The forefathers of modern Native American nations such as the Hopi, Zuni, and Zia, the Ancestral Puebloans created a vast and complex civilization, including a trading network that extended to the Pacific Ocean in the west, the Great Plains in the east, and Central America in the south. Some of the cliff dwellings they constructed nearly a millennia ago are still standing, along with Puebloan petroglyphs and pictographs adorning the canyon walls. This rich cultural cache tells a story of religious, hunting, agricultural, and astronomical events. Exploring the twisting canyons of Cedar Mesa is like walking through a giant open-air museum.

In following these ancient paths, it's easy to feel a kinship with the people that lived here so long ago. They likely feasted, sang, laughed, prayed, worked, and looked up to the heavens with the same feelings of awe and wonder. Although Cedar Mesa offers visitors a singular window into their history, it also provides us with a reminder that the more things change, the more they stay the same.

↖ The Ancestral Puebloans lived in the Cedar Mesa area from the late centuries BC to the late 1200s AD.
↑ A lonely butte.

"This rich cultural cache tells a story of religious, hunting, agricultural, and astronomical events. Exploring the twisting canyons of Cedar Mesa is like walking through a giant open-air museum."

← An ancient pictograph in Grand Gulch.
↓ A room with a view.

GOOD TO KNOW

START / FINISH
Kane Gulch Ranger Station, Utah
Bullet Canyon Trailhead, Utah

HIGHEST / LOWEST POINT
Kane Gulch Ranger Station
(2,000 m [6,500 ft])
Junction of Grand Gulch and Bullet Canyon
(1,650 m [5,400 ft])

SEASON
April to May and October to November are the ideal times to visit Cedar Mesa. Spring features wildflowers, mild temperatures, and longer daylight hours. Autumn typically sees fewer people, crisp daytime temperatures, and cooler nights.

PERMITS
Permits are available online or in person at the Kane Gulch Ranger Station between March 1 and June 15 and again from September 1 to October 31. The ranger station is closed outside of these prime seasons, but during this period all charges can be paid at self-serve kiosks, with no reservations needed.

HELPFUL HINTS

TRANSPORT BETWEEN TRAILHEADS
11 km (7 mi) separates the two trailheads. If your hiking group doesn't have two vehicles (or if you are solo), your options are hitching, walking, or perhaps leaving a bicycle at the Bullet Canyon Trailhead in order to ride back to your vehicle at the Kane Gulch Ranger Station (where safe overnight parking is available).

CEDAR MESA ETIQUETTE
As always, respect should be paid when visiting these historic sites. Don't touch the fragile art or take any artifacts such as pottery. Cedar Mesa still sees pilgrimages from the descendants of the Ancestral Puebloans, who consider the area to be sacred.

GUIDEBOOK
A Hiking Guide To Cedar Mesa by Peter Francis Tassoni provides a comprehensive overview of the archeological sites and canyons in the area.

SUPPLIES & ACCOMMODATION
The town of Blanding, Utah, is located approximately 60 km (37 mi) away from Cedar Mesa and provides lodging, groceries, fuel, and other supplies. Note that this traditional Mormon town sees many of its business closed on Sundays, the notable exceptions being convenience stores and gas stations.

BACKGROUND

EDGE OF THE CEDARS STATE PARK AND MUSEUM
Located in Blanding, this world-class museum is an excellent capstone to your time in the area. It boasts an impressive Ancestral Puebloan dwelling on site, as well as a comprehensive collection of artifacts and trade goods from as far away as modern-day Mexico.

STAR GAZING
The nearby Natural Bridges National Monument (20 km [12 mi] away) is an International Dark Sky Park (IDSP) that offers camping and remarkable geological wonders. Some of the darkest skies in the continental United States are found here due to its remote location.

AUTHOR'S ANECDOTE

SOLITUDE AND SOLEMNITY
I went to Cedar Mesa by myself during the winter of 2018; I had the gift of time, and I wanted to use it. The appropriate clothing, equipment, and copious amounts of hot drinks at night meant that not only did I make do in the below-freezing temperatures, but I greatly enjoyed my time in the canyons.

I didn't see anyone for four days. I'm not sure of the total distance I traveled, as I spent most of the trip exploring hidden dens and crevices off the path of the main canyon. While wandering, I found cliff dwellings, rock art depicting a crescent moon and planets, and pottery shards that originated from faraway lands.

On my last day I stumbled upon a kiva, a center of worship for the Ancestral Puebloans and their descendants today. Upon entering the kiva, I saw a shaft of light shine through the ladder opening of the ceiling from where I had just come. My immediate surroundings were illuminated with a golden hue, and I experienced the defining moment of my trip. A time and place full of mystery, beauty, wonder, and a feeling of the sacred in the wild places.

BONUS TRACK

A ROOM WITH A VIEW
Although the main purpose of a kiva was to serve as a center for rituals, these rooms also acted as meeting places for political and social gatherings. The walls of the kivas were often adorned with vivid murals, and the round shape of the earliest examples stood in contrast to the typical rectangular and square designs of Puebloan residences.

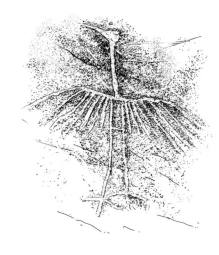

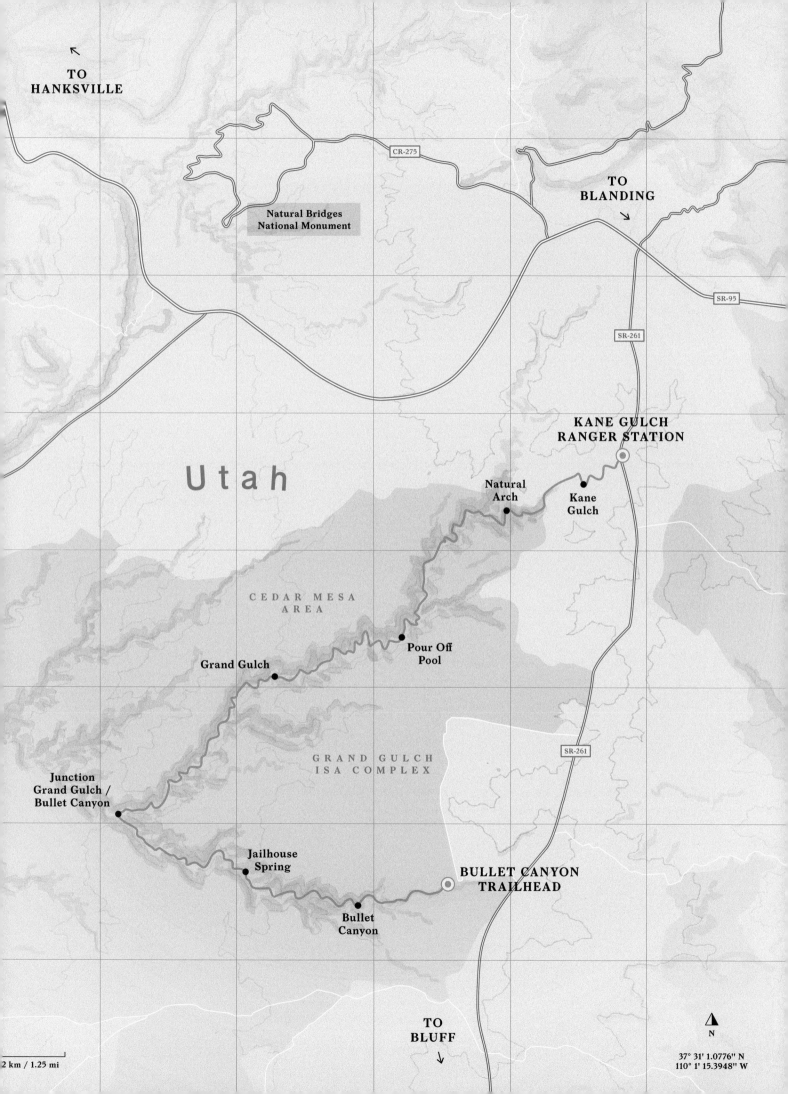

TO
HANKSVILLE

CR-275

Natural Bridges
National Monument

TO
BLANDING

SR-95

SR-261

KANE GULCH
RANGER STATION

Utah

Natural
Arch

Kane
Gulch

CEDAR MESA
AREA

Pour Off
Pool

Grand Gulch

SR-261

GRAND GULCH
ISA COMPLEX

Junction
Grand Gulch /
Bullet Canyon

Jailhouse
Spring

BULLET CANYON
TRAILHEAD

Bullet
Canyon

TO
BLUFF

N

2 km / 1.25 mi

37° 31' 1.0776" N
110° 1' 15.3948" W

Wanderlust USA

ALASKA

Everything about Alaska seems big—its mountains, rivers,
glaciers, animals, distances, stories, and beards are all of
oversized proportions. The same goes for the backpacking
possibilities, which are just a wee bit shy of limitless.

THE GLACIER BEHIND THE LITTLE LAKE

The Panhandle
ALASKA

ABOUT THE TRAIL

→ <u>DISTANCE</u> 16.7 km (10.4 mi)

→ <u>DURATION</u> 6 to 8 hours

→ <u>LEVEL</u> Moderate

Juneau is the sole capital city in the United States that can't be reached by road. Cut off from the rest of Alaska by the Pacific Ocean, the Coast Range, and the Juneau Icefield, it's only accessible by air or sea. This isolated character, combined with its spectacular mountain and marine landscapes, have long made it a mecca for hikers. And one of the best trails from which to take in the city's abundant natural wonders is the climb to the top of Mount McGinnis.

Beginning at the West Glacier Trail Trailhead, 21 km (13 mi) from downtown Juneau, the Mount McGinnis Trail is a tale of two sections. The first part of the hike is congruent with the popular West Glacier Trail (5.5 km [3.4 mi]) and suitable for ramblers of all experience, age, and fitness levels. Well maintained and easy to follow, the pathway extends from the trailhead parking lot to a scenic rocky ledge (436 m [1,430 ft]) that offers fantastic views of Juneau's most famous attraction, Mendenhall Glacier.

Approximately 21 km (13 mi) long and 2.4 km (1.5 mi) wide, Mendenhall Glacier is one of 38 glaciers that flow down from the massive Juneau Icefield (3,885 sq km [1,500 sq mi]). Its original names were *Sitaantaagu* (the Glacier Behind the Town) and *Aak'wtaaksit* (the Glacier Behind the Little Lake) according to the Tlingit, the region's indigenous peoples. The glacier's terminus is Mendenhall Lake, which was formed in the early 1900s due to its namesake's regression. In recent times its rate of retreat has accelerated dramatically, and as a result, the lake continues to grow in size, now measuring 2.4 km (1.5 mi) long, 1.6 km (1 mi) wide, and 65 m (220 ft) deep.

"The 360-degree panorama is one of Alaska's finest—which is saying a great deal. On a clear day, hikers can see Auke Bay, Douglas and Admiralty Islands, the Chilkat Range, the Juneau Icefield, and the star of this extraordinary ice-age production, Mendenhall Glacier."

↖ Bears frolicking on the shore of Mendenhall Lake.
↑ An archway of ice.
← A mist-shrouded forest near Juneau.

281

Mendenhall Glacier as seen from the Mount McGinnis Trail.

To return to our tale of two sections, the rocky lookout over the massive river of ice is the turnaround point for the West Glacier Trail, but for those who plan to continue to the summit of McGinnis, this is where the hike really begins in earnest. The mountain's apex is still another 3 km (2 mi) and about 853 m (2,800 ft) of elevation gain away. From here to the summit, the trail transforms into a sporadically marked route. Due to its exacting nature, it should only be attempted by fit and well-equipped hikers (see info box) with a good sense of direction.

Tracing the mountain's eastern ridge, tree line is reached at approximately 701 m (2,300 ft). For the remainder of the ascent, the route passes through an enchanting alpine landscape of flowery meadows, picturesque ponds, lingering snowfields, and soothing streams. For those who would like to overnight on Mount McGinnis, this is the area in which to do so. Campsite options abound, with sunsets and sunrises from this lofty perch adding another dimension to an already classic hike.

After approximately three to five hours of climbing, you will arrive at the top of Mount McGinnis. The 360-degree panorama is one of Alaska's finest—which is saying a great deal. On a clear day, hikers can see Auke Bay, Douglas and Admiralty Islands, the Chilkat Range, the Juneau Icefield, and the star of this extraordinary ice-age production, Mendenhall Glacier. If you have spent any time traveling around the United States, the summit vista will confirm that Juneau is not only America's most isolated state capital, but also its most scenic.

↑ Killer whales frequent Alaska's bays and inlets 12 months a year.
↓ Reflections on Auke Lake.

"Juneau is the sole capital city in the United States that can't be reached by road. Cut off from the rest of Alaska by the Pacific Ocean, the Coast Range, and the Juneau Icefield, it's only accessible by air or sea."

↑ Mendenhall Ice Caves.
← Aurora Borealis over Juneau.

GOOD TO KNOW

START / FINISH
West Glacier Trailhead (out-and-back to the summit of Mount McGinnis)

TOTAL ELEVATION GAIN
1,273 m (4,177 ft)

SEASON
Mid-June to September. On average, it rains 222 days per year in Juneau. As a result, the hike to the top of Mount McGinnis, particularly once it leaves the West Glacier Trail behind, is usually muddy and slippery. Be sure to pack a rain jacket and wear shoes with good traction (See below, Gear Recommendations).

PERMITS
You do not need a permit to hike the Mount McGinnis Trail.

CAMPING
If you have the time, doing the Mount McGinnis Trail as an overnight excursion is highly recommended. Excellent camping options are available between tree line and the summit.

HELPFUL HINTS

GEAR RECOMMENDATIONS
Rain jacket, trail running shoes, gaiters, insulation layer, beanie, map, compass/GPS, bear spray. A lightweight pair of binoculars is also a good idea for wildlife spotting and glacier gazing.

WATER
H_2O can be found in the ponds and streams of the alpine meadows just above tree line. Bring a filter or chemicals to purify.

JUNEAU'S FIVE FAMOUS PEAKS
Mount McGinnis is one of five popular "walk-up" peaks in the Juneau area. The other four are Mount Juneau, Mount Roberts, Thunder Mountain, and Mount Jumbo. Each member of the quintet is easily accessible from the town center, requires nothing in the way of technical climbing gear, and can be done as a day hike by most reasonably fit hikers. As with the Mount McGinnis Trail, each of the other four peaks offers a combination of lush temperate forests, fascinating wildlife, and spectacular vistas of glaciers, islands, and the surrounding coastal range *Note: Mount McGinnis is the highest and toughest of the five climbs.*

FLORA & FAUNA

You may encounter bears, porcupines, bald eagles, deer, and ptarmigans (the state bird) along the way. Keep an eye out for mountain goats at the summit.

BACKGROUND

THE ALASKAN HOTEL & BAR
If you're looking for a place to enjoy a post-summit celebration, it's hard to go past the iconic Alaskan Hotel & Bar. Established in 1913, the Alaskan Hotel is the oldest operating hotel in Juneau. According to legend, the original proprietors tied the hotel's keys to a helium balloon, which they subsequently released to signify that the hotel would remain open in perpetuity.

AUTHOR'S ANECDOTE

DELPHINE OF THE MOUNTAINS
It was on the Mount McGinnis Trail in June 1998 that I met Delphine, a young French lady who hailed from Chamonix. After hiking and chatting together for most of the day, I ended up traveling around Alaska and the Yukon with her for the next month. More than two decades later, I have yet to meet a more genuinely enthusiastic hiker.

Delphine literally sprang out of her sleeping bag every morning. Each meal, no matter how basic (we're talking plain porridge and water), was appreciated as if it was her last. Flora, fauna, and landscapes were uniformly taken in with childlike wonder. She was one of those people who was simply made to be outdoors. I call them "wilderness lifers."

I haven't seen Delphine since 1998. After corresponding for a year or two (back in the days when people still sent letters), we drifted out of contact. However, I'd like to think that after all these years she is still regularly wandering the hills and valleys of her beloved French Alps. Now in her early 40s, her elven-like step may be a little slower (or not!), but I bet the unconditional love she felt for the natural world remains undiminished.

BONUS TRACK

GLACIERS
Alaska is home to 616 named glaciers, with thousands more unnamed glaciers dotted throughout the state. Glaciers are formed when more snow accumulates than melts over the course of many years; eventually this compacts into ice. There are two types of glaciers: alpine glaciers and continental glaciers. The former begin on mountainsides and flow downward through valleys, whereas the latter are larger and not limited to alpine areas. They tend to spread in all directions, and in the process envelope all of their surroundings—whether it be plains, mountains or valleys—with a thick blanket of ice. The largest sub-category of continental glaciers are known as ice sheets, and they extend over an area of more than 50,000 sq km (19,305 sq mi). The only two ice sheets in the world today are in Greenland and Antarctica. By itself, Antarctica constitutes more than 90 percent of the world's glacial ice, in which is contained approximately 70 percent of the earth's fresh water.

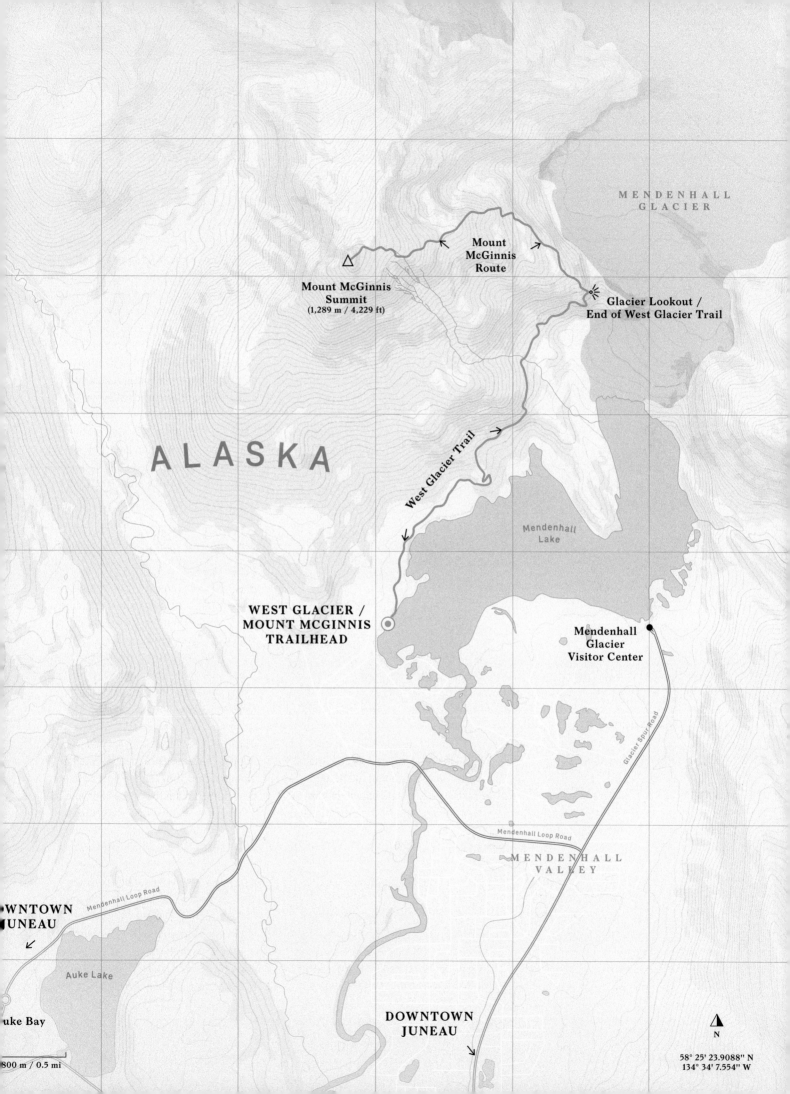

MENDENHALL
GLACIER

Mount
McGinnis
Route

△ Mount McGinnis
Summit
(1,289 m / 4,229 ft)

Glacier Lookout /
End of West Glacier Trail

ALASKA

West Glacier Trail

Mendenhall
Lake

WEST GLACIER /
MOUNT McGINNIS
TRAILHEAD

Mendenhall
Glacier
Visitor Center

Glacier Spur Road

Mendenhall Loop Road

MENDENHALL
VALLEY

DOWNTOWN
JUNEAU

Mendenhall Loop Road

Auke Lake

uke Bay

800 m / 0.5 mi

N

58° 25' 23.9088" N
134° 34' 7.554" W

DENALI NATIONAL PARK

THE CROWN JEWEL
OF THE NORTH

The Interior
ALASKA

Alaska. The name conjures up images of pristine wilderness and outdoor experiences like no other. A land in which everything seems to be of proportions fit for a Russian novel—the mountains, the myths, the rivers, the glaciers, the beards, and the wildlife. And that brings us to Denali National Park and Preserve, the embodiment of these larger-than-life Alaskan qualities. Known as the "crown jewel of the north," Denali is bigger than the state of New Hampshire and the country of Slovenia. It's also home to Mount Denali, which, at 6,190 m (20,310 ft), is the tallest peak in North America and the centerpiece of the park that bears its name.

While Denali may be blessed with a bounty of space (24,464 sq km [9,446 sq mi]) and natural wonders, two things it doesn't have in abundance are roads and trails. Regarding the former, there is just a solitary 148 km (92 mi) ribbon of a dirt road (Denali Park Road) in and out of the park's interior. As for the latter, within six million acres of Denali National Park, there are only 56 km (35 mi) of maintained pathways. The reason behind this dearth of tourist infrastructure? In the words of Don Striker, the park's superintendent: "Denali is a place that has been set aside to connect people to America's past, a place that protects present wildlife and amazing landscapes for your enjoyment and that of future generations."

The primeval character of Denali makes it an extraordinary place to visit, and there's no better way to familiarize yourself with its untamed wonders than to go backpacking. Unlike with day-hiking excursions (see info box), you will need to obtain a backcountry permit, carry a bear canister, and submit a trekking itinerary if you intend to venture into Denali's remote interior. All of this is done in advance with the help of rangers at

"The primeval character of Denali makes it an extraordinary place to visit, and there's no better way to familiarize yourself with its untamed wonders than to go backpacking."

← Denali Park Road (148 km [92 mi]) is the only road into and out of the national park's interior.
↓ Mother Nature's light show.

the national park's headquarters. Once the red tape has been taken care of, use Denali's excellent shuttle service to get to your chosen starting point, and then walk out into the wild.

Upon leaving the park road and all vestiges of civilization, a subarctic environment of massive river valleys, frigid tundra, vast glaciers, and windswept ridges awaits. The absence of trails means that backpackers overnighting in the Denali wilderness should be proficient navigators, in addition to possessing other basic wilderness skills such as the principles of campsite selection, layering, and how to ford a river. The Alaskan backcountry is no place for novices; the wilderness in this part of the world is as unforgiving as it is breathtaking.

The remote environment of Denali is home to an incredible array of wildlife. Among the many animals that roam the park, the "big five" are the ones that almost all visitors hope to see:

↑ Wide gravel bars and expansive alpine terrain—the view from near Polychrome Overlook.
↓ Wolves, caribou, moose, Dall sheep, and grizzly bears form Denali's "Big 5" mammals that all visitors hope to see.
→ Early morning campsite views of Mount Denali.

grizzly bears, wolves, moose, caribou, and Dall sheep. Observing these remarkable mammals in their natural habitat is one of the highlights of any excursion into the Alaskan wilderness, evoking a mixture of awe, fascination, and trepidation (at least for some!).

During any multi-day hiking excursion in Denali, seeing a wide range of fauna is almost guaranteed. However, what isn't a sure thing is viewing the Denali massif itself. Situated near the center of the Alaska Range, Denali, which means "the Great One" or "the High One" in Koyukon, is so large that it creates its weather, and can only be seen approximately 30 percent of the time. When it does peek through its shroud of low-lying cloud, the massive form is an inspiring sight to behold. It is not only the highest mountain on the continent but also a sacred place that's central to the creation myth of the region's original inhabitants, the Koyukon Athabascans.

For seasoned hikers, a backcountry trip in Denali National Park is a not-to-be-missed experience when visiting Alaska. Here, away from the crowds, you will find your chance to unplug and embrace nature sans safety net. No trails. No huts. No signs. Just raw wilderness. The way Denali has always been—and will hopefully continue to be for many generations to come.

↑ ↑ Soaking in the seasonal change from summer to autumn.
↑ Toklat River.

GOOD TO KNOW

SEASON
Mid-May to mid-September

PERMITS
A backcountry permit is required (along with a bear canister) for all overnight trips in the national park's interior. Permits are obtained at the Denali National Park Visitor Center with the help of Park Rangers, who can also assist with any other information you may require in regards to snow conditions, river fords, and wildlife. Denali is divided into 87 backcountry units, 41 of which have a quota on the number of campers per night; thus permits are subject to availability.

HELPFUL HINTS

PRECAUTIONS FOR BACKPACKING IN BEAR COUNTRY

The following tips apply both for Denali National Park, as well as other areas frequented by black and grizzly bears:

1. **Don't cook where you camp.** A bear's sense of smell is approximately seven times greater than a bloodhound and 2,100 times better than humans. By cooking in the same place you intend to sleep, you may as well ring a dinner bell for any bruins that happen to be in the vicinity. When backpacking in bear country, cook your main meal either at lunch or at least 30 minutes before setting up camp.
2. **Avoid popular campsites.** Whenever possible, try to avoid camping at popular campsites or campgrounds.

Bears aren't stupid. It doesn't take them long to make the association between lots of careless campers and a potentially easy meal. By far the majority of bear "encounters"—all estimates are over 90 percent—occur at popular park campgrounds (e.g. Yosemite and Yellowstone National Parks). If you have no choice but to overnight at an oft-frequented area, utilize bear lockers or bear poles whenever available.

3. **Wild Camping:** The alternative to camping at popular sites is known as "wild" or "stealth" camping, which is the modus operandi of all backcountry trips in Denali. Basically it means camping in an unused spot, away from trails and even water sources, which bears tend to frequent at dawn and dusk. When wild camping, the onus is even greater to practice "Leave No Trace" camping principles. This is important both for the bear's safety—bears that become habituated to human behavior are either put down or relocated—as well as the welfare of those backpackers that come after you.
4. **Noise:** When hiking through bush or thick forest, be sure to make some noise. Belt out some songs, talk loudly—whatever floats your boat. The objective is to negate the element of surprise. If bears hear you coming, chances are they will want to avoid an encounter as much as you do.
5. **Bear-proofing a campsite:** Through a combination of using pristine/stealth sites and not cooking where you camp, you greatly minimize the chances of a bear encounter occurring. The next step is to bear-proof your campsite by protecting your food and any other items in your kit that may give off unnatural odors (e.g. toothpaste, sunscreen, insect repellent, even the clothes you cooked in). In the backcountry of Denali National Park, this means using a bear canister. You can either borrow one for free from the Park Service, or bring your own.

WHAT TO DO IF THE PRECAUTIONS DON'T WORK?
In the unlikely scenario that a close encounter does occur, here are some guidelines to follow. *Note: These tips also appeared in the Kluane National Park chapter of* The Hidden Tracks, *the second installment of this Wanderlust series:*

1. **Observe and stay calm.** If you see a bear from a relatively close distance, stay calm and observe its movements. If it doesn't run off the moment it spots you, speak to the bear in a strong, calm, and even tone. Raise your arms to make yourself look bigger and (in theory) more intimidating.
2. **Slowly back away.** If the bear stands its ground but otherwise seems disinterested, slowly back away while keeping the bear in sight. Do not turn your back on the bear.
3. **Don't run.** In the event that all your else fails and you find yourself being charged by a bear, whatever you do, don't run. That can cause the bear to think of you as prey, and subsequently trigger an instinctive reaction to chase.

4. **Bear spray:** Most bear charges are bluffs (i.e. a bear will run toward you and at the last moment veer off); however, if it becomes apparent that the charge is not a bluff, use bear spray as a last resort. Wait until the bear is within 10–15 m (32–49 ft). Make sure you are not aiming the spray into the wind.

FLORA & FAUNA

BEYOND THE BIG 5

When it comes to spotting wildlife in the park, Denali's big five—grizzly bears, moose, caribou, wolves, and Dall sheep—tend to garner most of the attention. However, the park is also home to many smaller, but no less impressive, creatures including wolverines, lynx, marmots, foxes, pikas, golden eagles, willow ptarmigans (Alaska's state bird), and the wood frog, the park's lone amphibian.

BACKGROUND

DENALI VS. EVEREST

When people talk about a mountain's height, they are usually referring to its highest point above sea level. By that criterion, Mount Everest in the Himalaya (measuring 8,848 m [29,029 ft]) is the tallest mountain in the world. However, when measured from base to summit, the world's tallest mountain is actually Denali (5,500 m [18,000 ft]); Everest's vertical rise from base to peak comes in at 3,700 m (12,000 ft).

THE "DENALI" RESTORATION

Denali ("the Great One" or "the High One") is the name Native Koyukon Athabascans attributed to North America's highest mountain. But for almost 100 years of recent history, the peak's official name was Mount McKinley in honor of the former American president William McKinley (who never visited Alaska). During this period, there were repeated attempts by U.S. Congress to restore its original name, but they were continually blocked by Ohio lawmakers (McKinley's home state). The situation was finally rectified in 2015, when the Obama administration, under an order signed by Secretary of the Interior Sally Jewell, restored the mountain's native name, thus recognizing "the sacred status of Denali to generations of Alaska Natives."

AUTHOR'S ANECDOTE

SLEEPING HIKER, CHARGING BEAR

On the fourth day of my Denali hike (July 1998), I decided to call an early end to proceedings. A wide-open grassy expanse bordered by a crystal-clear stream was an invitation I could not pass up. Not long after establishing camp, I drifted off to sleep while cloud gazing outside my tent. Less than 30 minutes later, I was awoken from my slumber as the ground beneath me began to shake violently.

"Earthquake?" "Are there buffalo in Denali?" Before I had a chance to clear my head, I felt a huge whoosh not more than two meters to my left, as a fully grown grizzly bear ran past at high speed. With eyes popped and cheeks puckered, I watched, transfixed as the charging bruin ran off into the distance, apparently having been spooked by a small low-flying aircraft, no doubt full of deep-pocketed tourists wanting to get as close as possible for a photo op.

ACTIVITIES

BIRDING IN DENALI NATIONAL PARK

Although its terrestrial animals garner most of the attention, Denali has also long been recognized as a haven for ornithologists. Over 160 species of birds have been recorded in the National Park, including golden eagles, ravens, horned grebe, yellow rumped warbler, trumpeter swans, snow buntings, magpies, and gray jays. Broadly speaking, Denali's avifauna consists of migratory birds and hardy year-round residents. The former (around 80 percent of the total species) arrive in the spring and depart in the autumn, meaning that summer is primetime for birdwatchers in Denali. Winter pickings are much slimmer, but well rugged-up enthusiasts are able to observe northern goshawks, Canada jays, gyrfalcons, pine grosbeaks, and different types of ptarmigans, the largest and most abundant of which is the willow ptarmigan (Alaska's state bird).

DEEP ROOTED

THE LEGEND OF DENALI'S CREATION

According to Athabascan legend, a powerful but lonely young man by the name of Yahoo journeyed west in his canoe to find a wife. He found the woman he was looking for in a village ruled by a ruthless raven war chief. While fleeing with the young lady, Yahoo was pursued by the chief, who created a tempest in order to stop them. In response, Yahoo managed to momentarily calm the storm by throwing a magical stone into the water ahead of him. Increasingly infuriated, the wrathful chief continued his attack by hurling his great spear (which had never missed its mark) at Yahoo's back. Seeing the glint of the spear come toward him, Yahoo was able to react in time by creating a huge wave, which, as it rose into the sky, transformed into a mountain of stone that deflected and shattered the spear. Blinded by his anger, the chief and his canoe crashed into the base of the rocky wall, at which time he transformed into a raven and flew to the mountain's summit. Yahoo and his soon-to-be-wife then traveled safely back to his home in the east, where they subsequently had many children. It was these descendants who named the mountain created by Yahoo Denali, "the High One."

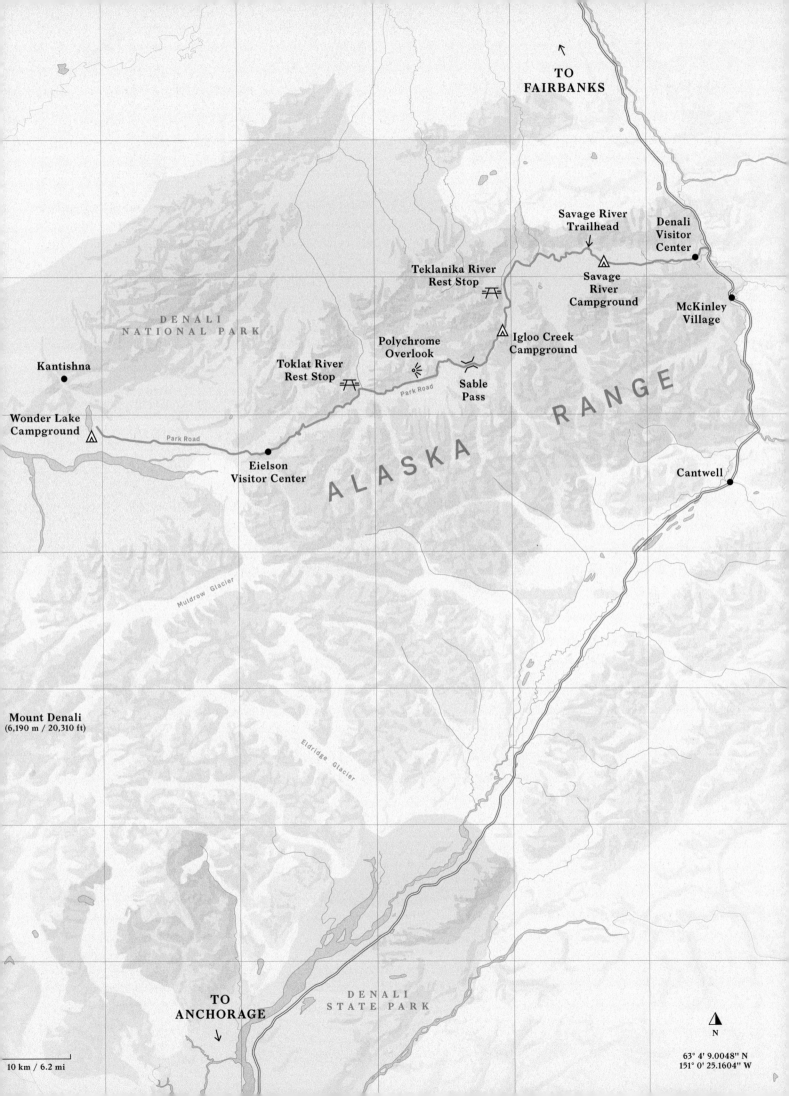

TO
FAIRBANKS

Savage River
Trailhead

Denali
Visitor
Center

Teklanika River
Rest Stop

Savage
River
Campground

McKinley
Village

DENALI
NATIONAL PARK

Polychrome
Overlook

Igloo Creek
Campground

Kantishna

Toklat River
Rest Stop

Sable
Pass

Park Road

Wonder Lake
Campground

Park Road

Eielson
Visitor Center

Cantwell

ALASKA RANGE

Muldrow Glacier

Mount Denali
(6,190 m / 20,310 ft)

Eldridge Glacier

DENALI
STATE PARK

TO
ANCHORAGE

N

10 km / 6.2 mi

63° 4' 9.0048" N
151° 0' 25.1604" W

HAWAII

Inimitable rainforests, yawning canyons, rugged coasts, and barren lava fields. Hiking in Hawaii is like nowhere else in the United States—an ocean-rimmed paradise marked by a tropical palette of lush greens, deep browns, and volcanic reds.

THE GRAND CANYON OF THE PACIFIC

Kauai

HAWAII

ABOUT THE TRAIL
→ <u>DISTANCE</u> 8 km (5 mi) round trip
→ <u>DURATION</u> 3 to 5 hours
→ <u>LEVEL</u> Moderate

Hawaii's Waimea Canyon is known as the "Grand Canyon of the Pacific." Situated on the island of Kauai, it's approximately 16 km (10 mi) long, 1,100 m (3,608 ft) deep, and is marked by a tropical palette of lush greens, deep browns, and volcanic reds. In a state renowned for its natural wonders, Waimea Canyon rates up there with the best, and there is no finer way to experience its dramatic topography than by exploring its depths via the Kukui Trail.

The origins of Waimea Canyon date back around four million years. At that time, part of the massive shield volcano that created Kauai island suffered a cataclysmic collapse while erupting. A giant lava-filled depression formed, and was subsequently sculpted and re-sculpted by rainwater from the slopes of nearby Mount Wai'ale'ale into what we know today as Waimea Canyon.

The Kukui Trail begins on Highway 550, 12.9 km (8 mi) north of the town of Waimea. It drops approximately 610 m (2,000 ft) to the canyon floor via a mostly well-defined pathway. During the first part of the descent, you'll be treated to sweeping views of the canyon and the winding Waimea River below. Equatorial hues mix together with crested buttes, tumbling cascades, and periodic rainbows to form an unforgettable panorama. Of the several waterfalls that can be seen on the eastern side of the canyon, the largest and most impressive is called Wai'alae Falls.

With an inordinate amount of rainfall hitting this part of Hawaii, Kauai is among the wettest places in North America. So although easy to follow, the Kukui Trail can often be muddy and loose. Regardless of the weather, lightweight, quick-drying trail running shoes with good grip are recommended. Additionally, due to the hot and humid conditions, drinking at least half a liter of water every hour is important for staying properly hydrated. It's possible to obtain H_2O from the streams along the way, but take note that waterborne diseases such as giardia are prevalent, so all water should be purified before consumption.

"Situated on the island of Kauai, it's approximately 16 km (10 mi) long, 1,100 m (3,608 ft) deep, and is marked by a tropical palette of lush greens, deep browns, and volcanic reds. In a state renowned for its natural wonders, Waimea Canyon rates up there with the best."

← Rolling clouds and lush vegetation.
↑ Descending the Kukui Trail.
← Hawaiian white hibiscus (Koki'o ke'oke'o).

Upon reaching the bottom of the canyon at Wiliwili campsite (see info box), enjoy a cooling swim in the Waimea River before undertaking the arduous ascent back to the rim. The shady and lush surroundings of the canyon's base hold a special place in the heart of many locals. According to folklore, it was here that two of Hawaii's most famous lovers were reunited against all odds. The story goes something like this:

Hiku and Kawelu were a young married couple. They had a happy relationship for the most part, but as with many newlyweds, they were not immune to the odd disagreement.

After one particular argument, Hiku left his wife and fled to the mountains. She patiently awaited his return, but when it seemed that he would not be coming back, she was struck with grief and committed suicide. When Hiku heard the news, he was full of remorse and set off on the dangerous journey to the Valley of the Dead (i.e. the base of Waimea Canyon) in order to bring his lost love back to the land of the living. He descended into the mighty gorge with a very long rope made of sturdy vines—there was no Kukui Trail back then! Upon reaching the canyon floor, Hiku spent days searching among the departed souls for his beloved Kawelu.

When he finally found her spirit, he professed his love and promised to never leave her again. As soon as Kawelu forgave her husband, her earthly body was restored, upon which the reunited couple climbed out of Waimea Canyon and lived happily ever after.

↑ **A secluded cascade.**
↓ **Kalalau Waterfall on the nearby Nā Pali Coast.**

↑ View from the Kalalau Lookout, a 15 km (9.3 mi) drive north from the start of the Kukui Trail.

↑↑ The Kalalau Trail on the Na Pali Coast.
↑ Winding river skirts the canyon cliffs.

GOOD TO KNOW

START / FINISH
Highway 550, about 1.2 km (0.75 mi) beyond the 8-mile marker

TOTAL ELEVATION GAIN
610 m (2,000 ft) down / 610 m (2,000 ft) up

SEASON
Year round

ACCOMMODATION & PERMITS
The Wiliwili campsite is located at the bottom of the Kukui Trail. Approximately 1.1 km (.66 mi) upstream from Wiliwili is a quieter, more isolated campsite by the name of Kaluahaulu. If you would like to camp in Waimea Canyon, permits need to be arranged in advance through the Hawaii State Parks' website.

HELPFUL HINTS

FROM CANYON RIM TO COAST
For those looking for something a little longer, it is possible to extend the hike by turning right once you reach the canyon floor. Heading south, the trail then follows the course of the Waimea River for 12.9 km (8 mi) to the historic seaport of the same name. Note that during the descent, the river will need to be crossed on multiple occasions; during periods of heavy rainfall it may not be passable due to high water levels.

FLORA & FAUNA

THE SPIRIT BIRD OF KAUAI
Throughout the Kukui Trail, you may spot wild goats, chickens, and one of Hawaii's most beloved creatures, the 'elepaio bird. Endemic to the Hawaiian Islands, 'elepaios are the sole members of the monarch flycatcher family (*Monarchidae*) in the United States. They also hold a special place in the archipelago's mythology, representing the guardian spirit of Hawaii's canoe makers.

BACKGROUND

MARK TWAIN & THE "GRAND CANYON"
Legend has it that Mark Twain was the first person to refer to Waimea Canyon as "the Grand Canyon of the Pacific." To this day, many Hawaiian tourism organizations attribute the quote to Twain. However, as is the case with many sayings associated with the legendary author and humorist, it isn't true. First, Twain never stepped foot on the island of Kauai during his visit to Hawaii in 1866. Second, the Grand Canyon wasn't called the Grand Canyon until 1869 (when it was named by the explorer, John Wesley Powell)—three years after Twain had left the Hawaiian Islands.

POINT OF VIEW

While nothing equals the immersive experience of descending into and out of Waimea Canyon on foot, a great way to experience this natural wonder from above is by driving the famed Kokee Road (HWY 550). One of the most scenic drives in all of Hawaii, the Kokee Road winds its way through the state park of the same name, and along the way boasts four incredible lookouts. The first one is the Waimea Canyon Lookout, located just past the 10 mile marker (see map). Here you will be treated to a sweeping panorama of the "Grand Canyon of the Pacific," and you'll even be able to spot where the Kukui Trail descends down to the river. Next up is the Pu'u Hinahina Lookout three miles further down the road. Smaller than its predecessor, the Pu'u Hinahina not only affords visitors a different perspective on Waimea Canyon, but also offers an unobstructed view of the massive chasm as it winds its way south to the Pacific Ocean. The next viewpoint on Kokee Road (mile 18) is perhaps the most famous of all: the Kalalau Lookout. It offers a wonderful vista of Kalalau Valley and the legendary Na Pali Coast, an area which is only accessible on foot via the classic Kalalau Trail. The fourth and final observation point of this scenic quartet, Pu'u O Kila, is just one mile further along, and it marks the end of Kokee Road. From here, the unimpeded views of Kalalau Valley are even better, and as a bonus, visitors can turn their gaze westward to take in the impressive sight of the Alakai Swamp, said to be the highest swamp in the world.

ACTIVITIES

Few things taste better on a hot summer's day than a chilled watermelon, pineapple, or papaya. And when it comes to fresh fruit (and vegetables), there aren't many places in the world to match Hawaii. Thanks to its rich soil and mild year-round climate, the growing season in Hawaii is long and bountiful, and approximately 30 percent of the state land usage is dedicated to farming. Other more uncommon delicacies found in the islands include rambutan, breadfruit, longan, canistel, and cainito.

The village of Waimea has several fresh markets—most of them operating on the weekends—to meet the demands of locals and tourists alike. Here are the most important ones:
· Waimea Mid-Week Market: Wednesdays between 9:00 a.m. and 4:00 p.m.
· Waimea Town Market: Saturdays

between 7:30 a.m. and 12:00 p.m.
- Waimea Homestead Farmers' Market: Saturdays between 7:00 a.m. and 12:00 p.m.
- Kamuela Farmers' Market: Saturdays between 7:30 a.m. and 1:00 p.m.

Most of these markets host around 20 to 40 local vendors. In addition to fruit and vegetables, you can also purchase flowers, coffee, handicrafts, and healthy breakfasts prepared on site.

PEAK PERFORMANCE: RECOMMENDED GEAR

Hiking in Waimea Canyon is often hot, humid, muddy, and slippery. Here are some gear tips to help with your trip preparation:

1. Lightweight, quick-drying trail running shoes with good tread are ideal for Waimea Canyon. If your ankles are strong and you're not carrying a heavy load on your back, good-quality sports sandals with a Vibram (or equivalent) sole can also work. Definitely leave the heavy boots at home when hiking in Hawaii.
2. Due to the prevalence of giardia in the water, bring either chemical drops/tablets or a filter to help purify water along the way. Plan on drinking at least half a liter of water per hour during the hike, particularly if you happen to be walking during the hottest time of the day.
3. Speaking of heat, the sun can be fierce in the tropics. Don't forget to bring a broad-brimmed hat, sunglasses, and sunscreen. An umbrella can also be a great multi-purpose option, providing portable shade when the sun is beating down, and shelter when it starts pouring. *Note: Kauai is one of the wettest places on Earth; nearby Mount Waiʻaleʻale receives more than 400 inches or precipitation per year, and on average it rains well over 200 days per year.*

4. Bring quick-drying shorts that perform double duty for walking and taking a cooling mid-hike swim in the Waimea River.
5. A lightweight pair of binoculars come in handy not only for bird watching during the hike, but also as a means of enhancing your views from the Kokee Road's spectacular lookouts.

DEEP ROOTED

SIX FACTS ABOUT HAWAII

1. Hawaii is the most isolated population center in the world. From the California coast to Hawaii is a distance of 3,846 km (2,390 mi). From Japan to the Aloha State it is 6,626 km (4,117 mi) as the crow flies.
2. The Hawaiian archipelago was first settled by seafaring Polynesians from other Pacific Islands between 300 and 600 AD.
3. The first European to "discover" Hawaii was Captain James Cook in 1778. He named them the Sandwich Islands, in honor of John Montagu, 4th Earl of Sandwich, who was one of his patrons. This moniker was used by foreigners and foreign governments up until the 1840s, when the local name of Hawaii became more widely accepted.
4. Before Hawaii was annexed by the United States in 1898 (through the Newlands Resolution), it was known as the Kingdom of Hawaiʻi. It remained a U.S. territory until August 21, 1959, when it became the 50th state in the union.
5. The state of Hawaii consists of 137 islands, with the eight major ones as follows: Niihau, Kauai, Oahu, Maui, Molokai, Lanai, Kahoolawe, and the Big Island of Hawaii.
6. From Kure Atoll in the north to the Big Island of Hawaii in the south, the state of Hawaii stretches some 2,414 km (1,500 mi), making it the second widest of America's states (after Alaska), as well as the longest island chain in the world.

NEARBY: KALALAU TRAIL

Coastal hiking does not get much better than the Kalalau Trail, located on Kauai's north shore. There are pristine beaches, cascading waterfalls, lush valleys, and jaw-dropping 180-degree vistas over the Pacific Ocean. Linking all of these natural wonders together is a sometimes precarious pathway along one of the world's most dramatic coastlines.

The Na Pali Coast is a jagged mountain range of towering cliffs that rise to a height of 1,200 m (4,000 ft). Its imposing character and unbeatable setting has long made it a popular backdrop for dozens of Hollywood movies, including Steven Spielberg's Jurassic Park and the legendary original version of King Kong from 1933. The only way into and out of this dramatic coastal realm is via the Kalalau Trail (KT).

First established in the late 1800s, the KT measures 35 km (21.7 mi) out-and-back, and takes place entirely within the boundaries of the Na Pali Coast State Park. During its course, it passes through five lush coastal valleys and negotiates several cliff-hugging sections of butt-clenching, palm-sweating narrow pathway. Although it's possible to hike the KT in one long day, it's recommended that you take two or three. The Na Pali Coast is not that easy to get to, and if you've come all this way to hike, you may as well enjoy it for as long as you can! During your hike be sure to take the 7 km (4.3 mi) side trip from Hanakapiʻai Beach up to a beautiful waterfall in Hanakapiʻai Valley.

As the crow flies, it's less than 30 km (18.6 mi) from Waimea Canyon to Keʻe Beach, the starting and finishing point of the Kalalau Trail. However, due to the fact that the northwest region of Kauai is mostly road-free protected wilderness, the circuitous drive between the two is approximately 116 km (72 mi) and takes just over two hours.

The Kalalau trail is one of 32 treks featured in *Wanderlust: Hiking on Legendary Trails*, the first installment of this Wanderlust book series.

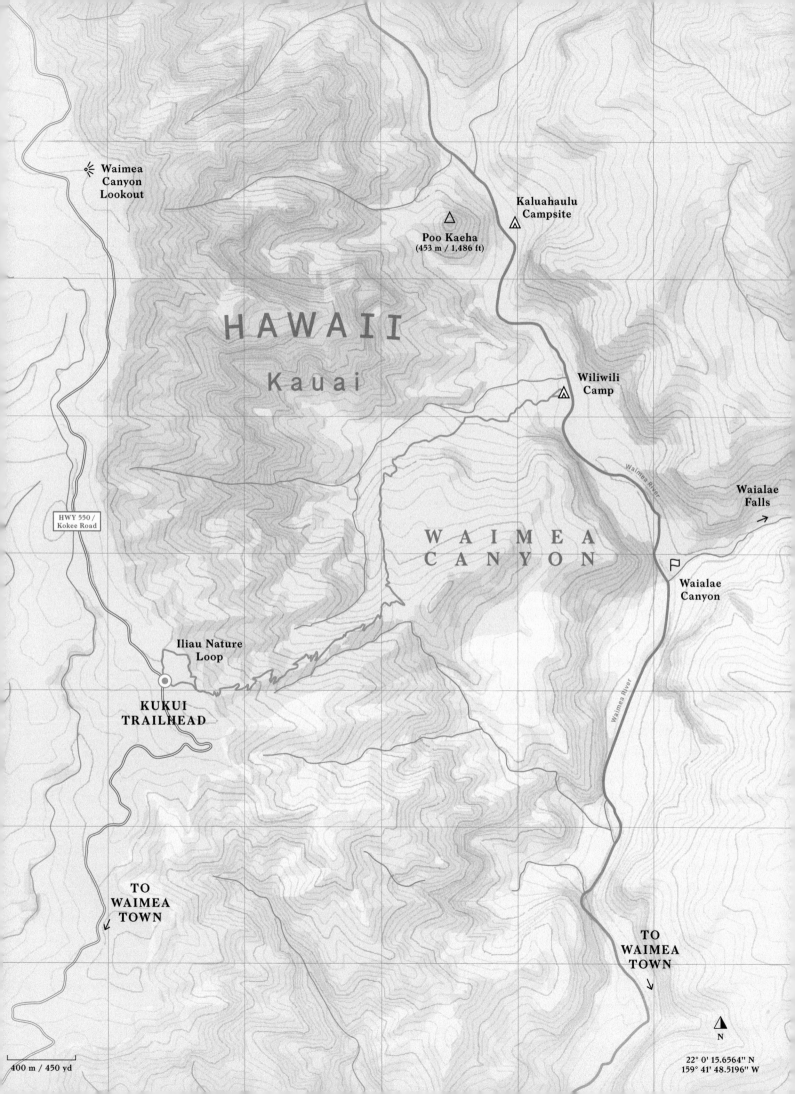

Waimea
Canyon
Lookout

Kaluahaulu
Campsite

Poo Kaeha
(453 m / 1,486 ft)

Wiliwili
Camp

HAWAII

Kauai

Waimea River

Waialae
Falls

HWY 550 /
Kokee Road

WAIMEA
CANYON

Waialae Canyon

Iliau Nature
Loop

Waimea River

KUKUI
TRAILHEAD

TO
WAIMEA
TOWN

TO
WAIMEA
TOWN

N

400 m / 450 yd

22° 0' 15.6564" N
159° 41' 48.5196" W

LOOKING FOR SOMETHING MORE?

"Deserts, rainforests, mountains, or coasts;
I've never had a preference. If I'm out in the wilderness
with everything I need in the world on my back,
chances are my smile is wide and my thoughts are clear."

—
CAM HONAN

CHIEFS HEAD PEAK

SCALING NEW HEIGHTS IN THE ROCKIES

Rocky Mountain National Park, Colorado

ABOUT THE TRAIL
→ <u>DISTANCE</u> 27 km (17 mi)
→ <u>DURATION</u> 8 to 12 hours
→ <u>LEVEL</u> Challenging

This little-known out-and-back hike works its way from Sandbeach Lake Trailhead to the summit of the third-highest mountain in Rocky Mountain National Park. Mostly off-trail and with more than 3,048 m (10,000 ft) of total elevation gain and loss, the trek to Chiefs Head Peak is far from a cakewalk. However, once you reach the top, you will be rewarded with an otherworldly 360-degree panorama, which includes spectacular views of Glacier Gorge, along with Longs Peak, Pagoda Peak, and Mount Meeker. During the hike, you may spot moose, bears, and elk. Fun fact: In 1976, Rocky Mountain National Park was designated by UNESCO as one of the first World Biosphere Reserves.

TIMBERLINE TRAIL

CIRCUMNAVIGATING MOUNT HOOD

Oregon

ABOUT THE TRAIL
→ <u>DISTANCE</u> 67 km (40 mi)
→ <u>DURATION</u> 2 to 3 days
→ <u>LEVEL</u> Moderate

Circumnavigating Mount Hood (3,429 m [11,249 ft]), one of Oregon's most iconic volcanoes, the Timberline Trail is a long-time favorite of Pacific Northwest hikers. During its course, the trail passes through luxuriant old-growth forests, wildflower-filled meadows, and rough volcanic landscapes. Majestic vistas of glaciers and waterfalls abound. Perhaps the most challenging aspect of the Timberline Trail is the fact that you must ford many glacial rivers along the way. This holds particularly true during early summer, when snowmelt is at its peak.

ARIZONA TRAIL

THRU-HIKING THE GRAND CANYON STATE

Arizona

ABOUT THE TRAIL
→ <u>DISTANCE</u> 1,315 km (817 mi)
→ <u>DURATION</u> 40 to 50 days
→ <u>LEVEL</u> Moderate to challenging

One of America's 11 designated National Scenic Trails, the Arizona Trail (AZT) is a 1,315 km (817 mi) non-motorized pathway that spans the entire length of the Grand Canyon State. Highlights of the trail include the Superstition Mountains, the San Francisco Peaks, a wide variety of wildlife (e.g. Gila monsters, javelinas, roadrunners, elk, coyotes, and desert tortoises), and the chance to hike across one of the seven natural wonders of the world, the Grand Canyon. Tip: The best time to hike the AZT is in the spring, when water sources are plentiful due to snowmelt.

← Scrambling along the summit ridge of Chiefs Head Peak (4,139 m [13,579 ft]).

→ A symbol of America's Southwest, the saguaro (*Carnegiea gigantea*) is the largest cactus in the country.

TAHOE RIM TRAIL

AROUND AMERICA'S LARGEST ALPINE LAKE

Sierra Nevada, California

ABOUT THE TRAIL
→ <u>DISTANCE</u> 266 km (165 mi)
→ <u>DURATION</u> 10 to 13 days
→ <u>LEVEL</u> Moderate

The Tahoe Rim Trail (TRT) is a well-marked and well-maintained trail that circumambulates beautiful Lake Tahoe in California's Sierra Nevada. Following ridgetops for most of its course, it affords magnificent vistas of not only the lake, but also Nevada's Great Basin to the east and the Sierra Crest to the west. Situated 1,897 m (6,225 ft) above sea level, Lake Tahoe is the largest alpine lake in North America, and, with a depth of 501 m (1,645 ft), it's also the second-deepest on the continent after Oregon's Crater Lake. Fun fact: The Tahoe Rim Trail shares about 80 km (50 mi) of its treadway with the Pacific Crest Trail on the western side of the lake.

TETON CREST TRAIL

A GLACIER-SCULPTED MASTERPIECE

Grand Teton National Park, Wyoming

ABOUT THE TRAIL
→ <u>DISTANCE</u> 63 km (40 mi)
→ <u>DURATION</u> 2 to 3 days
→ <u>LEVEL</u> Moderate

The Teton Crest Trail (TCT) is an exhilarating high-level route through the heart of Grand Teton National Park. In the space of 63 km (40 mi) it showcases towering granite peaks, majestic glaciers, glistening alpine lakes, and terraces with sheer cliffs. In regard to wildlife, there are grizzly and black bears, moose, wolves, and bison. As a bonus, due to its proximity to Yellowstone National Park (less than an hour's drive north), it's easy for TCT hikers to combine their time in the Tetons with a few days of exploring Yellowstone's geothermal wonders.

PINNELL MOUNTAIN TRAIL

INTO THE INTERIOR

Alaska

ABOUT THE TRAIL
→ <u>DISTANCE</u> 44 km (27 mi)
→ <u>DURATION</u> 2 days
→ <u>LEVEL</u> Easy to moderate

The Pinnell Mountain Trail (PMT) is an above-tree line trek through the sparse Alaskan interior. Located 172 km (107 mi) east of Fairbanks, it traverses windswept ridgelines and passes by some of the state's oldest rocks. Dating back to the Cambrian and Precambrian periods (700 million–2 billion years ago), these rocks have been sculpted by the elements into fantastical shapes. The PMT is managed by the Bureau of Land Management (BLM), and is one of the few maintained pathways in Alaska's interior. This makes the trail ideal for inexperienced hikers who want to experience raw wilderness but aren't sure if they're ready for an off-trail overnight excursion. Tip: June is an excellent time to do the Pinnell Mountain Trail. It's the prime season for wildflowers, and from June 18–25, you can witness the natural phenomenon of the midnight sun.

HALEAKALA CRATER TRAIL

SUNRISE OVER MORDOR

Haleakalā National Park, Hawaii

ABOUT THE TRAIL
→ <u>DISTANCE</u> 17.9 km (11.1 mi)
→ <u>DURATION</u> 6 to 8 hours
→ <u>LEVEL</u> Moderate to challenging

Lava flows, cinder cones, and a dormant 3,055 m (10,023 ft) volcano—the out-and-back trail to Haleakala Crater is one of the most unique day hikes in America. Reminiscent of Tolkien's Mordor, the stark and desolate character of Haleakala's surroundings is such that NASA sent the Apollo astronauts here in the 1960s in preparation for their moon landings. A pre-dawn start provides the opportunity to catch the sunrise from the volcano's rim. Tip: Bring a warm jacket, as dawn temperatures on the rim can be chilly.

MID STATE TRAIL

A METRIC TRAIL IN AN IMPERIAL COUNTRY

Pennsylvania

ABOUT THE TRAIL
→ <u>DISTANCE</u> 527 km (327 mi)
→ <u>DURATION</u> 20 to 30 days
→ <u>LEVEL</u> Moderate

The Mid State Trail was the first hiking trail in the United States to employ the metric system on trail signage, and to this day it remains one of the only ones to do so. Measuring 527 km (327 mi), it spans the length of Pennsylvania from the border with New York to the Mason-Dixon Line. Passing through a combination of state-designated parks, forests, and game lands, it's often said that the Mid State Trail is the "wildest" footpath in Pennsylvania; but in reality, it is very much a "green corridor," with accessible roads rarely more than two to three kilometers (one to two miles) away.

DEVIL'S GARDEN LOOP

THE NATURAL BRIDGE CAPITAL OF THE WORLD

Arches National Park, Utah

ABOUT THE TRAIL
→ <u>DISTANCE</u> 11.6 km (7.2 mi)
→ <u>DURATION</u> 5 hours
→ <u>LEVEL</u> Easy

Within its 310 sq km (76,679 acre) boundaries, Arches National Park boasts more than 2,000 stone arches. The longest of these natural bridges is known as Landscape Arch, measuring an amazing 88.4 m (290.1 ft) in length—almost the same size as a football field! This and many other red-rock delights such as fins, pinnacles, and balancing rocks can be found on the Devil's Garden Loop, a family-friendly day hike that ranks as one of the finest trails in Arches National Park. Tip: Go early in the morning or late in the afternoon to avoid the crowds.

← ← The view over Dicks Lake from the Tahoe Rim Trail.
← The Teton Crest Trail has an average elevation of over 2,438 m (8,000 ft).
→ The red rock delight that is Arches National Park.

ACROSS THE ROCKY MOUNTAIN STATE

Colorado

ABOUT THE TRAIL

→ DISTANCE 789 km (490 mi)
→ DURATION 30 to 40 days
→ LEVEL Moderate to challenging

The Colorado Trail (CT) begins in the foothills just outside of Denver and extends 789 km (490 mi) across the Rocky Mountain State through to the historic town of Durango. Along the way it passes through eight mountain ranges, six wilderness areas, five major river systems, and six national forests. One of the finest alpine trails in the world, the CT is well marked and maintained throughout its course, and its average elevation of 3,139 m (10,300 ft) makes it the highest of America's 11 designated National Scenic Trails. Thanks to its many accessible trailheads, the CT is also a great option for those who don't have the time to do an entire thru-hike, but are interested in doing shorter sections. Tip: The summer months constitute monsoon season in the Rockies, and electrical storms generally occur in the afternoons and/or evenings. Try to avoid exposed ridges and hilltops at these times of day.

IN THE FOOTSTEPS OF THOREAU

Massachusetts

ABOUT THE TRAIL

→ DISTANCE 13.7 km (8.5 mi)
→ DURATION 4 to 6 hours
→ LEVEL Easy

Follow in the footsteps of famed author and naturalist Henry David Thoreau, who walked the entire 40.2 km (25 mi) eastern shore of Cape Cod over three days in 1849. The 13.7 km (8.5 mi) section between Eastham and Newcomb Hollow Beach retraces the initial day of Thoreau's walk while traversing a coastal landscape of sand dunes and salt marshes. The sweeping views of the Atlantic Ocean are breathtaking, and given that Cape Cod's seashore has been under the jurisdiction of the U.S. federal government since 1961, it remains almost as peaceful and development-free as it was during the time of Thoreau.

GIANT ESCARPMENTS AND PARTING WATERS

Bob Marshall Wilderness, Montana

ABOUT THE TRAIL

→ DISTANCE 97 km (60 mi)
→ DURATION 4 to 6 days
→ LEVEL Moderate

Beginning and ending at the South Fork Sun Campground (50 km [31 mi] west of Augusta), this scenic loop hike in the Bob Marshall Wilderness circumambulates one of Montana's most spectacular geological features, the Chinese Wall. Measuring about 35 km (22 mi) in length and with an average height of 300 m (1,000 ft), this imposing limestone escarpment forms part of the Continental Divide, meaning that water flowing down from its eastern side drains into the Atlantic Ocean (via the Gulf of Mexico), and water flowing down from its western side drains into the Pacific Ocean.

↑ Walking the Chinese Wall in the Bob Marshall Wilderness.
← A crystalline alpine lake on the Colorado Trail.

OREGON DESERT TRAIL

TRAVERSING THE HIGH DESERT

Oregon

ABOUT THE TRAIL
→ <u>DISTANCE</u> 1,207 km (750 mi)
→ <u>DURATION</u> 40 to 45 days
→ <u>LEVEL</u> Challenging

The Oregon Desert Trail (ODT) is a little-known backcountry hiking route across Oregon's remote High Desert region. With harsh, exposed terrain and little in the way of dedicated signage, the ODT is a hike best suited to adventurous and experienced ramblers who are accustomed to solitude. During its rugged course, it links some of the state's most impressive natural features, such as the Hart Mountain National Antelope Refuge, Steens Mountain, and the amazing Owyhee Canyonlands. It also offers abundant opportunities for wildlife viewing in the form of mule deer, pronghorn antelope, coyotes, American badgers, and hundreds of bird species. Tip: The Oregon desert receives minimal precipitation, and due to its isolated location, there is not much artificial light to be found. As a result, the night skies are spectacular. Take advantage whenever you can and sleep under the stars!

↘ The sunrise over Stephens Pond in
   the Adirondack Mountains.
↓ The Owyhee Canyonlands of eastern Oregon.

REDWOOD CREEK TRAIL

IN THE SHADOW OF GIANTS

Redwood National Park, California

ABOUT THE TRAIL
→ <u>DISTANCE</u> 25.1 km (15.6 mi)
→ <u>DURATION</u> 7 to 10 hours
→ <u>LEVEL</u> Easy

This moderately trafficked out-and-back jaunt is Redwood National Park's signature hiking trail. It can be done as either a day hike or as an overnight backpacking trip to take in the scenery at a slower pace—a good choice if you have the time. The trail follows a lush riparian corridor through hemlock, spruce, bigleaf maples and, of course, old- and second-growth redwoods. The turnaround point and scenic highlight is the Tall Trees Grove, a remarkable collection of ancient redwoods that was famously featured in National Geographic magazine in 1963. The widespread attention created by the article helped the area to eventually be designated a National Park in 1968. Fun fact: The world's tallest tree, a coast redwood (*Sequoia sempervirens*) called Hyperion (115.5 m [379 ft]), is located in a secret location in the Redwood Creek watershed.

NORTHVILLE-PLACID TRAIL

TREKKING AMERICA'S ORIGINAL WILDERNESS

Adirondack Mountains, New York

ABOUT THE TRAIL
→ <u>DISTANCE</u> 214 km (133 mi)
→ <u>DURATION</u> 7 to 10 days
→ <u>LEVEL</u> Easy to moderate

The Northville-Placid Trail (NPT) is the premier long-distance trek in New York's Adirondack Mountains. Traversing some of the most remote valleys on the Eastern Seaboard, it meanders by an enchanting collection of ponds, lakes, and cascades; look out for the impressive Wanika and Millers Falls. Along the way, you can either camp or utilize the more than 40 lean-to (three-sided) shelters that dot the length of the well-maintained pathway. Most of the NPT lies within peaceful forests, but for those in search of jaw-dropping mountain views, it's possible to connect the trail with the spectacular High Peaks Wilderness Area near the trail's northern terminus—historic Lake Placid. Tip: The NPT is at its best in the fall, when the forests transform into a kaleidoscopic wonderland of autumnal shades.

OZARK HIGHLANDS TRAIL

A JOURNEY THROUGH THE INTERIOR HIGHLANDS

Arkansas

ABOUT THE TRAIL
→ <u>DISTANCE</u> 266 km (165 mi)
→ <u>DURATION</u> 10 to 12 days
→ <u>LEVEL</u> Moderate

The Ozark Highlands Trail is an infrequently trodden 266 km (165 mi) route that traces the wide and rocky backbone of Arkansas's Ozark National Forest. Stretching from Lake Fort Smith State Park in the west to Woolum on the Buffalo River in the east, it lopes its way along scenic ridgelines and through deep hardwood forests, passing by an impressive collection of seasonal waterfalls, sandstone bluffs, and giant boulders. Along with the neighboring Ouachita Range, the Ozark Mountains form part of the Interior Highlands, the highest region in the United States between the Appalachian and Rocky Mountains. Tip: During the hot summer months, there are lots of water holes along the trail where you can go for a cooling swim.

BENTON MACKAYE TRAIL

A HIDDEN GEM OF SOUTHERN APPALACHIA

Georgia, Tennessee, and North Carolina

ABOUT THE TRAIL
→ <u>DISTANCE</u> 463 km (288 mi)
→ <u>DURATION</u> 17 to 22 days
→ <u>LEVEL</u> Moderate

Named after the founder of the Appalachian Trail, the Benton MacKaye Trail (BMT) is a hidden gem of the southern Appalachian Mountains. It measures approximately 463 km (288 mi) in length, and during its serpentine course passes through three states and eight federally designated Wilderness and Wilderness Study Areas. The BMT receives only a fraction of the foot traffic of its more famous and much longer neighbor, the Appalachian Trail, making it an excellent option for solitude-seeking hikers looking to avoid the crowds. Tip: The BMT is best done in the spring or fall in order to enjoy the wildflowers or autumnal colors.

ZION TRAVERSE

HIGH PLATEAUS AND ECHOING CANYONS

Zion National Park, Utah

ABOUT THE TRAIL
→ <u>DISTANCE</u> 77.7 km (48.3 mi)
→ <u>DURATION</u> 3 to 5 days
→ <u>LEVEL</u> Moderate

The Zion Traverse (ZT) is made up of a series of interconnected trails, and takes hikers on a journey to parts of Zion National Park that day trippers rarely visit. Equally popular as a route for ultra-marathoners (the record is less than seven hours!), the ZT winds its way through hanging gardens, echoing canyons, sandstone monoliths, and high plateaus. Wildlife viewing opportunities abound, and sharp-eyed ramblers may spot bighorn sheep, mountain lions, bobcats, canyon tree frogs, golden eagles, and great blue herons. Tip: Be sure to do the short side trip to Angels Landing, which boasts one of the most incredible lookouts on the entire Colorado Plateau.

FOOTHILLS TRAIL

A WATERY WONDERLAND IN THE CAROLINAS

South Carolina and
North Carolina

ABOUT THE TRAIL

→ <u>DISTANCE</u> 122 km (76 mi)

→ <u>DURATION</u> 5 to 7 days

→ <u>LEVEL</u> Moderate

The Foothills Trail is a 122 km (76 mi) National Recreation Trail in the Appalachian Mountains of the Carolinas. A popular pathway that can be enjoyed all year round, its serpentine course extends between Table Rock State Park in the east and Oconee State Park in the west. Water is the dominant theme of the Foothills Trail, and during its length you'll encounter a collection of spectacular cascades, quaint ponds, and meandering streams. During the warmer months, there are lots of opportunities to swim and float in the Chattooga River, which is famous for its white water rafting and trout fishing.

LAKESHORE TRAIL

SAND DUNES AND SHIPWRECKS IN THE UPPER PENINSULA

Pictured Rocks National Lakeshore, Michigan

ABOUT THE TRAIL

→ <u>DISTANCE</u> 68.2 km (42.4 mi)

→ <u>DURATION</u> 3 to 4 days

→ <u>LEVEL</u> Moderate

The Lakeshore Trail is a classic pathway along the southern shore of Lake Superior in Michigan. Bookended by the waterside towns of Munising and Grand Marais, the scenic pathway encompasses lighthouses, sand dunes, shipwrecks, sheer cliffs, lonely beaches, and spectacular views of Lake Superior. The trail traverses the length of Pictured Rocks National Lakeshore, the first to be designated a National Lakeshore in 1966 by U.S. Congress. Tip: Transport for this point-to-point trail is easy, thanks to the regular shuttle service between the park's western and eastern ends. The shuttle is run by ALTRAN, the Alger Transit Authority.

← ← A scenic lookout over the Ozark
Mountains of Arkansas.

← A misty river valley on the Benton
MacKaye Trail.

→ Views over Lake Superior from the
Pictured Rocks National Lakeshore.

Wanderlust USA

The Great American Hike

This book was conceived, edited, and designed by gestalten.

Edited by **Robert Klanten**
Editor-at-Large: **Santiago Rodriguez Tarditi**
Contributing Editor: **Cam Honan**

Texts by **Cam Honan**
Text for Outer Mountain Loop (Big Bend National Park) &
Grand Gulch – Bullet Canyon Loop (Cedar Mesa) by **Paul Magnanti**
Text for Cedar Run – Whiteoak Canyon Loop
(Shenandoah National Park) by **Alan Dixon**
Text editing by **Rachel Sampson**

Editorial Management by **Britta Gimmini**
Photo Editing by **Madeline Dudley Yates, Mario Udzenija**

Design by **Britta Hinz**
Layout and cover by **Ilona Samcewicz-Parham**
Illustrations by **Florian Bayer**

Map research by **Cam Honan**
Map design by **Bureau Rabensteiner**

Typeface(s): Larish Neue by **Radim Peško**,
Zimmer by **Julian Hansen**

Cover image by **Simon Prochaska @simon.prochaska**
Backcover image by **Christopher Zebo**
Salesheet images by
Maroon Bells **Steven Shattuck/@Shattuck311** (top left)
Pacific Crest Trail **Ryan Choi/@choirizo** (top right)
Grand Canyon **Raja Hamid/rajahamid.com** (middle)
Pacific Northwest **Ashley Hill/sobohobo.com** (bottom)
Alaska Spread images by **Brian Browitt/
brianbrowittphotography.smugmug.com**

Printed by Grafisches Centrum Cuno, Calbe
Made in Germany

Published by gestalten, Berlin 2019
ISBN 978-3-89955-985-9

3rd printing, 2021

© Die Gestalten Verlag GmbH & Co. KG, Berlin 2019

For more information, and to order books, please visit www.gestalten.com

Bibliographic information published by the Deutsche Nationalbibliothek. The Deutsche Nationalbibliothek lists this publication in the Deutsche Nationalbibliografie; detailed bibliographic data is available online at www.dnb.de

None of the content in this book was published in exchange for payment by commercial parties or designers; gestalten selected all included work based solely on its artistic merit.

This book was printed on paper certified according to the standards of the FSC®.

Described by Backpacker Magazine as "the most travelled hiker on earth", **Cam Honan** has trekked in 61 countries across six continents, logging more than 96,500 km (60,000 mi) over the last three decades. He documents his journeys on his blog, *The Hiking Life*, and has written two bestselling titles for gestalten—*Wanderlust* and *The Hidden Tracks*.